The Social and Political
Thought of Archie Mafeje

The Social and Political Thought of Archie Mafeje

Bongani Nyoka

WITS UNIVERSITY PRESS

Published in South Africa by:
Wits University Press
1 Jan Smuts Avenue
Johannesburg 2001

www.witspress.co.za

First published 2020

http://dx.doi.org.10.18772/12020095942

978-1-77614-594-2 (Paperback)
978-1-77614-598-0 (Hardback)
978-1-77614-595-9 (Web PDF)
978-1-77614-596-6 (EPUB)
978-1-77614-597-3 (Mobi)

Project manager: Alison Lockhart
Editor: Monica Seeber
Copyeditor: Alison Lockhart
Proofreader: Lee Smith
Indexer: Marlene Burger
Cover design: Hybrid Creative
Typeset in 11.5 point Crimson

To my paternal grandmother, Nonzwakazi Nobanzi Ntuli (1918–2001),
and my mother, Nomsa Mtsaka

Contents

Acknowledgements ix

Introduction xi

Part I: A Critique of the Social Sciences

1 From Functionalism to Radical Social Science 3

2 A Totalising Critique 29

3 Reading Mafeje's *The Theory and Ethnography of African Social Formations* 59

Part II: On Land and Agrarian Issues in Sub-Saharan Africa

4 The Land and Agrarian Question 103

5 Peasants, Food Security and Poverty Eradication 135

Part III: On Revolutionary Theory and Politics

6 Neocolonialism, State Capitalism and Underdevelopment 173

7 Liberation Struggles in South Africa 201

Notes 229

Bibliography 251

Index 261

Acknowledgements

This book would not have been possible without the generous support of many individuals and institutions. For financial support, my thanks are due to the Academic and Non-Fiction Authors' Association of South Africa (ANFASA) and the Johannesburg Institute for Advanced Study (JIAS).

I am equally grateful to the Wits University Press team, particularly Roshan Cader and Kirsten Perkins. I would like also to thank Alison Lockhart who proficiently managed this book project. I owe a special debt to my editor, Monica Seeber, who addressed the manuscript with perspicacity and professionalism.

A shorter and somewhat different version of chapter 7 appeared in the journal *Social Dynamics* in 2020. Thanks to the publisher Taylor and Francis for permission to reuse the article.

I wish to acknowledge my indebtedness to Jimi Adesina, who not only introduced me to African scholarship when I was an undergraduate student, but also supervised both my Master's and doctoral theses.

I must express my gratitude to Sifiso Mxolisi Ndlovu for advice and assistance at various stages of preparing the manuscript. I am grateful also to Michael Cross and Bongani Ngqulunga. I cannot forget to thank Patrick Mlangeni who drew the pre-colonial map of the Great Lakes region that appears in this book.

Naturally, all remaining errors in this book are entirely my own.

Bongani Nyoka
Tshwane
April 2020

Introduction

A spectre is haunting the South African academy, the spectre of knowledge decolonisation. Academics and university students are calling for decolonisation, but what they call brilliant is not new, and what they call new is not brilliant. As early as the nineteenth century, the South African poet William Wellington Gqoba grappled with the impact of Western education on black people; in the early twentieth century, Benedict Wallet Vilakazi and Herbert Isaac Ernest Dhlomo were debating the role of language and modernity in South Africa. Equally, the works of Cheikh Anta Diop on sources of knowledge and social history, Kenneth Onwuka Dike on African historiography and Ngũgĩ wa Thiong'o on language and decolonising the mind point to a longer genealogy of outstanding work on decolonisation discourse and a critique of Eurocentrism. In South Africa, mainstream social scientists in the 1980s and 1990s were talking about reform, while in the 2000s they were talking about transformation – but throughout the 1990s and 2000s, other voices, alternative to the mainstream, were talking about the Africanisation and the indigenisation of knowledge.

These ideas – reform, transformation, Africanisation, indigenisation – continue to this day, but the idea of decolonisation has gained more traction than any of them.[1] All the same, the inability to transcend the call and to get into the actual business of decolonising means that the call itself has taken on a life of its own. It is what I call the politics of suspension; talking about decolonisation for so long without engaging in the actual process means that the term loses its content and becomes irrelevant. It is also what I call epistemic posturing, for talking about the need to engage in knowledge decolonisation is not itself the act of decolonising knowledge – nor does it constitute a rupture with old knowledge systems. Eurocentrism has long been an object of critical analysis by African scholars, so to speak of Eurocentrism and coloniality in the social sciences is at this point merely to state the obvious.

In this book, when talking about knowledge and epistemological decolonisation, I refer to tapping into the African knowledge archive. I use the term in a narrow sense to refer to engaging with the works of African scholars and in a broad sense include taking seriously what Jimi Adesina calls the 'ontological discourses and narratives' of African people.[2] In other words, I use the term to mean generating theoretical insights from the lived experiences of African people, rather than importing theory in order to understand them. Based on these two senses, this volume shifts the discussion from talking about decolonising knowledge to the actual process of doing so. A critique of Eurocentrism and coloniality is necessarily built in to the process of tapping into the African knowledge archive and engaging with the ontological narratives of African people. I do this by deep engagement with the works of Archie Mafeje and the African societies he wrote about.

Archie Mafeje was born on 30 March 1936 in the village of Engcobo, in what was then the Cape Province (now part of the Eastern Cape). He studied at the University of Cape Town (UCT) from 1957 to 1963 and left South Africa in April 1964 with a Master's degree in social anthropology to pursue doctoral studies at the University of Cambridge. He completed his PhD in social anthropology in 1968 and applied for a teaching position at his alma mater, UCT. He got the job on merit, but could not take up the offer because the apartheid government exerted pressure on UCT to rescind his appointment – because, the government said, a black man could not teach at a 'white' university. This became a cause célèbre, the 'Mafeje Affair', which led to student protests in South African universities and in other parts of the world. He became a wandering exile, living in The Hague, Dar es Salaam, Copenhagen and Rome, before settling in Cairo. In the 1970s, he married the Egyptian feminist intellectual Shahida El-Baz and taught sociology at the American University in Cairo from the 1970s until he retired in the mid-1990s. He returned to South Africa in 2002 and died in 2007 in Pretoria. His life in exile meant that his work was not known or read in the country of his birth and he is much better known in other parts of the world.

This book is about the works of Archie Mafeje. It is the first comprehensive engagement with the entire body of Mafeje's scholarship. It excavates his intellectual ideas and shows the nexus between them and his political environment. Mafeje's work can be categorised into three broad areas: a critique of epistemological and methodological issues in the social sciences; the land and agrarian question in sub-Saharan Africa; and revolutionary theory and politics. Following his death, there has been a great deal of interest in his work. Leftists and liberals alike study Mafeje's life and work, but most writings on him are inadequate – where they are not merely superficial, they are misleadingly inaccurate. Whereas his work is widely respected throughout the African continent and in other parts of the world, his intellectual prowess is treated by many South African academics and intellectuals as something of a rumour. There are two main camps. The first is of social scientists such as Andrew Bank, Leslie Bank and Lungisile Ntsebeza, who have not only written about Mafeje's life history, but also, casually and superficially, about his work. The second camp is of black intellectuals such as Fred Hendricks and others who are interested primarily in Mafeje's debates and strange notions of Africanity as a combative ontology. While the 'life history' camp treats Mafeje as an *enfant terrible*, the 'debates and Africanity' camp treats him as a combative warrior – but the tie that binds these two camps is that they generally write about Mafeje through the biographical medium. This caricature of Mafeje in South African intellectual circles is unfortunate because he was someone whose academic career traversed five decades and gave rise to six books, nine monographs and 140 peer-reviewed journal articles and book chapters, apart from the numerous research reports he wrote as a consultant to the Food and Agriculture Organization (FAO) of the United Nations from 1976 to 1999.

There is a third camp, which, through the works of Adesina and his students, treats Mafeje as the serious scholar that he was. They engage with his work at the level of ideas. My book contributes to the third camp. It consists of three main parts. In the first part I have devoted three chapters to explicating Mafeje's analysis of epistemological and methodological issues in the social sciences. Chapter 1 focuses on his intellectual development through his shift from liberal functionalism to a radical social science and, in particular, on his work on the sociopolitical role of *imbongi* (a sociopolitical commentator or a poet) and his assessment of tribalism and its counterpart, ethnicity. A discussion of Mafeje's critique of the ideological function of tribalism is important for a number of reasons. First, his essay on tribalism effectively established a radical break with his early liberal functionalism,[3] although it constitutes a thematic critique of anthropological concepts, rather than a programmatic critique of the social sciences as such. Second, his analysis of the concept of tribe has been widely misunderstood; this chapter discusses precisely what he had in mind. He did not reject the entity or the institution of tribe as non-existent; rather, he rejected it as an anachronism. The object of his critique was, essentially, the ideology of tribalism.

The second chapter is concerned to dispel the conventional view that Mafeje's critique of the social sciences was limited to a polemic on the discipline of anthropology. The chapter demonstrates that such a view is a partial reading of his work. His argument was that *all* the social sciences are Eurocentric and imperialist. Importantly, chapter 2 shows that to claim Mafeje's critique centres on anthropology makes a reformist of him, rather than the revolutionary scholar that he was. The object of this chapter is to emphasise that his critique of the social sciences is best understood as programmatic (concerned to interrogate the social sciences as social sciences), rather than thematic (concerned to interrogate specific concepts and categories).

The third chapter shows how Mafeje attempted to break with epistemology, but it also demonstrates what he meant when he spoke of ethnography. For that reason, this chapter discusses in detail his magnum opus, *The Theory and Ethnography of African Social Formations*. This book was his most incisive theoretical and methodological statement as well as his attempt at making good on his objective to 'overthrow paradigms themselves'.[4] It underlines the fact that Mafeje did not offer a negative critique of the social sciences but, rather, sought to deconstruct and reconstruct a social science that speaks to the realities of the African continent. Without understanding Mafeje's inductive theoretical and methodological approach to the social sciences – the idea of generating theory from African societies on their own terms – one cannot hope to understand his substantive work on the land and agrarian question and on revolutionary theory. In this sense, all the aspects of Mafeje's work are interrelated and in this book I piece them together. I suspect that Mafeje took the connection between the different aspects of his work for granted, because he did not make the connection explicit in his writings. My aim is to make this connection explicit and to characterise it more fully.

Having laid the foundation with Mafeje's theoretical and methodological approach, I take up his substantive work on land and agrarian issues in sub-Saharan Africa in Part II of this book. It begins in chapter 4 with the problem of land and agriculture on the African continent, using the case of colonial Buganda in Uganda for a deeper understanding of the agrarian revolution and the land question, and moves to a discussion of the agricultural crisis, also discussing the dynamics of African land tenure systems. The next chapter looks at small African producers, or peasants, and their responses to agrarian challenges, which I link to agrarian reform and notions of poverty eradication.

Part III focuses on Mafeje's work on revolutionary theory and politics. Chapter 6, devoted to the post-independence period in the global South, discusses neocolonialism and underdevelopment. The chapter is also concerned with understanding the notion of state capitalism and looks closely at Mafeje's critique of the notion of dual economies. The final chapter attends to his contribution to revolutionary theory and politics, in the context of South and southern Africa. Although in 1978 Mafeje published a paper on the Soweto uprising, much of his work on South African politics appeared from the mid-1980s to the late 1990s. I advance a critique of the popular notion that apartheid South Africa was a case of 'colonialism of a special type' or 'internal colonialism'.[5] I deliberate on the national question in South Africa, Mafeje's call for a socialist democracy and the socialist conception of the national democratic revolution.

What makes Mafeje's ideas so powerful and original is that he was not content with reiterating received or orthodox theories. In all aspects of his work he avoided giving ready-made slogans and easy solutions to complex problems. His ability to combine his political commitment with his intellectual work is what makes his ideas so enduring. Archie Mafeje was in a category by himself.

This book presents an opportunity to tap into some of Mafeje's ideas and considerable intellectual legacy, in order to look at our society anew. Although some of his ideas may be deemed outdated, given that he began writing in the 1960s, they nevertheless stimulate us to think about socio-political and economic issues in different ways. The most important reason why we need to read Mafeje's work is precisely because we need ideas not only here in South Africa, but also throughout the African continent. Mafeje had very important things to say about decolonising knowledge and knowledge production, and about race and class issues, all of which are hugely relevant in South Africa today. We would lose a great deal by not taking seriously some of his and other African intellectuals' ideas. At the moment South African intellectual debates are stale. This is partly because we do not reflect on old ideas, and to freshen up our debates we should revisit the ideas of intellectuals like Mafeje and his peers. The point is not to take Mafeje's ideas slavishly, but to react to them critically and to debate them. Returning to Mafeje's ideas will have an impact on current and future generations of readers. With this book, my goal is not to exhaust discussion of Mafeje's work, but to point out that it exists.

Part I
A Critique of the Social Sciences

1 | From Functionalism to Radical Social Science

From his high school days in the 1950s Archie Mafeje was a member of the Non-European Unity Movement (NEUM), later renamed the Unity Movement of South Africa (UMSA), a radical Marxist political organisation. He was therefore versed in classical Marxism and other radical theories. Yet his early work, published as a postgraduate student at the University of Cape Town (UCT) in the early 1960s, is written from the functionalist anthropological perspective fashionable at the time. This suggests that he was a radical Marxist in Unity Movement circles, while steeped in liberal and functionalist anthropology in his academic work – which indicates the bifurcated existence that still afflicts a good number of black students in South African universities today.

His famous essay of 1971, 'The Ideology of "Tribalism"', established a radical break with his early liberal functionalism, yet constitutes a thematic critique of anthropological categories, of particular themes or concepts within the social sciences, rather than an all-encompassing critique of the social sciences themselves.[1] Notwithstanding his otherwise compelling critique of the ideology of tribalism, his handling of the concept of tribe has been widely misunderstood. Mafeje did not so much reject the entity of tribe, or claim it was non-existent – he rejected it for being anachronistic. In *The Theory and Ethnography of African Social Formations*,[2] he laments this misreading of his work.[3] What Mafeje set out to analyse was the ideology of tribalism, as the title of his 1971 essay clearly indicates; the problem lies in his concession that the entity of tribe existed in Africa at an earlier period. Jimi Adesina's objection is that such a view is not borne out by history or archaeology.[4] There was always migration, movement and intermingling on the African continent. This was interrupted by colonialism and the implementation of arbitrary colonial borders. I believe it is because of this fact that Mafeje says that Europeans invented tribes in Africa.

Mafeje's argument turns on four key issues. First, his understanding of the 'ideology of tribalism' is that it was European in origin: colonial administrators used it in their policy of divide and rule on the African continent. Second, the ideology of tribalism was used by European social scientists not only to explain conflicts in Africa, but also to rationalise colonialism. Third, African leaders have used it for political ends. Finally, insofar as ordinary Africans came to believe in it, tribalism is false consciousness.

Early functionalist writings

Mafeje began his academic career at UCT in 1957 as an undergraduate student, studying biological sciences, with majors in botany and zoology. But because of his poor academic performance in these subjects, in 1960 he switched from the biological sciences to the social sciences, majoring in social anthropology and psychology. From November 1960 to September 1962, Monica Wilson employed him as a research assistant to carry out ethnographic research in the township of Langa, Cape Town. His field notes led to a book co-written with Wilson, *Langa: A Study of Social Groups in an African Township*, published by Oxford University Press in 1963. In the same year, Mafeje completed his Master's degree in social anthropology, his thesis titled 'Leadership and Change: A Study of Two South African Peasant Communities'. The book on Langa seeks to answer two questions: (i) what are the effective social groups in Langa? and (ii) when and why do they cohere, and when and why do they split or dissolve? The second question, the authors argue, leads to one of the 'fundamental problems in social anthropology': what is the basis for the coherence of groups?[5]

Typical of liberal academics, Wilson and Mafeje confess that although South Africa of the 1960s was in a political crisis, they did not ask political questions of their research participants. They attribute this to the banning of the two major political organisations at the time, the African National Congress (ANC) and the Pan Africanist Congress (PAC), but there is a sense in which their explanation is misleading. The research began long before Mafeje was hired as Wilson's assistant. A.R.W. Crosse-Upcott was Wilson's fieldworker from July 1955 until March 1957, some five years before the ANC and PAC were banned in 1960. So Wilson and Mafeje's claim that they could not pose political questions 'because that would have aroused political suspicion' is a rationalisation after the fact. Nor is there a valid reason why Wilson could not ask political questions during Crosse-Upcott's tenure as fieldworker. Silence on political issues highlights one of the major problems with liberal anthropological writings – the tendency to pretend to remain neutral in the face of important political developments, often a reflection of a political commitment antagonistic to the demands and objectives of the suppressed group. It is about acquiescence with the oppressor group, even if they disagree on minor issues. This commitment says more about Wilson than Mafeje, even at this early stage.

The theoretical objectivity (assumed neutrality) of liberal functionalist anthropology does not necessarily mean that its practitioners are apolitical. On the contrary, that anthropologists remain silent on matters political in favour of value-free scientific inquiry is itself a political manoeuvre typical of liberal academics. On the pitfalls of liberalism Adesina observes that it has a tendency to acquiesce with injustice and inequity in order to preserve class, race and gender privileges and that the preservation and defence of these privileges is usually in the form of arguing against government encroachment on individual freedom and liberty. In universities, this takes the form of academic and intellectual freedom.[6]

In anthropological writings certain questions – of slavery, conquest, land dispossession, exploitation and oppression – are hardly ever posed. When they are, they receive rather perfunctory treatment. In Bernard Magubane's view they 'constitute a historical totality of horror, whose structures are bound together in such a way that any one of them considered separately is an abstraction'.[7] In the 1960s, 1970s and 1980s anthropology and history shared the same problem of abstraction. Magubane observes that 'what is striking about the historiography of

South Africa is that each generation seems to think that history began only yesterday and what happened a day before yesterday is "ancient history" that has no relevance for today's problems'. Magubane could see, in the discipline of anthropology, a sinister political project, which, in spite of its purported neutrality, was designed to enable colonial administration and apartheid. He recognises that in the colonial situation anthropologists studied Africans as though they were 'people without history'. Magubane maintains that anthropology became an applied discipline that sought to manage Africans for the purposes of control and exploitation. He contends that although anthropological writings spoke of social change in Africa, they could not account for change because 'failure to account for change was built into the subject as a theoretical discipline'.[8] In the eyes of anthropologists, Magubane writes, Africa serves as 'raw material for anthropological studies'. Because of the ahistorical nature of anthropology, it was unable to account for the changes taking place in Africa since the advent of colonialism, and to the extent that it did, it did so in ethnocentric and mechanistic terms. Anthropological research findings described black people's behaviour and needs, but overlooked the historical and structural context that gave meaning to those needs. Following C. Wright Mills, Magubane refers to such undialectical and seemingly apolitical analyses as 'savage neutralism'.[9]

It was because of Mafeje's participation in the study of Langa that certain of these problems were avoided in his book with Wilson. For example, he uses the terms that research participants used for themselves. Mafeje's first article, 'A Chief Visits Town', is concerned to 'illustrate the attitude of townspeople in Cape Town to chiefs'.[10] In 'townspeople' he includes both black migrant workers and permanent residents. Mafeje is interested in the first group in particular. 'Migrant workers,' he reasons, 'regard themselves as country people and most of them have their families in the country. Their reaction in any given political situation is of particular interest, as it gives the sociologist an opportunity of seeing how the people's aspirations fit in the government's policy of increasing the power of Bantu authorities in the country, and appointing chiefs' representatives in towns or establishing urban Bantu councils.' In particular, Mafeje sets out to describe the arrival in Cape Town of Chief Zwelihle Mtikrakra, the third chief of abaThembu. Beyond the descriptive nature of the article, its theoretical thrust is that by the 1960s there were no tribes to speak of in South Africa. The absence of tribal entities in South Africa means that, contrary to liberal functionalist anthropology, there is no absolute divide between rural and urban settings – owing to the migrant labour system, the Africans in the countryside were already incorporated into the British colonial state by the end of the nineteenth century and the classification 'tribe' is an anachronism. By the time the apartheid government took office, some Xhosa chiefs in Cape Town (such as Chief Joyi) were not only ordinary labourers, but had also transcended ethnic identities in order to fight racial oppression. In his 1963 article, Mafeje notes that Chief Joyi believed that 'the chief is a chief by the grace of the people'.[11] Although Chief Mtikrakra himself was not really well received in Cape Town, and although a certain section of the Langa population regarded chiefs as *oomantshingilane* (police spies) or government stooges, some chiefs had a 'chance of acquiring a position in the national struggle, if they are still, as individuals, acceptable to the modern political leaders'.[12] This is a political reality with which anthropological writings had failed to grapple.

Mafeje's subsequent article, 'The Role of the Bard in a Contemporary African Community', was part of his thematic critique of the anthropological anachronism that reduced African societies to tribes.[13] He uses the English term 'bard' interchangeably with, or to translate, the isiXhosa word *imbongi* because he saw a similarity between *imbongi* and the bard in medieval Europe.[14] In anthropological literature and linguistics, the bard is reduced to a praise-singer. Mafeje concludes that this is a misplaced assessment because bards are sociopolitical critics more than praise-poets and argues that anthropologists and linguists are 'over-emphasising the wrong aspect of the institution'.[15] There is a functional difference between bards and individual members of society who compose praise-poems for themselves or their loved ones. Anthropologists saw the difference only in status: those who act as praise-singers as a calling and those who do so for personal reasons. The former have greater political significance while the latter act for self-entertainment. As a result of the seriousness of the institution of *imbongi*, not every member of society can stand up at public gatherings and recite a poem, either for a chief or the general public. Those who do might do so for personal gain or recognition, but that is hardly the central function of the bard. In arguing that *imbongi* is a sociopolitical critic, Mafeje does not deny that *imbongi* might from time to time praise the chief (every political institution has its legitimisers). The point was to call into question the view that *imbongi* is primarily a praise-singer.

Although the terms 'poet' and 'bard' are often used synonymously, Mafeje contends that the latter is a term of Celtic origin used to designate ancient Celtic poets who enjoyed certain privileges and functions. The term 'bard' comes from the Latin *bardi*, a title for national poets and minstrels among the people of Gaul and Brittany. Although the institution disappeared in Gaul, there is 'evidence of its continued existence in Wales, Ireland, Brittany and Northern Scotland, where Celtic people survived the Latin and Teutonic conquests'.[16] In Wales, an organised society with hereditary rights and privileges, the bards were akin to royal families and were exempt from tax and military service. Their duty was to celebrate victories and sing hymns of praise, and they gave poetic expression to societal sentiments. In this sense, they were very influential. In Ireland, too, bards were a distinct social category, and also enjoyed hereditary rights. They were divided into three types, each of which had a distinct role: those who celebrated victories and sang hymns of praise; those who chanted the laws of the nation; and those who gave poetic genealogies and family histories. In South Africa the role of *imbongi* is to interpret and organise public opinion. If *imbongi* is unable to do so, he cannot attain the status of a national poet. The major difference between the South African bard and his European counterpart is that the former does not enjoy hereditary rights and privileges such as tax exemption. South African bards are not an organised society. They pursue their endeavours as individual members of society. *Imbongi* is self-appointed and his success depends largely on how people respond to him. If the people respond positively, *imbongi* could be elevated to the level of *imbongi yakomkhulu* (the poet of the main residence) or *imbongi yesizwe* (the poet of the nation). In the latter sense, he transcends 'tribal' identities.

For Mafeje, there were three key issues that characterised both the South African and the European bards: they usually emerged from the ranks of commoners (were not of royal blood); their role and substance depended on how they were received by the people; and they had freedom to criticise (overtly or covertly) those in power. Having laid this historical and conceptual background at the beginning of 'The Role of the Bard', Mafeje goes on to analyse the poems of *imbongi* known as Melikhaya Mbutuma, who was *imbongi* of abaThembu's paramount chief, Sabata Dalindyebo. Mafeje followed Mbutuma as part of his fieldwork in what was then the Transkei for his Master's thesis in 1963.

The methodological lessons to be drawn from Mafeje's article on the role of the bard relate to literary, archival research, ethnography and textual analysis. The poems are in isiXhosa; Mafeje first reproduces them in the original and then translates them into English to make their meaning apparent to the reader – but also to subject them to critical scrutiny. Although the process of translation is prone to clumsiness, his translation is accurate and the meaning is not lost. *Imbongi yosiba* (the poet who writes down his poems) is usually distinguished from *imbongi yomthonyama* (the poet who recites his poems from memory), but Mbutuma's poems were in written form, 'except some of the shorter ones which I wrote down as he recited them in public gatherings'.[17] Mbutuma's poems cover political events in the Transkei region from 1959 to 1963.

In citing these poems, Mafeje illustrates the role of the bard as a mediator between two social categories, the ruler and the ruled. Although the poems are political in content, Mafeje's goal is not to show Mbutuma's political astuteness, but to highlight the role of the bard as a mediator (although to mediate in the events of the Transkei of the late 1950s and early 1960s was *ipso facto* to play a political role), but when the situation fails to resolve, *imbongi* is forced to abandon his role as a mediator and join forces with either side. If he sides with the ruler whose authority is being questioned, he loses his social status, which depends more on acceptance by the people than on the ruler.

A reader of Mafeje's article will not fail to notice his political fidelity to the people, which is quite evident in his analysis of the poems and the general political developments in Transkei of the 1960s. Moreover, unlike social anthropologists such as Isaac Schapera,[18] Mafeje clearly demonstrates that the people were not merely impressed by the form of the poems from *imbongi* – they were impressed by the content or substance, and when they asked for *imbongi* who 'says worthwhile things', or when the chief's entourage took away the microphone from *imbongi* who was critical of the chief, everyone knew that this was testament to Mbutuma's political astuteness.

On the ideology of tribalism

Mafeje's argument is that few social scientists had been able to write about Africa without invariably making reference to tribalism and it was not clear whether this was a distinguishing feature of the African continent. He argues that from the viewpoint of the sociology of knowledge, objective reality is not easily distinguishable from subjective dispossession. In this sense, social scientific categories are hard to separate from the ideological baggage of their peddlers. It is not by accident, therefore, that when African scholars write about their societies they tend to reach conclusions and to deploy concepts different from those of their Euro-American counterparts. According to Mafeje, liberal idealists, Marxist materialists and African converts alike tended to assign nomenclature that was fundamentally at odds not only with African history, but also with the present day. The problem with social scientific writings in Africa was not necessarily one of concrete realities, but one of ideology – particularly the ideology of tribalism.

The phenomenon of tribalism is traceable to European colonialism and its ideological reconstruction of African realities. Europeans regarded the African continent as distinctly tribal, and European social scientists were unable to transcend the colonial categorisations of Africa used by colonial administrators – precisely because their studies were the handmaidens of colonialism. The assumption that Africa was tribal produced certain 'ideological predispositions that made it difficult for those associated with the system to view these societies in any other light'.[19] Colonial anthropologists, and some of their African counterparts, wrote about

Africa as if there were no significant economic and political changes on the continent by the turn of the twentieth century. It thus stands to reason, Mafeje maintains, that if tribalism is uniquely African, then the ideology that perpetuates it is distinctly European.

While some European social scientists sought to exonerate themselves by arguing that they did not use the term 'tribe' to denigrate Africans, but because Africans themselves tended to use it,[20] it is significant that the term surfaced only when English was spoken, as Mafeje argues. Even if it were true that Africans use the term, social scientists are not bound to use the same terms as their objects of inquiry, and their argument ends up as phenomenological affirmation of what the objects of inquiry say, instead of a critique rooted in historical and wider contexts. At any rate, the question stands: From where did the 'natives' derive these categories in the first place? Sometimes, adopting the terminology of the objects of inquiry would be useful and even desirable, but it could also perpetuate stereotypes, particularly if the researcher uses derogatory terms uncritically to mimic the objects of research. Things are not always what they are called. In South Africa the word 'tribe' has no equivalent in local languages. People tend to speak of a nation, clan or lineage, or simply identify themselves according to the territory from which they originate.

Mafeje considers that tribes, noticeably the central unit of analysis in anthropological writings, were, by and large, created by colonial authorities and were a result of the setting of colonial borders, which hindered the free flow of African people. That anthropologists were uncritical or otherwise unable to transcend the notion of tribe says something about their complicity in colonial domination and the structuring of African societies. Anthropological studies were serviceable to colonial administrators; it is not surprising that Africans, who are still shaped by colonial distortions, continue to use the term in spite of its connotations. The negative images that Africans come to have about themselves cannot be understood outside this historical and sociological context. In *The German Ideology*, Karl Marx and Friedrich Engels observe that in every period in history the ruling ideas are always those of the ruling class. This means that 'the class which is the ruling *material* force of society is at the same time its ruling *intellectual* force'.[21]

Significantly, Mafeje reasons, anthropologists had ignored any noticeable changes in Africa by the turn of the twentieth century. The essentialist and purist nature of the assumption that there were no changes in Africa conveniently depoliticised the colonial intrusion that forced African people into migrant labour. This is the period in which Africans were being ensnared into the web of extra-economic and political relations. Even when Africans were residing in urban areas, anthropologists always sought to re-tribalise them by tracing their rural roots or by drawing invidious tribal distinctions among them through perpetuating stereotypes.[22] This was not the only method they adopted, since they sought also to draw distinctions between urban-based and rural-based Africans, the former purportedly aspiring to a 'Western way of life', 'Europeanisation' or 'civilisation' while the latter were referred to as 'red people' or 'pagans'. Aspiring to a Western way of life meant that Africans paid the heavy price of deculturation. Such changes in African societies, emanating as they did from extractive economic and political relations, led to studies of social change.

Curiously, while anthropologists saw that African societies were not as static as they had hitherto thought, they did not dispense with tribe as a unit of analysis. The concept became an organising framework in a different way. Initially considered a rural phenomenon, it was now discovered that tribalism persists in urban areas as well – colonialists and anthropologists re-tribalised Africans while at the same time seeking to 'civilise' them. The rural/urban divide was, of course, a false dichotomy since the urban African was the same as the rural African. Sociologically, people adjust or adapt to the environments they find themselves in.

Mafeje saw Arnold Epstein as one of the few anthropologists willing to dispense with the concept of tribe.[23] Epstein contends that Africans living in urban areas were not necessarily affected by tribalism; in the copper mines of Zambia, miners refused to accept 'tribal elders' as their representatives or leaders in negotiations with mine management. Waged workers were suspicious of salaried leaders. Having noted this, Mafeje concludes that this 'was another instance of class formation among Africans'.[24] I believe that this is a controversial point, which some may wish to dispute and to argue that Mafeje mistook social stratification for class – that gradations within the same stratum need not admit class differentiation and the so-called salariat is not a class apart from the proletariat. For Mafeje this was a known datum, however, in that he did not declare the miners to be a class proper, but rather that they were gaining class consciousness. Enthusiastic about such developments, Mafeje was moved to assert that these were winds of change that were fast becoming a reality. He mentions political scientists who came with notions of modernisation in what they considered to be modernising states. That such theories were no different from anthropological civilising missions is not something Mafeje offers to discuss. He goes on to argue, however, that anthropologists were incorrigible in their use of the term 'tribe' as an analytical category, only this time they were more determined to buttress the 'persistence and resilience' of tribes, rather than their disintegration or disequilibrium. While anthropologists initially sought the tribe in rural areas, they now sought to identify its resilience and persistence in urban areas. This represented, according to Mafeje, a shift (although not a change) in the ideological standpoint of anthropologists. For them, modernisation was not incompatible with tribalism or traditionalism. They thought 'tribal values' were an explanation for Africans' reluctance to embrace modernity and that Africans would fully modernise once they had dispensed with tribalism.

Mafeje says that unlike anthropologists who wholeheartedly embraced the tribal ideology to explain both the successes and failures of modernisation in Africa, political scientists and African nationalists used the ideology of tribalism only to account for failures in modernisation and, unlike anthropologists, preferred to speak of problems of integration, penetration and mobilisation. In spite of this, political scientists had conceptual problems much bigger than those of anthropologists. They lacked the ethnographic detail of knowledge available to anthropologists and their use of the tribal framework made it difficult for them to account for similar problems in other parts of the world. As a result, they fell victim to Eurocentrism in the same way as their anthropologist counterparts. The only difference is that anthropologists have *ab initio* been engaged in tribal studies.

Having discussed the political antecedents and ideological function of the concept of tribalism, Mafeje turns his attention to its conceptual problems. His question, one that immediately arises, is whether tribalism exists without the existence of tribes. Anthropologists typically described tribes as societies that were 'self-contained, autonomous communities practising subsistence economy with no external trade'.[25] In the 1940s, Meyer Fortes and E.E. Evans-Pritchard introduced new terms such as 'centralised states', 'stateless' and 'acephalous' societies.[26] Yet it is odd to suggest that African societies were, by the twentieth century, still self-contained, autonomous communities that were practising subsistence economy. Thus, Mafeje reasons, the continued use of the word 'tribe' is a contradiction in terms.

Instead of dispensing with the concept altogether, the social anthropologist Isaac Schapera shifted the proverbial goalposts by redefining tribes as 'separate "political communities", each claiming exclusive rights to a given territory and managing its affairs independently of external control'.[27] This is a loosely formulated definition; if this is what passes for a tribe, then surely an array of societies, including nation states, are tribes. The constituent elements of a tribe outlined in Schapera's definition are to be found in many places even to this day. In this regard, anthropologists, following Schapera's definition, were not only contradicting themselves, but were also, as evidenced by the double standard of the definition, performing an ideological role. It is noteworthy that according to Mafeje the concept of culture never figured in the foregoing definitions of tribe until the arrival of pluralist sociologists and political scientists. Moreover, by 1969, anthropologists had dispensed with the term and sought, once more, to redefine it. By then, Philip Hugh Gulliver had defined a tribe as 'any group of people which is distinguished, by its members and by others, on the basis of cultural-regional criteria'.[28] Again, this is not an airtight definition. There is no reason to suppose that the same cannot be said of European societies. Moreover, the notion of a tribe had, in Gulliver's view, become a subjective perception.

Having mounted a critique of colonial anthropological writings, Mafeje concedes that 'although their reasons are suspect, anthropologists *may have been right* in insisting that traditional or pre-colonial African societies, large or small, were tribes'.[29] Although Mafeje concedes that anthropologists might have been right, there is very little evidence, on the basis of the definitions he enumerates, that this was actually the case. If I am reluctant to endorse what he says, it is not because I believe that Mafeje was wrong; it is simply that he himself was uncertain about the veracity of what he said – 'anthropologists *may* have been right'. In his second impression on the concept, Mafeje concedes unambiguously that a 'careful analysis of African social formations would indicate that tribal formations *did* exist in Africa but that they were not characteristic of *all* regions of the continent'.[30] Adesina questions the validity of this. He argues that 'the problem is that Mafeje pursued his line of thought at the expense of conceding that the category might have been valid at an earlier time. Not only does Anthropology deal with its objects of enquiry outside of history, it is ill-equipped to address the issues of history.'[31] Mafeje goes on to say that he did not deny the existence of tribal sentiments and ideology on the African continent. His argument is that this ideology and sentiment has to be reconceptualised in the post-independence period. Mafeje says we have to make a distinction between someone who tries to preserve the traditional integrity, customs and autonomy of their tribe and someone who invokes tribal ideology in order to maintain power, not in a rural but in an urban setting, and thereby undermines and exploits fellow Africans. For Mafeje, 'the fact that [the ideology of tribalism] works, as is often pointed out by tribal ideologists, [was] no proof that "tribes" or "tribalism" exist in any objective sense'.[32]

That tribalism seems to work in Africa is not a sign that the term exists objectively but, rather, an indication of false consciousness on the part of Africans. This is so because in subscribing to tribalism, which leads them to ignore the real causes of their suffering, they unwittingly submit to voluntary servitude. Tribalism is of great benefit to African leaders who peddle tribal rhetoric because it leads away from a correct comprehension of reality and, in the process, conceals the exploitative role of the African elite. It is 'an ideology in the original Marxist sense', something that the African elite share with their 'European fellow-ideologists'.[33] Mafeje points out that if tribalism per se does not matter, the ideology of tribalism does – for three reasons. First, it performs a capitalist, colonialist and imperialist function that obscures the nature of economic and power relations domestically (it also performs the same function between Africa and capitalist countries of the West). Second, it is not only divisive among Africans, but also between Africans and people from outside the continent. Third, it is an outdated concept that thwarts analysis and cross-cultural comparisons. Elsewhere, Mafeje argues that '"tribalism" is more an ideological reflex than an index of some concrete existence in Africa',[34] and he laments the fact that his earlier critique of tribalism was taken to mean a denial of the existence of tribes in Africa. That is not so, Mafeje argues. His original argument 'was that the idea that all African societies were "tribes" was a result of the colonial legacy on the continent' and he concedes that the problem with this misunderstanding may be a result of the fact that 'the original paper was not definitional and was concerned mainly with exposing the falsity of that assumption [that all African societies were tribes] by pointing to contrary cases'.[35]

Mafeje maintains that '"tribes" refer to particular forms of political organisation which are kin-based. The chief is the most senior man of the most senior lineage of the founding clan, whether putative or real'.[36] Mafeje was only shifting the deckchairs here. First, if 'kin-based relation' is what makes the political organisation a tribe, how many of abaThembu, for example, are abaThembu because of consanguinity? Consanguine relations and political structure relate to entirely different elements of social life. Second, if this is what defines a tribe, what is a clan or lineage? It is not uncommon to use the label 'tribe' to define people who share a common language – even if the sub-variations of the language are such as to make aspects of communication mutually unintelligible. If, as Mafeje argues, the word 'tribe' does not exist in the indigenous languages, what is the point of African intellectuals seeking to sustain the idea? What makes 11 million amaZulu a tribe and 5.3 million Scots a nation?

In his second impression on the concepts of tribalism, Mafeje writes that African intellectuals believe that the European assumption that there is tribalism in Africa reflects the usual European stereotypes derived from colonialism.[37] Significantly, this leads to an ideological and epistemological disjuncture between African intellectuals and their Western counterparts. Mafeje goes on to argue that the problem 'is not to decry a spurious category called "tribalism" but to confront the problem of *cultural pluralism* within modern nation-states which, deriving from the European historical antecedent, are supposed to be unitary. What is called "tribalism" in Africa is often an attempt by disadvantaged sociocultural groups to gain more social space within the given political and economic setup. In the circumstances, democratic pluralism is at issue rather than a dictatorial insistence on misconceived unitarism.'[38]

Mafeje suggests that with democratic pluralism tribalism would wither away; yet this ignores the patent reality that democracy does in fact facilitate a resort to narrow jingoism in mobilising support or articulating grievances. There is little evidence that democracy necessarily attenuates tribalism. Mafeje modified his earlier position on tribalism; he oscillated between cultural pluralism and democratic pluralism. It is far from clear that the two are the same or that the existence of one necessarily entails the existence of the other. Mafeje did not quite spell out what he really had in mind when he invoked the notion of pluralism. In an article titled 'The Bathos of Tendentious Historiography', he says that 'in recent years there has been an observable social drift toward *democratic pluralism* ... Democratic pluralism is more of a social than a political concept. For instance, it does not mean "multipartyism" but, rather, the right of people(s) to form their own organisations for self-fulfilment and for having a direct input in the formulation of national policy regarding things that affect them.'[39] He did not use pluralism as it was used by anthropologists and subsequently criticised by Magubane.

As early as 1969, Magubane had questioned the notion of pluralism and its anthropological counterpart, tribalism. According to him, anthropological writings on pluralism and tribalism were too tentative and superficial to explain what was taking place in Africa during colonialism.[40]

Symptoms were treated as underlying causes. For Magubane, the problem with pluralism is that it treats social cleavages as though they are innate or as though societies are static. In this regard, the pluralist anthropologists could not construct what Magubane calls, following Perry Anderson, 'a totalising history'.[41] Magubane's objection is that conflicts in Africa should be historicised and contextualised and not reduced to psychological variables like tribalism or the purportedly innate hatred between ethnic groups. It remains the case, of course, that for societies to be considered societies they ought to have some degree of coherence and stability. However, there are no societies without internal divisions and frictions. The issue, for Magubane, is to explain these frictions in depth and contextually (that is, finding their root causes). Magubane maintains that, properly understood, present-day conflicts stem from colonial and imperial rule. The administrative personnel may have changed, but the economic and institutional structures remain.

The problem with pluralist anthropology is to isolate ethnic conflicts and other social features in space and in time.[42] For Magubane, the pluralists were reluctant to situate problems in Africa in the wider context of the colonial situation or as an extension of the capitalist metropole. To the extent that African societies were brought together through arbitrary colonial borders, they were robbed of the opportunity to develop organic institutions that would foster unity and solidarity. The notion of pluralism failed to explain the role of governments in denying societies the opportunity to foster organic unity. Because some pluralists considered tribalism to be the source of conflict, they assumed that African societies will always be ridden by conflicts since, in their view, tribalism was the state of nature in Africa. In many respects, the concept of pluralism as was used did not take into account economic and social analysis of Africa – what it did do was to brush aside core issues and make conflict and tribalism seem natural. Ultimately, Magubane observes, this led to the view that these conflicts would sort themselves out or die a natural death.

Magubane further contends that the use of such concepts as tribalism and pluralism in explaining conflicts in Africa was a case of stereotypes prevailing over reality; to understand the true nature of these concepts one had to consider colonial maladministration and neocolonialism. Parochial loyalties existed and at times manifested themselves in ethnic terms, but such loyalties were typically based on *perceived material interests by those who exploit them*.[43] To the extent that pluralists invoked history, it was only to invoke prejudices, many of which were devoid of analysis of present-day problems in Africa. Pluralists simply appealed to notions of an African as a tribesman in an essentially primitive state. The focus – even when aided by empirical research – was on epiphenomena, not the core socio-historical and structural realities. Epistemologically, pluralist anthropologists, inspired by John Furnivall, misread his argument.[44] Magubane argues that 'despite the limitations of the concept of pluralism as used by Furnivall, among the recent pluralists the concept becomes not only a distortion of the social realities but a despairing philosophy … Pluralism, as used in this sense, covers such disparate social and economic historical formations that it loses validity.'[45]

Magubane's central critique of pluralism is that it merely described a multiplicity of ethnic groups within a particular nation state, yet it said very little about the relationship between the said groups – save when they were in conflict. Pluralism on the part of anthropologists only meant 'multi' and was never qualified or accompanied by reference to concrete historical situations.

On ethnic groups, ethnic divisions and ethnicity

Mafeje considered that the terms 'tribalism' and 'ethnicity', typically deployed interchangeably by social scientists, were used as 'things in themselves'; the terms are 'illusory and need to be deconstructed and replaced by radical or transcendent thought-categories'.[46] In an article on the use of tribalism in Africa, Peter Ekeh notes that 'while it now appears that the term "ethnic group" has replaced the disparaged concept of "tribe" in African scholarship, there is no clear statement about the relationship between the two – whether, especially, there has been transition from one to the other and whether there is persistent relevance in the previous analysis of tribes for our understanding of ethnic groups in modern Africa'.[47] Ethnicity was the successor to tribalism in part because it was considered

less offensive. Mafeje claims that the two concepts have the same ideological connotations. The advantage the term 'ethnicity' has over the term
'tribalism' is that Africans have no objection to its usage, but although 'ethnicity' has gained currency among African scholars, this, Mafeje realises,
does not explain why it is correlated with the crisis of state power in Africa
and elsewhere. He contends that ethnicity may not be what it is presumed
to be – as far as he is concerned the term is a metaphor. Although in his
classic text *The Theory and Ethnography of African Social Formations* Mafeje
denies the existence of tribalism but not of tribes, in the essay 'Multi-
Party Democracy and Ethnic Divisions in Africa', while conceding that
the idea of ethnicity is a pervasive problem in Africa, he denies that it is
attributable to the existence of ethnic groups: 'In our interrogation, while
acknowledging the fact that "ethnicity" has become a pervasive problem
in Africa, we will try to dispel the supposition that it is attributable to
the existence of a multiplicity of natural units of affiliation called "ethnic
groups" within African countries.'[48]

Mafeje returns to classical sociology on the distinction between a social
group and a social category. A social group is characterised by necessary
patterns of social interaction (a lineage, an association, a religious sect)
whereas a social category, although characterised by a common identity,
has no necessary or regular patterns of interaction. He believes that the
same was true of the so-called ethnic groups, members of the same race,
sex or faith. It might come as a surprise, he surmises, but the same is also
true of Africa's political elites. That they are dominant does not mean that
they are necessarily a coherent whole, or homogeneous. They are a category consisting of different social factions and in this sense they are a
loose category, yet for me there is reason to believe that this would apply
to any social group. I believe that it is shared characteristics that make
them a group, not face-to-face interaction or homogeneity. For Mafeje, it
is continued internecine conflicts among the elites that usually give rise
to labels such as 'tribalism' or 'ethnicity'. My view is that Mafeje's argument limits the problem to the political elite and misses the possibility
that contestations and tensions that give rise to jingoism exist at the level
of ordinary citizens. Controversially, Mafeje argues that members of the

African elite are too loosely organised and their interests too personalised to constitute a class in itself and for itself. The social category of elite is not the same thing as class.

In support of the foregoing claim, Mafeje contends that 'historically, it is unimaginable that members of a hegemonic class would engage in unbridled mutual extermination and preside over the destruction of their supreme instrument of social control, the state, as has become the order of the day in Africa'.[49] If that is the case, it is not clear how one should classify the African elite. Mafeje misses the target in this regard. What makes an elite an elite is its relations to other levels in society – social distance – and its relative size. Sub-divisions and intra-group conflicts are inherent in any social group. I am inclined to think that a distinction has to be made between contestation over control of the state between factions of the elite and situations where the legitimacy of the state and political society itself is at stake. Coherence is not an essential element in the characterisation of a group as a cultural, economic or political elite.

What matters, as was always the case with Mafeje, is to subject concepts to critical scrutiny. No theory or concept is taken for granted in his work. The question thus is whether or not such internecine struggles are neces-sarily a result of multi-ethnicity in African countries. Mafeje denies such an assumption and argues that the existence of ethnic groups or ethnic existence does not necessarily entail ethnicity. In his own words, 'exist-ence is not necessarily limited to systems of social classification'.[50]

Just as he makes a distinction between social groups and social cat-egories, Mafeje makes a distinction between categorical and structural relations. To the extent that 'systems of social classification are notional and taken for granted by their bearers they are passive and non-binding whereas socially structured relations are not only binding but are also purposeful and dynamic'.[51] People from different backgrounds or socio-cultural identities can live together in peace without discriminating against one another or exhibiting ethnicity. But 'in times of structural conflict not between whole categories but between interacting groups this could occur'. It is at moments such as these that 'perceived identities of difference are called into play'. Ethnic conflict (or ethnicity) is a result of greater interaction among people with sociocultural identities living in the same geopolitical space, a result of processes of state formation in post-independence Africa. Unlike pre-colonial and colonial wars, ethnic conflicts are not struggles for liberation but for relative advantage within the same sociopolitical framework. If anything, they are a distraction and do more harm than good; Mafeje concludes that they are not 'struggles for autonomy but for relative advantage within the same set-up. They are, thus, in theory *non-transcendent*.'[52]

But if this is the case, how does one understand secessionist movements or projects such as Biafra or South Sudan? Although intermittent or occurring not permanently but periodically, ethnic conflicts are nevertheless recurrent and are invoked typically at moments of crisis of state power. In this way, such conflicts become a political culture and an ideological tool to maintain or to gain power. Not only does this entail the centralisation of power, it also leads to ethnic competition. According to Mafeje, ethnic competition does not necessarily translate into ethnic conflict even when certain modes of existence or specialised fields of endeavour (pastoralism, arable agriculture, fishing) have become part of certain communities. With the possibility of competition for access to resources, such communities might also, by virtue of their specialisation, need to co-operate. From this perspective, ethnic diversity could contribute to social division of labour, but in post-independence Africa this is not to any extent the case, even if it might be true of pre-colonial Africa.

Mafeje claims that whatever conflict may arise in these situations, it is never widespread; that ethnicity does not occur at local level in mundane activities, but at national level where there is serious political competition. But this is not entirely accurate – when killings begin, they do so as local phenomena. It is significant, however, that ethnic antagonisms connote a state of national politics that deviates from the objectives of liberation movements and thus undermines nation building as envisaged at the moment of independence. For Mafeje, ethnicity is more the progeny of modern African politics than of African antiquity, and from a historical point of view it is hard to say that there is any organic link between the phenomenon of ethnicity and what are called ethnic groups. There are parallels between ethnicity and what people are called or what they call themselves. Ethnicity is peddled by African political elites in order to gain power or to maintain it. Only then do people embrace it as a result of classificatory systems or categorical identities. Political elites are fully aware of these weaknesses and proclivities, and take advantage of them to further their own ambitions.

Mafeje considers that ideology as false consciousness cuts both ways. This is so because the kind of falsity peddled by elites obscures objective reality such as class differentiation and group conflicts among the same people – and it also undermines co-operation among people of differing ethnic origins. Mafeje's claim, however, casts the political elites as all-knowing and consummate masters of history whereas sometimes they are both initiating and responding to social crises, and could be hapless beings swept up in the current of history, just like everyone else. Ultimately, the sorriest casualties of the ideology of ethnicity are the ordinary people and not the elites. The reproduction of ethnic identities is a work of serious indoctrination. As ethnicity may lead to disaster, the question that confronts sociologists is why African elites continue with what would suggest a level of irrationality in the elite mobilisation of ethnic jingoism. Self-aggrandisement on the part of the elites is not a satisfactory answer.

Part of the reason for this, Mafeje argues, is not just class interests, but sectional interests. Where class interests are vital to the class as a whole, sectional interests, if not managed carefully, could jeopardise the interests of the whole. Mafeje's claim does not really address the question. It would seem extraordinary that elites would want to jeopardise not only their opponents' interests, but their own interests as well, for sectional interests could threaten not just sections but also the whole. Mafeje does not immediately address this issue, but he argues that Africans in sub-Sahara have been the slowest in the world in developing an authentic class and although African ruling elites had bourgeois aspirations, they nonetheless demonstrated no consistent capitalist outlook, discipline and ethics. Instead, they plundered state resources and engaged in corrupt activities. Mafeje suspects that the real problem lay in their inability to 'convert states revenues into real capital'.[53] Tellingly, there is no qualitative difference in patterns of investment between mineral-rich and mineral-poor African countries.

Mafeje reasons that ethnicity is either an admission of failure or an excuse to cover up shortcomings. He calls this an 'ideological ploy' and not a class ideology. In the context of cunning manoeuvres by African elites, he considers the use of the term 'ideological ploy' more than justified, but the question is what makes it ideological – and it is ideological because of its ideational or cognitive impact on the people. What the elites believe or do not believe is somewhat irrelevant – it is the impact of what they say to their target constituencies that matters. This, in Mafeje's language, is an ideological reflex and not ideology itself. Although he said this, Mafeje still believed in the explanatory value of ideology in the classical sense, and by ideology he refers to the rationalisation of class interests, which, in the main, applies to hegemonic classes since they wish to remain dominant. The term 'rationalisation' refers to both practical considerations and normative claims to justify them; ideology can be used in a positive sense and also in a negative sense. Given this ambiguity, Mafeje reasons that it is difficult to tell what the guiding ideology of the emergent African elites is supposed to be. The absence of a broader societal and regional vision has led to the 'degenerative political culture' of ethnicity and to petty dictators. In this sense, African elites have no competitive advantage over others in the world. The disintegration of African states and economic decay can be explained similarly. The effects of ethnicity are typically acknowledged, but are hardly seen as ideology per se – it is ethnic-consciousness, instead, that is seen as ideology proper, and ethnicity is seen in negative terms because it is used to gain power by manipulating people's sentiments. In this sense, it can be described as antipathetic. Mafeje thought that it was important to note that there exist sympathetic forms of organisation among people of the same ethnic origin. He gives examples of mutual-help associations, burial associations and social clubs, which tend to be inward looking and are usually found in urban areas where newcomers might suffer alienation and anonymity, and social and emotional insecurity.

In colonial anthropological parlance these organisations are called tribal associations; anthropologists refer to them as voluntary associations.

Yet they miss the contradictory nature of such a label in that, by their own admission, tribal organisations are prescriptive while voluntary organisations are discretionary insofar as individuals have freedom to choose. Voluntary organisations were seen as affirmations of the discourse of social change, the supposed progress from barbarism to civilisation. Aside from these colonial epithets, Mafeje notes that the underlying issue here is that the so-called tribal associations are people's organisations and not intended for exploiting or oppressing others. From the members' point of view the value of the organisations 'was instrumental rather than ideological'; 'their relations were personal rather than categorical'.[54] Mafeje considers it is incorrect to refer to solidarity of their kind as ethnicity since this term connotes an evocative, impersonal and pernicious force. Above all, it could be argued that ethnicity is the exact opposite of these associations because it militates against their mundane and innocent interest.

Mafeje analyses what he calls, in anthropological terms, 'exegetic texts', authored by living subjects in their own context, excerpts and quotations based on views from ordinary people who were involved in ethnic conflicts in Africa, specifically the Bahutu-Batutsi clash that led to the Rwanda genocide and the *majimboism* in Kenya.[55] Having discussed these texts, or verbal reports, which, he concedes, are 'very scanty', Mafeje notes that the problem in Africa is not necessarily the existence of multi-ethnicity but, rather, that African leaders supposedly dealing with the national question in their own countries are the very people at the root cause of political conflicts. African elites are the cause, or 'authors' in Mafeje's language, and not the bearers of ethnic identity because socially, economically and politically they are too far from and free of the conflicts they fuel. Mafeje reiterates that ethnic identity on its own was innocuous and there was nothing to it that could be said to be intrinsic since in many ways it can be replaced with other identities such as religion, race or regionalism. On the African continent there has been a blanket approach to conflict resolutions, which relate to liberal notions of rational negotiations – but although negotiations are important in their own right they tend to run against vested interests, and here Mafeje criticises liberal social scientists for failing to recognise the concept of contradiction in political conflicts. He does not say much about the concept but, given his partiality to revolutionary theory, he is invoking Mao Tse-Tung's antagonistic and non-antagonistic contradictions. Simply, the former speaks to irreconcilable differences between those waging the struggle and their enemy, while the latter refers to reconcilable differences among the comrades and fellow travellers waging the struggle (in any case, the powerful political elites would rarely be willing to negotiate away their power and comparative advantages). In this way, wars or conflicts of resistance are not at all irrational. Additionally, they are not likely to be solved by conflict resolution or negotiations unless and until their root cause has been effectively dealt with.

In this sense, conflict resolutions tend to deal with symptoms rather than causes. Because liberal ideals of negotiations tend to dominate the discourse of conflict resolutions in Africa, it could be said that the symptomatic reading of problems is to be expected. In another sense, there is the old question of the superstructure and the material base, which remains unaddressed. Although Mafeje does not mention it, it is nevertheless latent in his analysis – for example, he questions issues of superstructure such as the law and state institutions, which are usually invoked to solve problems of ethnic conflicts. Yet these issues, despite their importance, hardly succeed in solving societal problems. It is only later in his argument that Mafeje speaks about the material base of ethnic social formations in Africa, arguing that it has been undermined by modern developments in the process of which ethnic identities are used as tools to mediate or forge new social relations and for promoting new social interests. Against Claude Ake and Okwudiba Nnoli, who argue that lack of commoditisation of social relations in Africa is one of the reasons for the persistence of ethnic identities, Mafeje argues that the opposite is true because if there is anything that capitalism successfully introduced on the continent it is the market system – which necessarily includes the sale of labour power.[56] Mafeje contends that in the African market system, trade or circulation competes with agriculture not only in national, but also in regional economies and national and regional trade means that people of different ethnic origin would have to learn each other's languages. This then leads to what he calls acculturation. 'As far as this is concerned, it is quite possible that African peoples are ahead of their ruling elites.'[57]

If one were to excuse the awkward term 'acculturation', which Mafeje uses quite freely, the issue in the foregoing quote is that through inter-action or intermingling ethnic identities tend to be irrelevant (although sometimes latent) until they are used or manipulated by political powermongers. This idea, in typical left discourse, sees the masses – when they engage in acts that the intellectuals consider contradictory to their assumed interests – as hapless victims manipulated by their elites, and yet because of their perceived interests, people participate enthusiastically in the extermination of others who are of different hues, creed or other iden-tities. Mafeje's denunciation of the African elites is in this sense typical of the class-centric discourse of the left.

In the context of processes of social integration it becomes important to decentralise power. Decentralising power gives space for local initiatives so that people can express themselves in various ways. Mafeje contends also that decentralising power does away with fragmentation among ordinary citizens and brings them together. This may, however, not be the case because such fragmentations simply play out at the local level. The contradictions that manifest as national phenomena are typic-ally experienced at local levels, in which segments of a local government or even a town can become the basis for new fragments invented in the process of competition over resources. Mafeje argues that 'strategically and in the long term, there is no advantage in fragmenting the existing African states'.[58] When he talks about decentralisation he had in mind the delegation of authority and responsibility to provincial and local governments – something neither new nor novel. One might argue that even in centralist states such as the United Kingdom substantial work and autonomy happens at local levels. One would be hard-pressed to find an African country where all powers and decision making are concentrated at the national level. Several African countries are federations, yet Mafeje does not advocate a federal structure such as in the United States, states within a state. Such a model, he says, could increase regional antagonisms, especially where regions coincide with ethnic maps.

In many African countries prospects for nation building were undermined by the 'bourgeois form of government adopted at independence'.[59] The claim that Africans are generally incompetent, autocratic and corrupt does not, on its own, suffice as an explanation since many African leaders who have the potential to make changes have been imprisoned, banned, exiled, assassinated or murdered, often with the help of imperialist Western powers. Mafeje concedes that ultimately the use of concepts such as ethnicity, ethnic groups or multi-partyism is prejudicial and quite Eurocentric. For one thing, multi-partyism is not the same thing as democracy; for another thing, to equate the term with democracy mistakes form for substance. Moreover, it is analogical in nature, with very little regard for qualitative differences in sociocultural context.

Mafeje contends that there is greater ethnic integration in Africa than ever before, attributed to migration and intermarriages. If anything, 'sociologically-understood, the so-called ethnic conflict or ethnicity is a sign of the imperatives of greater integration or social pressures arising out of a shrinking political arena'.[60] He continues: 'If by "shrinking political arena" is meant increasing crisis of democracy, then it becomes clear that in the absence of other ideological predispositions the corollary of this is intensified "ethnicity". If intensified ethnicity is an index of absence of democracy, then it stands to reason that our starting point is not the imagining of ethnic divisions, nor their ideological manipulation in the form of ethnicity but the question of democracy itself.'

Mafeje's general conclusion is that ethnic divisions in Africa are, by and large, imagined and encouraged by the elites who stand to benefit from them. This is ideological manipulation, which should be called ethnicity and 'not innocent, self-imposing identities which people acquire by historical accident'.[61] In the final analysis, what makes people who they are is not the labels attached to them, but what they do to reproduce themselves.

2 | A Totalising Critique

When I went to Langa to do fieldwork in 1961, I was armed with an essentially ahistoricist and overly functionalist question: Why and how do social groups cohere or split? Historically, it is necessary not to accuse me of inanity but simply to acknowledge the fact that I should have known that ebbs and flows are the very movements of which the dialectic of history is made, and, as such, are permanent features of collective existence.

Archie Mafeje, 'Religion, Class and Ideology in South Africa'

By the late 1960s and early 1970s, Archie Mafeje had managed to reconcile his Marxist political convictions with his academic work.[1] He had moved on from his liberal functionalist work of the 1960s to write from a Marxist perspective and also to advance a programmatic critique of the social sciences.[2] Yet those who are enthusiastic about polemic tend to reduce his evaluation of the social sciences to a polemic on anthropology. Theirs is the standard or conventional view, which holds that he single-handedly demolished anthropology as a discipline, or that he single-handedly destroyed the science of anthropology. This conception of Mafeje's work is misleading in at least three respects. First, while it is true that the discipline of anthropology underwent a crisis for at least two decades, its system of thought shaken, it is not true that it was demolished – for all its problems, anthropology is still a thriving academic discipline. Mafeje, Bernard Magubane and Francis Nyamnjoh would not, as late as the twenty-first century, have felt the need to analyse a discipline dead and buried. Second, the idea that Mafeje 'single-handedly' demolished anthropology is factually and historically incorrect – there were a number of other radical social scientists who dissected anthropology from the late 1960s to the 1980s. Third, the suggestion that Mafeje only criticised anthropology made him seem a reformist scholar. However, a careful reading of his analysis of the social sciences more broadly suggests that he was in fact a revolutionary scholar. Mafeje understood what other radical social scientists did not: that all the social sciences are Eurocentric and imperialist and the focus on anthropology to the exclusion of other disciplines is founded on reformism. He called for the adoption of a thoroughgoing commentary of the social sciences, which would lead to the emergence of what he called 'non-disciplinarity'.[3]

Thus the excessive focus on Mafeje's assessment of anthropology is a one-sided and partial reading of his *oeuvre*. Mafeje traced the development of anthropology and its impact on Africa in relation to the other social sciences. Having traced anthropology's role in colonialism and imperialism, he acknowledged that it was bound to be plunged into deep crisis precisely because of anti-colonialist and anti-imperialist struggles. Mafeje thus advocated the importance of the study of ethnography in the social sciences in Africa.

Sociology of knowledge and the 'totalising critique'

Mafeje's 1975 essay 'Religion, Class and Ideology in South Africa' is not only a brilliant analysis of social change, but also a pioneering work in the sociology of knowledge. Together with 'The Ideology of "Tribalism"', it marks a significant departure from standard anthropological and sociological writings on Africa. The 1975 essay, moreover, constitutes an auto-critique of his earlier work with Monica Wilson on Langa. Evaluating some of the themes pursued in *Langa*, Mafeje focuses in particular on those aspects that dealt with religion; outlining his theoretical matrix, he singles out a controversial question in the epistemology of the sociology of religion. The question turns on whether it is possible to reconcile a belief in an 'extra-societal source' – the transcendental viewpoint – and a belief in a positivist conception of science.[4] In other words, the conflict seems to be about whether belief systems are a reflection of concrete realities – experience – or an outcome of higher or divine intervention. This challenge compelled secular theorists to make a distinction between sociologists of religion and religious sociologists. For Mafeje, this reinforced the positivistic notion of value-free or non-partisan science. Just as materialists are confronted with the problem of consciousness and empirical history, positivistic idealists are similarly confronted with the problem of theodicy. As a result of the functionalist approach, South African sociology of religion was confined to narrow studies of churches and tribal rites and their function in society. Yet, 'the preoccupation with institutions has meant a narrowing of context to a point where some of the more general ramifications of belief systems and some nascent forms of commitment are made to appear as something apart'.[5] This is Mafeje insisting on taking into account history and the wider sociopolitical context – his argument is that functionalist analyses of social phenomena or 'functionalist organicism' interpret social change as if it only meant 'a substitution of one set of institutions with another' because of the tendency to study social institutions as if they were disconnected, rather than to focus on societies as a whole.[6] At the descriptive level, this may well be valid, but at the substantive level it serves as what Mafeje terms an 'ideological mystification' of underlying societal issues. Accordingly, social change, such as is understood by functionalist and positivist sociologists, does not necessarily connote the radical historical transformation advocated by Marxists. In analysing social change, Mafeje appeals primarily to the sociology of knowledge and attempts to relate sociological phenomena to its material substratum, class and ideology.

Writing in response to Magubane's well-known essay on the review of social change, 'A Critical Look at Indices Used in the Study of Social Change in Colonial Africa', Philip Mayer says: 'The considerable interest of Magubane's paper seems to me to lie in its contribution to the sociology of knowledge rather than to the theory of change. The author's own "existential" situation is therefore of some relevance, especially as such single-minded onslaught of "colonial anthropology" seems almost anachronistic in 1970. He is speaking out of personal experiences which have clearly affected his perspective.'[7] There is a lot riding on this quote. First, Mayer is not praising Magubane, or if that was his intention, the compliment is surely backhanded. Second, Mayer sets up a false dichotomy between the sociology of knowledge and contribution to the study of social change. In the process, he disdainfully discards the relevance of one's existential experiences in the process of knowledge making and, in so doing, confirms both Mafeje's and Magubane's commentary on, respectively, the positivistic nature of social anthropology and sociology in Africa. Mayer wrote as though social scientists write neutrally and objectively, without being influenced by the sociological baggage of their socio-historical backgrounds. His argument accords with the issues raised by Lewis R. Gordon when he says that such treatment as black intellectuals get from their white counterparts, where it is not patronising, is so contemptuous that they are seen as providers of experience, rather than as knowledge makers in their own right.[8] Yet taking seriously one's lived experiences is precisely what enabled both Mafeje and Magubane to see through the colonialist and imperialist nature of the social sciences in Africa. Third, Mayer is unable to see through the colonial nature of anthropology, even as late as the 1970s – which is precisely because of his failure to acknowledge the importance of one's own socio-historical and biographical experiences. By contrast, however, and in taking seriously the sociology of knowledge, Mafeje was able to understand the totality of South African history without getting entangled in the idealistic arguments that characterise the works of liberal functionalist and positivist sociologists and anthropologists in South Africa. This is what he calls a totalising critique.

The holistic historical approach is important for Mafeje because, as he says, 'a sociology of knowledge that operates outside of particular historical contexts seems futile'.[9] In acknowledging the importance of history and context, Mafeje parts ways with liberal idealists who only focused on what he terms minor contradictions and perversions of South African society. For Magubane, colonial anthropologists – in refusing to acknowledge that colonialism is an essential dimension of the present social structure – assumed that its general characteristics are already known and therefore one could conduct research without situating these characteristics in their historical context. What is essential in understanding social change, Magubane argues, is 'a total historical analysis'.[10] In accounting for changes in African urban and rural settings, colonial anthropologists spoke of 'Europeanisation', 'Westernisation' or 'acculturation'. In so doing, Magubane says, they thought Africans were aspiring to a Western way of life and did not take into account that Africans were deprived of their being and knowledge systems. Colonial anthropologists, according to Magubane, played down the fact that the purported acculturation of Africans hinged on three stages. First, there was a period of contact between the coloniser and the colonised, in which the latter were defeated through physical force. Second, there was a period of acquiescence during which some Africans were not only alienated from their societies, but also acquired the 'techniques and social forms of the dominant group', such as religion and education. Third, there was a period of resistance in which Africans 'developed a "national" consciousness that transcends "tribal" divisions and confront the colonial power with the demands of national liberation'.[11]

There is an overlap in these stages. But they must all be taken into account if one is to survey social change in Africa in a meaningful way. Thus, for Magubane, colonialism had at all times to be the natural starting point. Social anthropologists and sociologists tended to ignore the fact that the different stages of change in Africa were accompanied by force and coercion, and to focus on appearances and superficial issues that do not scratch beneath the surface, so that many of the conclusions reached were no more than impositions of dominant values on Africans. These studies also tended to take on micro units of analysis, such as individual behaviour, rather than society at large, whereas the study of social change requires that one examine not only the victims of oppression, but also the structure of domination itself and the methods used by the oppressor to maintain the oppressive structure.

Anthropologists have a tendency to create a dichotomy between rural and urban communities. For Mafeje, there is a dialectical link between the two settings. Based on the fieldwork he conducted in Langa township and the rural Transkei for his Master's thesis, he argues that, sociologically, town and country are not polar opposites – the 'Christian atmosphere' that permeates Langa township is also to be found in the rural hinterland of All Saints, an Anglican mission station in the Engcobo District. The same can be said of cultural practices – the migrant worker who lives in Langa is the same man who goes home to perform cultural rituals during holidays or for subsistence farming in his retirement and, furthermore, the so-called pagans of the Transkei are to be found in the migrant worker barracks in Langa. Mafeje writes: 'In South Africa after 1½–2 years I was able to interview in the Transkei, a rural area, the same men as I had interviewed in Cape Town. In Uganda before I had finished my 15-month survey some of the poorer farmers had disappeared to the city for employment or were commuting by bicycle.'[12]

According to Mafeje, what becomes 'a curious logic of colonial history' is the fact that the pagans, or *amaqaba*, who were once considered conservative insofar as they refused to give up their African ways of living, became latter-day militants through the sheer force of their resistance to Christianity and the Western way of life. They found allies in the urban-based militant youth who rejected Christianity and racism by appealing to an African God. Mafeje finds that the youth in Langa were not only indifferent to the church, but were also dissatisfied with it – and that was partly why they condemned Christianity as a ploy by whites to oppress and exploit black people. The grievances and feelings of the youth 'are genuine and they explode with anger and frustration'.[13] Mafeje says there may have been a difference between the two – the militant youth (who rejected Christianity and spoke of an African God) and *amaqaba*, the rural dwellers (who rejected Christianity and the Western way of life) – at the level of theoretical self-consciousness, but there were also affinities. The rural-urban thesis, much loved by anthropologists and sociologists of social change, was no more than a false dichotomy, for the same white supremacist ideology was found in both settings – in the church, white liberal ideology reproduced itself through missionary work and education. Mafeje is, however, too quick to find positive features in this colonial arrangement when he says: 'While at first this represented a *progressive* force, by introducing the arts of writing and universalising metaphysical concepts in small pre-literate societies which relied on simple theoretical paradigms for explanation, later it became *reactionary*, precisely by failing to come to terms with the contradiction of its own emergence in peculiarly South African conditions.'[14]

Mafeje unwittingly accepts the 'civilising mission' of the missionaries, but fails to locate its logic in its wider sociological and historical context. The sheer enormity of pain and oppression accompanying this 'civilisation' simply overshadows the supposed 'progressive force' about which Mafeje speaks. The colonial project, suitably interpreted, was about plundering, looting and subjugating. Civilisation, if it must be so called, is a by-product and not the driving force of colonialism. Mafeje is here pandering to the social change theory of colonial social scientists. Once again, Magubane's work is instructive in this regard. Magubane argues that because social scientists of the time were reluctant to criticise colonial governments, they chose to play it safe and did not expose the truth about colonial rule or touch on matters political, but simply focused on anodyne issues such as blacks speaking English, wearing European-style clothes or buying expensive cars. To the extent that they touched on colonialism, they depicted it as a necessary stage in history and considered how its long-term effects benefited African people. They ignored altogether the suffering, exploitation and degradation of Africans and their value systems. Thus, when the theory of social change accounts for social change in Africa, it does so in mechanistic and ethnocentric terms. When social scientists saw change, they saw tribesmen who were becoming Europeanised, mistaking appearance for reality. In this respect, they saw the fulfilment of white supremacist ideals – hence the notion that the African was being 'civilised'.

Notwithstanding Mafeje's claim about the progressive nature of liberal ideology, he nevertheless acknowledges that being civilised did not necessarily mean automatic acceptance of the white liberal middle-class cosmic view. Liberal theory, which has always taken for granted its own supposed progressiveness, was put under the spotlight and its hypocrisy exposed by Mafeje. It was unable to transcend itself insofar as it treated black people as perpetual subordinates in need of tutelage. The liberals sought to produce 'black "carbon-copies" of white Christian orthodoxy in South Africa'.[15] Mafeje posits that, from the point of view of the sociology of knowledge, the liberal might not be able to transcend their own ideological limitations. Following Max Weber, Mafeje reminds sociologists of knowledge that ideologies cannot be transcended because they can be both objective and subjective at the same time. The best that people can do is to endure ideologies 'stoically'. Insofar as Weber accepted the view that ideologies cannot be transcended, Mafeje admits that Weber 'paid the price of being radical without being revolutionary'. In invoking the sociology of knowledge, Mafeje's attempt was to build a case against the supposed value-free or non-partisan positivist belief generally, and functionalism particularly.

On positivism and functionalism in anthropology

The issues above were not unique to the social sciences in South Africa, but were characteristic of the social sciences more generally. Indeed, anthropologists and sociologists in other parts of the world had, by the 1960s, begun to question the status of anthropology as a discipline as well as the categories anthropologists used in understanding Africa and other 'less-developed' societies. In the essay 'The Problem of Anthropology in Historical Perspective', Mafeje surveys the diverse manner in which critics of anthropology in the North aired their views on the status of anthropology and found that in the American academy criticisms of anthropology were largely ideological, rather than theoretical. In Britain, on the other hand, he found the discussion less ideological, so as to give it respectability in the name of an academic dialogue.

These discussions and revisions led to what Mafeje calls 'neopositivist conceptions' of the French anthropologists.[16] Neopositivism was to be found in Lévi-Straussian structuralism or in liberal relativism, which was couched in neo-Marxist jargon. According to Mafeje, this was an ideological tactic all of its own. Unlike in the United States and the United Kingdom, in France there was a sharp divide between Marxist and non-Marxist anthropology. Although the scholars attempted to place on the table issues that plagued anthropology as a discipline, Mafeje nevertheless felt that the problematic they grappled with was badly formulated from the start. Characteristically, the critics of anthropology in the United Kingdom lacked a totalising critique and sought to rehabilitate anthropology by suggesting that it was not always in the service of colonialism and imperialism. The 'militantly critical anthropologists', on the other hand, allowed their analyses to remain at the level of ideology and polemic, the upshot of which was self-contradictory appellations such as 'radical anthropology' or 'socialist anthropology'. Yet, as Mafeje eloquently argues in his essay on the problems of anthropology, 'it is as hard to fit socialist clothes on an imperialist offspring as it is to transform positivism by radicalising it'.

In short, the two sides of the divide are best understood as reflective of the complicity of opposites. They take different routes only to arrive at the same conclusion: there is a better side of anthropology, which can be rescued. Magubane, a critic of anthropology himself, was not spared Mafeje's criticism. Mafeje reminded Magubane of the importance of the sociology of knowledge in shaping one's ideas. Not only was Mafeje censuring Magubane, he was also conducting auto-critique, arguing that in singling out colonial anthropology as *the* problem, its critics were undialectical and thus created an epistemological impasse. They identified, in anthropology, functionalism and imperialism, but failed to link these to the 'metropolitan bourgeois social sciences which are equally functionalist and *imperialist*'.[17] They failed to advance the totalising critique about which Mafeje spoke. As far as he was concerned, the problem of anthropology was primarily theoretical ('universal') rather than ideological ('colonial'), for merely to point out that anthropology was a handmaiden of colonialism was to present the argument in a partial and ideological way – that it was colonial could not have been its single diagnostic attribute. Epistemologically, its biggest crime was positivism, functionalism and alterity.

The Enlightenment, out of which anthropology and the other social sciences were born, was inherently bourgeois and sought to universalise anthropological viewpoints. This then laid the foundation for the European civilising mission of the nineteenth century – 'the highest point of European colonialism'.[18] The European civilising mission was not a noble endeavour. In the main, its rationale was 'economic plunder, political imposition and other inhumane practices'. While these practices took extreme forms in the colonies, they had in fact started in Europe and were an expansion of European capitalism. Magubane argues that the first colony of England was Ireland, where the English first tested colonialism and put it into effect. For Fanon: 'The well-being and the progress of Europe have been built up with the sweat and the dead bodies of Negroes, Arabs, Indians and the yellow races.'[19]

The European expansionism about which Mafeje speaks served as a source of inspiration for European scholars of the Enlightenment. This, then, is the substratum that served as a basis for the philosophies and ideologies of European expansionism from which metropolitan bourgeois social sciences cannot be separated and it is important at all times to connect it with anthropological writing in Africa. Having laid this foundation, Mafeje reasons that functionalism, which is a particular paradigm within the social sciences, is the natural starting point. Although functionalism had been discussed, few anthropologists had analysed its ideological status in the age of European expansionism. Those who attempted to do so fell into the trap of associating functionalism only with the discipline of anthropology and with the historical epoch of colonialism. Yet, as Mafeje says: 'In the same way that capitalism, as a specific mode of accumulation, had to exist before imperialism could manifest itself, likewise functionalism, as a theoretical rationalisation of the epoch, had to exist in the metropolitan countries before it could be used in the colonies.'[20] Moreover, 'in its paradigmatic form functionalism is a product of nineteenth century Western European bourgeois society, and was never limited to a single discipline called "anthropology". On the contrary, it straddled all the life sciences.' In the nineteenth century, functionalism relied mainly on analogies derived from physical and biological sciences to account for complex social phenomena. The other version of functionalism, rationalist-utilitarian, 'was a reflection of the logic of the industrial revolution in England and France' and the two pioneers of modern functionalism, August Comte and Herbert Spencer, came from France and

England respectively. For them, rationality, utility and functional value, order and progress were foundational to a bourgeois European society. These principles affirmed its achievements and justified its continued existence. Such theories in the works of Spencer and Comte served as an inspiration for Émile Durkheim, who synthesised them and came up with structural-functionalism. If it were not for the synthesis of Spencer and Comte in Durkheim's work, structural-functionalism 'would not have emerged in anthropology in quite the same way that it did'.[21]

The Spencer-Durkheim theoretical nexus laid the foundation for the works of British anthropologists such as Bronisław Malinowski and Alfred Radcliffe-Brown, who both owed their greatest intellectual debt to Durkheim primarily and to Spencer and Comte secondarily. For Malinowski, the premium was on the psychological and biological needs of the individual, so that social and cultural institutions were merely a response to the said needs – a Spencerian understanding of society. Radcliffe-Brown, on the other hand, following Durkheim, stressed the autonomy of social institutions and sought to understand how disparate social elements and institutions were instrumental in maintaining the social whole. But Radcliffe-Brown remained faithful to Spencer's use of biological analogies, as did Malinowski. Malinowski's and Radcliffe-Brown's writings greatly influenced American functionalist sociologists such as Talcott Parsons, George Homans and Robert K. Merton.

The foregoing description does not, in my opinion, complete the picture. For one thing, sociologists have also been influenced by Max Weber, Durkheim's contemporary, whose work reminds them that not all positivist sociology is functionalist. Weber rejected the use of biological or natural science analogies in explaining social phenomena. He appealed to individual subjective meanings by using 'ideal types' and 'normal types' as suitable methods of sociological analysis. Mafeje says: 'For him, unlike Talcott Parsons, adaptive behaviour on the part of individuals was no measure of the "functionality" of the system. Rather, systems functioned because they had an internal logic, whether it was good or bad individuals – a question which Weber treated as a purely subjective matter.'[22] Mafeje believed that ideas and social forms are shaped by particular nations and bourgeois classes at any particular time. Positivism and func-tionalism are examples of such ideas. It is not clear, therefore, whether bourgeois writers such as Spencer could espouse neutrality and 'positive science' and still be faithful to their class interests. For Mafeje, this was an attempt on their part to gloss over social contradictions that were mani-fest in Europe, where there was inequality, exploitation and unmitigated sociological individualism – the upshot of capitalism.

Having discussed the link between the Enlightenment and func-tionalism, I now turn to how the latter found expression in the col-onies through anthropology. It should be remembered that, for Mafeje, anthropology was in the colonies what other social sciences were in the metropolitan countries – and to single out anthropology and leave out the other social sciences is a form of mystification. Moreover, function-alism was the prevailing paradigm in both the metropole and the colonies. That anthropologists lent their support to colonial governments was not Mafeje's main contention; the issue, for him, was the ontology upon which the intellectual efforts of anthropologists are premised. Equally, it is beside the point whether any anthropologists were opposed to colo-nialism. In the final analysis, the contours of anthropology are as much colonially determined as they are informed by functionalism; the oppos-itional anthropologist and the colonial anthropologist are in unison with regard to the utility of social research institutes in Africa. Mafeje saw that it was significant that their units of analysis were the same: tribe, kinships and religious systems. On both sides of the purported divide, therefore, the anthropological enterprise was bourgeois *ab initio*.

For Mafeje, assessing the works of the older generation or the colonial anthropologists was not simply a reflection of a generation gap. It was a negation of negations. Just as functionalism is a negation of speculative his-tory in the Enlightenment, it is also an affirmation of bourgeois capitalist utilitarianism that oppresses the people of the global South and reproduces itself by producing native objects of study, who would later be identical to the 'knowing' subjects through the process of bourgeois conversion. In this regard, Mafeje said that he, along with Magubane, were products of colo-nial anthropology. The crimes of colonial anthropology were not merely based on descriptive and superficial writings about modernising Africans who sought European status. The crimes lay in its ahistoricity, which failed to retrace the problems confronting African people to colonialism. Mafeje believed that he and Magubane had to be part of bourgeois functionalism in order to be its negation. Analogously, African revolutionaries had to be part of colonialism in order to experience its frustrations. To ignore these factors, said Mafeje, was to fall victim to undialectical presumptuousness. Although anthropologists were among the first social scientists to arrive in the colonies, they should not be singled out as the only functionalists and academic imperialists. Functionalism and positivism were not unique to anthropology, but characterised all the social sciences. Mafeje's point is well taken. Yet it raises more questions than it answers. If the crime of social science lies in its being functionalist and positivistic, what would Mafeje have had to say about the social sciences that are not functionalist or positivistic in their epistemology? What would be said of the social sciences grounded in Marxist dialectical materialism – as Mafeje's analysis clearly is? In a sense, it appears that what Mafeje criticised was bourgeois social science, rather than social sciences as such.

Against this background, Mafeje was able to criticise anthropology without turning it into the 'black sheep' of the social sciences. Anthropology was the first to arrive in the colonies because the bourgeois metropole needed it in order to conquer the natives, about whom they were least informed. That it coincided with colonialism is hardly surprising since anthropology provided knowledge and access to hitherto unknown societies. Thus, to fixate on anthropology to the exemption of other social sciences – which were equally bourgeois and imperialist – is to engage in petty reformism, which does not take seriously history and the totalising critique.

Mafeje therefore advocates a holistic approach that transcends disciplines. Such an alternative is to be found, he suggests, in Marxism. He argues that there could be no disciplines within Marxism, and then he goes on to query the function of disciplines in society. He says that disciplines are there to illuminate problems of fragmented social existence and, in doing this, social scientists assume that it is for the benefit of 'uncomprehending ordinary people'. The assumption made by social scientists then leads to the bourgeois epistemology of subject-object relation. Mafeje clinches his argument by saying: 'If the function of bourgeois social science is to increase the awareness (or false consciousness) of uncomprehending objects, then when the people have become comprehending subjects, there will be no need for social science.'[23]

Mafeje's argument is not entirely convincing. This is an issue distinct from the critique of (bourgeois) social science. The non-disciplinarity that would emerge from transcending disciplines would still constitute social science. Marx was concerned with the ordering of society and social relations (the subject matter of social science) rather than biological or natural sciences. The paradox of the charge of Eurocentrism against functionalist-positivistic social science is that Marxism is itself fundamentally Eurocentric. The problematic that it sets itself is mainly Europe; speaking specifically to the European conditions – even if it could be appropriated (with considerable modifications) for the revolutionary projects in the (former) colonies.

In order to understand where Mafeje was coming from, one has to read him outside of the text. In other words, context is crucially important. In his search for alternatives, Mafeje was also limited by his background and environment. The issue is not whether Mafeje succeeded or failed in the very difficult task he set for himself. The point is to follow his line of thought and to see what insights African social scientists may garner from him in the quest for knowledge decolonisation. For a Unity Movement-trained Marxist such as he was, their internationalist outlook would have prevented him from adopting what he called an Africanist or even nationalist perspective on these issues. As far as he and the Unity Movement were concerned, to be Africanist or nationalist is to be reactionary.[24] He said at one point, for example: 'In the name of international socialism Pallo Jordan and I were trained to think that "nationalism" was narrow-minded, bourgeois, and, therefore, reactionary.'[25] If the sociology of knowledge is to be taken seriously, then this biographical detail and the context in which Mafeje wrote ought to be fully appreciated and not seen as a rationalisation of his argument.

Mafeje championed Marxism insofar as it does not recognise disciplines. Thus, according to him, even claims to Marxist anthropology or Marxist sociology are self-contradictory. Equally, Marxism cannot be interdisciplinary without being self-contradictory. The difficult question, then, is what the role of disciplines is in the social sciences. The answer is usually that the social sciences make complex sociopolitical issues apparent to uncomprehending laypeople. This is Mafeje's representation of it. The social sciences could well be for comprehending subjects. Most scholarly works are addressed to other scholars, in much the same way that the *Grundrisse* and *Das Kapital* are addressed to intellectuals, not the peasant or the factory worker (the complexity of scholarly writing had to be diluted in pamphlets to make it more comprehensible to the literate among the masses). According to Mafeje, the crux of the problem of the social sciences lies in their bourgeois epistemology of subject-object. Although it is said that the role of the social sciences is to increase the awareness of the unknowing objects, it is unlikely that this is so, for even when people become comprehending subjects, the social sciences still exist. In the final analysis, Mafeje argues, the role of the social sciences is politics and therefore ideological: 'Participation in the making and execution of decisions by either "knowing subjects" (experts, advisors and consultants) or liberated objects is a political process. Then Marxist theory which advocates revolutionary politics and which denies separation between subjects and objects, between theory and practice, between value and fact, and between science and history comes [into] its own. At the most fundamental level, it is the best anthropology that there is and the best candidate for future society.'[26]

Thus, 'if dialectical materialism is a theory of history, then historical materialism is its methodology'.[27] Marxists are acutely aware of the distinction between theory and practice – hence the idea of praxis. The fact that practice informs theory or vice versa is no reason to suppose that Marxism denies separation between the two. Although Mafeje declares that Marxism 'is the best anthropology that there is', he is willing to subject it to critical scrutiny when its categories do not adequately address the concrete cases they are meant to address.

On idiographic and nomothetic inquiry

In his essay 'On the Articulation of Modes of Production', Mafeje is concerned with understanding at least five important issues. The first is a question: Does idiographic inquiry yield deeper insights into societal processes than nomothetic inquiry?[28] He raises this issue specifically because he wants to understand whether traditional disciplines such as history and anthropology (both of which are idiographic) are the best candidates accounting for societal processes vis-à-vis Marxism, which makes nomothetic claims such as 'the theory of modes of production'. Mafeje's second issue is the mode of production as a unit of analysis, a worthy substitute for such concepts as tribe or nation, both of which are used by historians and anthropologists.[29] The third issue is that since Marxism tends to treat culture as purely a superstructural phenomenon (which has little influence on the base that produces the necessities of life), what is the relationship between cultural relativity and meta-theory? The fourth important issue asks what (if world history and anthropological philosophies are necessarily Eurocentric and therefore inadequate and unacceptable) counter theories one can generate from the global South. Finally, Mafeje's fifth issue, also a question, asks what – in an otherwise imperialist world – is the responsibility of the social scientist? These questions speak not only to the problem of theory, but also to the sociology of knowledge. Mafeje proposes to approach the general through the particular, and herein lies the genius of his approach. In grappling with these questions, Mafeje discusses the works of two Marxists, Harold Wolpe and Michael Morris, who wrote about South African capitalist relations and specific mechanisms of labour reproduction in the twentieth century.[30] In their attempts to understand South African conditions, they deployed Marxian categories such as class, mode of production, production relations, forces of production and social formation.

Mafeje wants first to clarify what it is that the two writers meant by these concepts, and then to understand how such concepts explain the concrete conditions they are meant to explain. Although he wants to clarify, he is equally concerned to comprehend the applicability of the concepts and their usefulness in different conditions. This is so because while the concepts seem theoretically reasonably precise, substantively they need further clarification. Wolpe, following Ernesto Laclau, made a distinction between a mode of production and an economic system, of which he sought to understand the constituent elements – capitalist modes of production, the African redistributive economies and the system of labour tenancy. For Mafeje, the latter two concepts were a deviation from Marxism and empirically unreliable.

For Morris, on the other hand, a mode of production was an articulated combination/structured combination or, more precisely, a determinate structure. On this score, a mode of production is combined precisely because modes of production do not follow one another sequentially, with one replacing the other; nor is a mode of production produced by movement or changes within it. To argue as Morris did is to ignore the Marxian dictum that the struggle is the motor of history. For Mafeje, this led to a theoretical confusion because there can be no theory of articulation between modes of production. According to Morris, contradictions occur in class struggles within a given social formation, not between modes of production or within a mode of production – but an argument of that sort abandons dialectical materialism altogether. Morris's thesis, Mafeje argues, could only be valid if class struggle (which is concrete) is used to mean the same theoretical or abstract construct (mode of production) used to explain it. In other words, a mode of production is a theoretical concept to explain the sociopolitically concrete. In Morris's account, however, the two are used somewhat interchangeably. According to Mafeje, Morris's thesis cannot be valid 'unless the material conditions of class struggle are accorded the same theoretical/logical status as the mode of production to which they refer. In orthodox Marxism this is provided for in the concept of "contradiction" within a mode or between modes of production.'[31]

Both Morris and Wolpe agreed that 'all modes of production exist only in the concrete economic, political and ideological conditions of social formations'.[32] But it is doubtful that Wolpe agreed with Morris's rejection of the articulation of modes of production; although Morris used the term 'social formation', he did not define it theoretically. Mafeje notes that in Wolpe's schema, on the other hand, the concept refers to specific 'mechanisms of social reproduction or the "laws" of motion of the economy'. By 'mechanisms of social reproduction', Wolpe meant a combination of modes of production. For Wolpe, 'the distinction between the abstract concept of mode of production and the concept of the real-concrete social formation conceived as a combination of modes of production constitutes the explicit or implicit presupposition of all these articles'.[33] Wolpe was referring here to chapters in the collection of essays he edited. To the extent that the distinction between the two concepts is either implicit or explicit in all the essays in the collection, Mafeje reasons that the authors had clearly ignored the view that the term 'social formation', even for Marx, can be both an empirical concept that refers to the object of concrete analysis and, as Étienne Balibar puts it, 'an abstract concept replacing the ideological notion of "society" and designating the object of the science of history insofar as it is a totality of instances articulated on the basis of a determinate mode of production'.[34] To this Mafeje adds that one ought to make a distinction between abstract concepts and the concrete referent that needs to be explained.

Having discussed these abstract concepts, Mafeje is keen to analyse the empirical issues they were meant to explain. Broadly speaking, Wolpe's thesis was that, with regard to the dialectic between urban and rural, the pre-capitalist mode of production ensured (or otherwise maintained) the reproduction of migrant labour. For Morris, it was the labour migration from white farms that maintained the reproduction of the labour-power of migrants. Although farmworkers were allocated pieces of land by the white farmer through the so-called labour-tenancy, they still sought work either on other farms or in the cities. This argument, such as was presented by Morris, that farmworkers could hold more than one job, 'is tantamount to [saying farmworkers supplement] *wage* with *wage*',[35] without giving a clear indication as to the supposed essential difference between the labour tenant on a white farm and his peasant counterpart in the rural areas who uses his labour power for his own subsistence.

This prompts the question as to the real difference between Wolpe's and Morris's theses of labour reproduction. For Morris, the difference between feudalist and capitalist relations of production lay in the difference between land rent and wage labour. Morris used the organising concept of 'relations of real appropriation' to understand this dynamic, but even so he oversimplified the social relations on white farms. The pre-capitalist South African case need not translate into feudalism by virtue merely of ground rent and landlordism. South African society was polyglot, unlike that of Russia. For Wolpe, the capitalist mode of production was linked to other modes of production, 'the African redistributive economies and the system of labour-tenancy and crop-sharing on White farms'.[36] Mafeje argues that this definition of a mode of production lacks rigour because 'labour-tenancy' and 'crop-sharing' connote two different things. Nor do they lend themselves to categories of 'feudalism' and 'capitalism'. Thus, when the colonial government ensured that Africans could never rise to the level of capitalist or commercial producers, they fought for their existing pieces of land and grazing rights for their livestock, and they sent family members to the rural areas with the stock they would have accumulated on white farms.

Those who engage in this practice, particularly in the Eastern Cape, are referred to as *amarhanuga*, those who go around collecting value (in the form of livestock) specifically from white farms, whereas those farm wage labourers uprooted from white farms are called *amaqheya*. Mafeje asks whether livestock could be thought of as property (means of production) or merely instruments of production. In the South Africa of the time, what did it mean to speak of property with reference to black people? For both Morris and Wolpe, property referred to land in the agricultural economy. Wolpe incorrectly said that land in the rural areas was held communally. Mafeje argues that this is inaccurate because arable land was individually registered at the magistrate's court, the head of the family accepting liability for annual rent. Strictly speaking, therefore, such land is owned by the state and not the individual. In this sense, peasant cultivators of the land are tenants of the state. The difference between peasants and tenants on white farms (*amarhanuga*) is that under the 'quit-rent' system, the former could pass down their registered plots under customary law. Registered plots could be inherited. This presented a problem for those theorists who talked about 'communal land'. Any family that had a plot could hold on to it perpetually, as long as they paid rent annually. This surely was no model of communally owned land.

The incorrigibility of the 'communally owned land' thesis, as opposed to the redistribution of land through kinship units, persists unabated in spite of the fact that theorists such as Claude Meillassoux and Pierre-Philippe Rey have written persuasively about the 'lineage mode of production', to which the notion of prestige goods is critical to an understanding of the social reproduction of lineages.[37] Mafeje contends that whether one is talking about white farms or the rural areas, cattle among South African peasants represent prestige goods, rather than property or means of production. As such, cattle are instrumental in lineage reproduction insofar as they facilitate, inter alia, issues of lobola or bride wealth. This invites questions about the role of livestock in subsistence farming and reproduction of labour.

In South Africa, the two do not necessarily coincide. Subsistence is met through cultivation of crops or wage labour. Livestock only entail means of lineage reproduction or are instruments of production. A related point is that what is usually owned communally in South Africa is grazing ground, not arable land as such.[38]

When Wolpe wrote about 'a development of classes in the reserves' he missed the fact that the possibility of such a process was thwarted by the Land Act of 1913, which was compounded when paramount chiefs, through the Bantu Authorities Act of 1951, were given farms as bribes by the state and thereafter bantustan government ministers helped themselves and their cronies to large portions of land. Still, this need not entail a growing land-owning class. Mafeje argues that 'to conduct class analysis we do not have to invent classes'.[39] The general lessons of this discussion are that a theory not adequately sensitive to concrete realities, however progressive, is likely to be as dangerous as its reactionary counterpart. Moreover, although Mafeje is advocating Marxism as the best answer to bourgeois social sciences, he is nevertheless willing to repudiate its categories if they do not accord with concrete realities. In saying this, I am not suggesting that Mafeje was an empiricist. Rather, I am saying that Mafeje took seriously ethnographic detail and the sociology of knowledge.

On the epistemological break and the lingering problem of alterity

Although anthropology has been criticised by a number of scholars located in different parts of the world, it has not yet dispensed with its problem of alterity – the 'othering' or the 'epistemology of subjects-objects' as Mafeje puts it. Reasons for this incorrigibility of alterity in anthropology go beyond questions of theory to speak to the sociology of knowledge. Knowledge making is as contested as politics. Mafeje says that epistemologies can be changed (though he does not specify the grounds under which such changes occur) and paradigms can be done away with. He is quick to point out that it is dangerous to assume that knowledge is a result of free inquiry. As far as Mafeje is concerned, new knowledge is usually won through struggle. In his discussion paper *Studies in Imperialism*, he writes: 'The requirements of social reproduction predicate that every society sanctions only such activities as are consistent with its overall mode of existence. Intellectual enquiry is no exception to this rule.'[40] Those who, like Mafeje, identified Eurocentrism in the social sciences have earned themselves labels such as angry, polemical or combative – once they have received these labels, they need not be taken seriously by the academic orthodoxy. Their 'anger' is managed by ignoring them. Social scientists who subscribe to the notion of value-free inquiry often miss the point that lived experiences play a crucial role in how one perceives the world and therefore how one constructs knowledge. Indeed, with characteristic eloquence, Mafeje argues: 'The separation between intellectuality and sociality is a result of European prejudice which we need not share. Intellectual activity is intrinsically social both in its constitution and in its practice. It can be stated emphatically that what puts intellectual issues on the agenda is social praxis.'

Mafeje continues: 'It would seem that intellectual systems are capable of a clean epistemological break.'[41] For example, there is no necessary affinity between Marxism and positivism or idealism. This raises the question of whether intellectual systems grow by accretion or by epistemological ruptures. If the latter were true, it would be difficult to explain why and how Mafeje was evaluating anthropology as late as 2001, when he and others had already done so in the 1960s and 1970s. Mafeje's repudiation of anthropology does not translate into its repudiation by all Africans, or even most Africans. This speaks precisely to the view that earlier analyses of anthropology do not necessarily entail a complete break with the discipline.

Mafeje argues emphatically that 'epistemological ruptures in sciences as well as in other forms of knowledge are usually preceded by crises'.[42] This is analogous to the Leninist notion of a 'revolutionary situation', which constitutes the necessary (though not always sufficient) condition for a revolution proper. Crises in the social sciences had long been identified by Mafeje, Magubane and others. The question was why this had not led to an epistemological rupture – particularly in Africa. Knowledge making in and about Africa was still very much centred in the West. Therefore, revolutionary crisis was a necessary but not a sufficient condition for a rupture. Revolutionary crisis in the social sciences had to be understood in the wider sociological context, which informed knowledge making – the working example being the skewed relations between the global North and the global South. Mafeje observes that 'social crisis occurs in society when the requisite processes of social reproduction cannot be attained by normal means i.e. means which are presumed to work because they have done so before'.[43]

It is still not obvious, however, whether Mafeje believed that, in spite of the analyses of the 1960s and 1970s, the social sciences had reached a point of an epistemological break. And it is not clear either whether African scholars missed the opportunity to capitalise on the momentum of the said crisis. Elsewhere, Mafeje argues that although social studies in African universities continued to be organised along disciplines, the critical studies of the late 1960s 'played havoc on disciplinary boundaries'.[44] He maintains that of all the social sciences that were subject to critical analysis, anthropology never fully recovered and underwent a crisis, particularly in the post-independence period.

There is a lot to tease out and reflect on in Mafeje's argument. First, it appears that anthropology has recovered from the crisis of the 1960s – Mafeje's re-evaluation of anthropology in the 1990s and 2000s suggests this. Second, it could be argued that although other disciplines were assessed by radical social scientists in the 1970s, they have survived the onslaught. Indeed, scholars of the global South would not now speak of Eurocentrism and the need for epistemological and curriculum decolonisation if the situation were as severe as Mafeje presented it. If anything, analyses of anthropology reflect a particular epoch, both intellectually and sociopolitically. In the age of neoliberal complacency there is now, more than ever, a need to revisit those critiques that have been overshadowed by conservative scholarship. To be fair, Mafeje was reflecting on the state of affairs in the 1980s and much has happened since. The consolidation of conservatism, both intellectually and sociopolitically, by an academic orthodoxy the world over, implies that what radical social scientists are pursuing now is the recovering of intellectual nerve about which Jimi Adesina speaks, rather than an epistemological break proper.[45] Mafeje said that one had to make a distinction between an epistemological break and the emergence of a new or alternative theory. Although methodologies can produce valid results, each methodology is limited by its underlying assumptions. According to Mafeje: 'It is when such underlying assumptions are found not to apply to an increasing number of observable instances that a theoretical crisis occurs.'[46]

The nagging question was why and how an epistemological break – or even an alternative theory – was reversed so that the gains already made lost their relevance. Mafeje's response to the question:

In the social sciences the ideological component, which earlier we referred to as intellectual prejudice, appears to be incorrigible, ultimately. For instance, irrespective of the evidence that might be brought to bear, there is no way in which social scientists in the imperialist camp could be persuaded that imperialism exists and is a major problem of development in the Third World. It is also noteworthy that it was only possible to convince the practitioners that there was *colonial* anthropology after colonialism had been fought and defeated.[47]

Formally, colonialism may have been fought and defeated but anthropology has not and, as Mafeje points out, 'while it is true that "modernisation theories" have been discredited, to assume that they have disappeared would be dangerous complacency'.[48] Although the social sciences may be deemed technical subjects, their theories do not change because of technical reasons that are inherent or internal to the social sciences. Revolutionary changes in the social scientific theories usually stem from social changes or crises. This means that the social sciences, more than the natural sciences, 'are strongly *ideologically-conditioned*'.[49] This notwith-standing, it is not always clear when such social crises occur or where the point is at which social problems amount to a societal crisis. Mafeje argues that social problems amount to a social crisis when they are no longer amenable to practical and theoretical rationalisations.

One way of objecting to Mafeje's argument would be to point out that it broke the old philosophical taboo on deriving 'ought' from 'is' – that X exists, or will exist, is no sufficient justification for its moral goodness. Such an assumption commits the naturalistic fallacy. Substantively, how-ever, such an objection may do little to dent the necessity of the societal crisis for historical changes, for it seems extraordinary that a rupture could simply come via spontaneous combustion. That notwithstanding, the moral or inherent goodness of societal crisis is still in doubt. This is so because the crisis in the social sciences in the 1970s has not neces-sarily led to an epistemological rupture. The incorrigibility of alterity in anthropology is a case in point. Yet it might be better to seek ruptures at meso levels instead of the level of totality of the social sciences. The works of Oyeronke Oyewumi on gender are representative of an epis-temological rupture in the global discourse of gender, particularly *The Invention of Women*.[50]

Although Mafeje was critical of anthropology as a discipline, he understood very well that all of the bourgeois social sciences are deeply implicated and he attempted to show that anthropology must be under-stood as consistent with the growth of functionalism and colonialism more generally. Anthropology, he said, was founded on studying the 'other'. Quite why the practice of othering persists even to this day is a question that exercised Mafeje a great deal. The lingering problem of alterity, it should be remembered, continues years after anthropology had gone through a crisis as a result of critical evaluations by Mafeje and other radical social scientists.

Three issues generally emerge from Mafeje's investigation: (i) the self-identity and role of African anthropologists in the post-independence period; (ii) the question as to whether there can be an African anthropology (not anthropology in Africa) without African anthropologists; and (iii) the question as to whether authentic representation on the part of African anthropologists would entail a 'demise of Anthropology as it is traditionally known'.[51] The general point is that deconstruction carries little weight if it does not entail reconstruction: negation without affirmation is meaningless. But attempts at reconstruction have always been difficult since much of it was conducted in the North, with only a few exceptions from the South. Mafeje captures something of this when he says: 'From a historical perspective, it could be said that in the main African anthropologists did not anticipate independence in their professional representations. What this would have entailed is an anticipatory *deconstruction* of colonial Anthropology so as to guarantee a rebirth or transformation of Anthropology.'[52]

In a review of Mafeje's *Anthropology and Independent Africans*, Godwin Murunga notes that in making these remarks, 'Mafeje overlooks the work of Okot P'Bitek in that the difference between [P'Bitek] and other African anthropologists is that P'Bitek declared anthropology dead in Africa and "redirected his energy into literature to the extent of championing the field of oral literature"'.[53]

In spite of the said deconstruction, or the so-called crisis anthropology went through, attempts at reconstructing or otherwise burying it altogether proved impossible. The lingering problem of alterity is a case in point. Elsewhere, Mafeje suggested that anthropology was on its deathbed, but not yet dead. Although Mafeje recommended in his earlier works that critical evaluations must be directed at all the imperialist social sciences, Helen Macdonald, in her article subtitled 'Subaltern Studies in South Asia and Post-Colonial Anthropology in Africa', has pointed out that Mafeje revised his position somewhat in the light of responses from his critics.[54] The most important thing, however, is that

Mafeje made a plea for non-disciplinarity, a case he had been building as far back as the 1970s with the essay 'The Problem of Anthropology in Historical Perspective'.

The issue turns on transcendence of disciplinarity as against the unification of disciplines. Adesina takes issue with Mafeje's rejection of disciplinarity and epistemology. He argues that not only did Mafeje mistake issues of pedagogy for those of research, but he also mistook epistemology for dogmatism. Adesina advances a well-considered, albeit brief argument against Mafeje, but it needs to be said that Adesina wrongly imputes to Mafeje the concepts of interdisciplinarity and transdisciplinarity.[55] Adesina's claim is that scholarship is interdisciplinary *ab initio*. No societal problems are purely social or purely economic. In terms of research, societal problems require one to tap into other disciplines. In Adesina's view, Mafeje's argument appeared misdirected. As regards pedagogy, Adesina argues, the danger with interdisciplinarity is that it leads to training students who have no methodological grounding in any discipline. This is a valid argument. But there is something to be said about Mafeje's advocacy of non-disciplinarity rather than inter- or transdisciplinarity. Mafeje's proposal has far-reaching consequences for both teaching and research.

The non-disciplinary approach makes proposals or has implications not only for transcendence of Euro-American epistemology and methodology, but necessarily holds true for teaching purposes as well. It has to be so, for the simple reason that if disciplinarity, such as is conventionally known, is to be transcended or otherwise dismantled for the purposes of knowledge production/research, the same must be true for teaching purposes. Thus Mafeje's new social science ought to entail new teaching or training methods as well. Mafeje did not use the concepts of interdisciplinarity and transdisciplinarity affirmatively. In recent articles Dani Nabudere and Helmi Sharawy both feel that Mafeje did not transcend the Western knowledge archive;[56] indeed, Mafeje 'does not uphold the idea of the End of Anthropology in order to liquidate an epistemological order, but rather to put in its place a more appropriate alternative to the concept, which, in his opinion, leads to anthropological theorising of another kind'.[57]

Again, here the question seems to turn on whether Mafeje succeeded or failed, and not on his attempt to liquidate an epistemological order, which is clear – the search for an epistemological rupture is a case in point. Mafeje's interlocutors are correct in claiming that he did not transcend the Western knowledge archive, but their reasoning is faulty. For example, they say he advocated interdisciplinarity. That is incorrect. A much more suitable example of Mafeje's failure to transcend the Western knowledge archive is his appeal to Marxism as the best anthropology there is. In this regard, Sharawy and Nabudere are onto something. But this is a position Mafeje modified in his later commentary on the social sciences, since he no longer appealed to Marxism per se. For example, in *Anthropology and Independent Africans*, Mafeje maintains that 'of interest to us in the present context is that all what is said above was not anthropological … Nor was it interdisciplinary … It was *non-disciplinary*.'[58] In his response to his critics, 'Conversations and Confrontations with My Reviewers', he argues that 'interdisciplinarity leads to theoretical hiatus. It will require a major epistemological breakthrough as good as positivism which instigated the rise of the disciplines and led to the fragmentation of social theory to achieve any coalescence.'[59] Earlier he had argued that 'the attack on Anthropology was heartfelt and justified in the immediate anti-colonial revulsion. *But it was ultimately subjective because the so-called modernising social sciences were not any less imperialist and actually became rationalisations for neocolonialism in Africa*, as we know now. However, the important lesson to be drawn from the experience of the African anthropologists is that Anthropology is premised on an immediate subject/object relation.'[60]

This is consistent with Mafeje's stance on the social sciences generally and on anthropology in particular. In the light of criticisms, however, Mafeje slightly revised his position. On the racist nature of anthropology he was consistent, but on the question of Eurocentrism in other disciplines he backtracked – an inconvenient afterthought that could have easily cost him the debate. Mafeje's belated concession that the other social sciences are less Eurocentric is a blunder that nevertheless does not diminish the overall substance of his assessment of the social sciences. Perhaps Mafeje might have been justified in making such a concession when one considers some of the pioneering works of African social scientists – Oyewumi's work in social science, for example, is hardly Eurocentric and Akinsola Akiwowo's sociology is just as far from Eurocentric.[61] Similarly, Ifi Amadiume's works fall within the social sciences but she rejects anthropology in favour of social history.[62] Nor are Cheikh Anta Diop's works in historical sociology Eurocentric. The point is that Mafeje was making a distinction between bourgeois Eurocentric social science and social science as such. His argument is that it is difficult to conceive of anthropology without racism (epistemology of alterity) whereas one can think of sociology or economics without being, *ipso facto*, racist. The anthropological inquiry is premised on the researcher as ontologically distinct from the subject of their inquiry, whereas Western sociologists study the subjects of their inquiry as ontologically similar to themselves.

Still, this does not explain why social scientists from the global South still speak today of epistemological decolonisation or curriculum transformation. That there exists less Eurocentric social science from African scholars is no reason to suppose that the social sciences are not overwhelmingly Eurocentric. To assume that the social sciences cannot be transcended, in the manner of Mafeje's non-disciplinarity, is to assume that the social sciences, as they are currently known, are transhistorical – they have been there since the beginning of time. That is not the case. Anthropology, for example, is the child of colonialism and imperialism. Mafeje's later position on anthropology centred on the lingering problem of alterity, years after the discipline underwent its epistemological crisis. In critically evaluating anthropology, and the social sciences generally, Mafeje was in search of an epistemological rupture and therefore new paradigms. Regardless of whether Mafeje backtracked in reviewing all of the social sciences, the substance of his analysis remains. He was not assessing anthropology (and other social sciences) for its own sake; he sought to replace it with something else. Hence 'deconstruction' and 'reconstruction'.[63] He saw such an undertaking as being accomplished through sound research and deep familiarity with one's ethnography and he says, for example: 'As our study on the interlacustrine shows, without a serious return to the study of African ethnography, it is not likely that any important breakthroughs will be made in African social science.'[64] What exists currently is anthropology in Africa as opposed to African anthropology. Mafeje uses the term 'ethnography' in two senses. First, ethnography as he conceives of it has sociocultural connotations – it is in fact his preferred substitute term for the nebulous concept of culture. Second, by using 'ethnography' he is referring to 'non-disciplinarity' and it became a substitute for the social sciences as they are conventionally known.

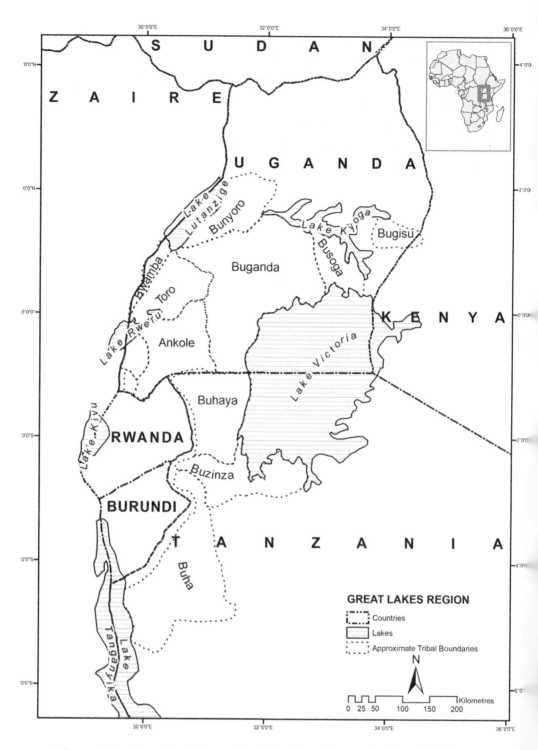

Figure 3.1. Map of interlacustrine kingdoms. Drawn by Patrick Mlangeni

3 | Reading Mafeje's *The Theory and Ethnography of African Social Formations*

In order to understand Archie Mafeje's critical approach to the social sciences, one should read and understand his magnum opus, *The Theory and Ethnography of African Social Formations*. This book is Mafeje's theoretical and methodological statement on what he meant when he spoke of a search for an epistemological break and non-disciplinarity. In this book, he moves between the abstract and the concrete with great aplomb. He discusses Marxian categories with deftness and subjects them to critical scrutiny using the pre-colonial Great Lakes region as a case study. It is a highly theoretical book and the issues he discusses are complex; the complexity, however, is to be found in his ideas and not in his prose. Mafeje wrote with great facility – exact and everywhere intelligible.

Concerning this book and Mafeje's monograph *The Agrarian Question, Access to Land and Peasant Responses in Sub Saharan Africa*, Samir Amin says: 'I consider these two contributions to be quite exceptional in terms of the quality of information provided and the rigour of their analysis.'[1] In this chapter I demonstrate the genius of Mafeje's project (the transcendence of Eurocentric knowledge systems) through a reading of his study of the interlacustrine kingdoms.[2] My point is to show how Mafeje successfully actualised his project of advancing new methodologies and epistemologies for the social sciences in Africa. In his study of the pre-colonial Great Lakes, he argues that a 'deeper ethnographic and historical awareness should give us enough confidence not to be tyrannised by concepts'.[3]

Mafeje believed that Africa is in a good position, as a site for research, to overturn Eurocentric theories and definitions. In *The Theory and Ethnography of African Social Formations*, Mafeje furnishes an original theory of African social formations with a new methodological approach. He overturns classical anthropological and developmental theories and in so doing analyses the relationship between political and economic power. According to Mafeje, pastoralism and agriculture in pre-colonial Africa need not necessarily represent different modes of production but, rather, different modes of social existence within the same mode of production. He rejects the articulation theory of modes of production and the concept of feudalism in pre-colonial Africa and then evaluates the impact of colonialism in the Great Lakes region and its impact on African societies.

The ethnography and social formations of the interlacustrine

Mafeje's starting point is to overturn the concept of ethnography as anthropologists generally use the term. He departs from the standard usage of the term in that he does not limit it to the study of 'tribes' or 'tribal identities'. Nor does he use it as a scientific description of races. Instead, he assigns to it cultural and social connotations. Unlike other anthropologists who have done something similar, Mafeje does not seek to isolate patterns of sociocultural organisation of communities. Such an approach is too narrow for him. His point is to relate communities to their wider sociological and historical context. For Mafeje, taxonomic categories tend to favour discontinuities, even where none exist. In this way, not only are they ahistorical, but they also tend to atomise societies.

It is true that different forms might entail different qualities or processes. But Mafeje was not interested in forms. He was interested in the similarities in processes or qualities, in the content of the essential characteristics of societies, the level at which similarities and differences become apparent. In their search for taxonomy, anthropologists who conducted research in the interlacustrine kingdoms tended to focus on forms as opposed to substance and the underlying features of those societies.[4] This led to speculative studies that border on racism. Colonial anthropologists tend to contradict themselves in that they identify a number of tribes, yet in spite of the diversity of the tribes, the anthropologists speak of ethnographic unity.

Mafeje's concept of ethnography relates to what he terms 'learnt habits', such as language, which facilitate social and cultural creativity. In his view, this has nothing to do with race or ethnicity, but is the concrete historical reality of the interlacustrine people. One of the major problems with anthropological research has been to conflate the notion of tribe (if by that one means a form of political organisation) and a linguistic group. For Mafeje, ethnographic evidence pointed to the contrary – the two do not always correspond. People may speak the same language, but still fall under different or independent chiefdoms.[5] The failure to appreciate the theoretical implications of this ethnographic detail leads to conceptual muddles, such as referring to the interlacustrine kingdoms as multi-kingdom tribes. On the other hand, in Bunyoro and Ankole, for example, there are unitary kingdoms in what are clearly ethnographically diverse communities. Thus, says Mafeje, for the anthropologist, 'the co-existence of the Bairu and Bahima in Bunyoro and Ankole or of the Bahutu and Batutsi in Rwanda and Burundi constituted something of an anomaly'.[6] Yet this need not be the case. These societies appeared anomalous precisely because of the anthropological atomisation of societies.

In *The Theory and Ethnography of African Social Formations* Mafeje gives two more reasons why his ethnography has little to do with race. First, people who comprise any one ethnic group would, under different circumstances or in a different time, fall under different groups or be known by a different name. Second, it is possible that the same group of people might, as a result of migration, ecological conditions and interaction with other groups – even within a given region and epoch – still account for ethnographic variation. Mafeje questions the distinctness and purity of ethnic or tribal identities and argues that distinctness of ethnic identities should never be overstated because fusion with other groups makes for cultural continuities and reproduction. As an example, the interlacustrine people had for some time ceased to view themselves as bounded societies or kin-based groups; by the fifteenth century the

Bunyoro ruling dynasties had sought to impose their authority on others in the region that had similar cultural, linguistic and modes of social organisation. This raises questions about the meaning of 'society' and the criteria used to ascertain its boundaries and, for Mafeje, the theoretical implications. For one thing, anthropologists use the term 'society' to designate bounded units that coincide with culture (or Mafeje's 'ethnography'). Marxists, however, reject the term as unscientific and ideologically laden and instead use the term 'social formation'. Mafeje did not consider a social formation to be the same as an articulation of modes of production. His use of 'social formation' differs from that associated with Étienne Balibar or Samir Amin.[7] For Balibar, the term 'social formation' referred either to 'an empirical concept designating the object of a concrete analysis, i.e., an *existence* ... or else an abstract concept replacing the ideological notion of "society" and designating the object of the science of history insofar as it is a totality of instances articulated on the basis of a determinate mode of production'.[8] Amin considered social formations '*concrete* structures, organised and characterised by a *dominant* mode of production which forms the apex of a complex set of subordinate modes'.[9]

For Mafeje, a social formation is characterised by an 'articulation of the economic instance' and 'the instance of power'. There are logical reasons why he avoided Balibar's and Amin's uses of the term. Logically, Mafeje maintains, 'we could not use an articulation of abstract concepts such as "modes of production" to designate the same concrete social reality they are meant to explain'.[10] One cannot define a concept and still have the very same concept within its definition. The economic instance has a concrete referent because it relates, primarily, to the level of production, not that of theory and abstraction. Equally, class struggle is a concrete reality occurring at the level of social relations and reproduction among members of competing classes or representatives of competing modes of production. This is the instance of power that ensures the continuation of struggles and ideological affirmations and it is not only applicable at the level of practice, but is also theoretically or universally applicable. Ethnography and social formation, as Mafeje conceives of the two terms, can be understood through a concrete historical analysis of the interlacustrine kingdoms. In his homage to Mafeje, Amin writes: 'I agree with Mafeje's definition of social formations as a bloc covering the economic and political realms. But it does not fully and necessarily substitute for the structuring of specific and differing modes of production.'[11] On the face of it, Mafeje's discussion of the ethnography and social formations of the interlacustrine is rather convoluted, yet it lays the foundation for his methodological and theoretical contribution.

Because of a lack of centralisation, the interlacustrine kingdoms were said to be segmentary or acephalous societies, their cultural practices characterised by lineages as a form of political organisation. Although this applies primarily at the local level, it remains the case even in the centralised kingdoms. In the pre-colonial period these societies were in transition from one form of political organisation to another, but the fixed anthropological binaries between segmentary/acephalous and centralised states obscure this historical process. Mafeje cautions that in describing these societies as transitional, he is not implying that they should be viewed in evolutionary terms – for example, not all segmentary societies in the interlacustrine kingdoms were destined to become centralised kingdoms as a form of political organisation but were, rather, exposed to centralising tendencies. The whole process should be understood in sociological and historical terms, rather than as 'natural' or biological evolution.

Mafeje continues by explaining that to fully understand this, one needs to consider the case of Bunyoro, Ankole, Buhaya and Rwanda, which were originally decentralised agricultural communities whose ways of living were modified 'by empire-building pastoralists who came from outside'.[12] The empire builders, however, need not have come from outside; good examples of empire builders and ruling dynasties coming from within include Buganda, Busoga and 'all other Bantu kingdoms, stretching from the Congo through Zambia, Zimbabwe and down to South Africa'. In fact, the rise of certain clans and lineages to establish royal clans and ruling dynasties is characteristic of the Bantu-speaking communities from the fifteenth century onwards. Further, Mafeje argues, pastoralism is quite common in Bantu-speaking communities in tsetse-free zones. Thus, the anthropological distinction between pastoralist invaders and native agriculturalists 'is, historically, not diagnostic'.[13]

In addition, the so-called Hamitic pastoralists, who were found mainly in the north, are archetypal segmentary societies. The question how and why, in their southward movement, the pastoralists came to establish powerful kingdoms has to be explained in sociological and not in racial terms. In addition, the notion of 'Hamitic' pastoralists and 'Nilotic' agriculturalists is historically inaccurate and theoretically unjustified since, through intermingling, these characteristics are to be found in both groups. Furthermore, long-horned cattle are not unique to Somalia and Ethiopia, but are to be found in countries such as Sierra Leone and Namibia. And pre-dynastic Egypt, from which the Hamitic pastoralists supposedly came, was not a pastoral society.

From the nineteenth century onwards, the interlacustrine region consisted of ten main kingdoms and three segmentary societies. All of them spoke Bantu languages. Although the kingdoms are said to have been ruled by dynasties of different ethnic descent, their constitutions contained more commonalities than differences. It is true that some were heterogeneous (Bunyoro, Ankole, Rwanda, Buhaya, Buha and Buzinza) while others were more homogeneous (Buganda and Busoga).

This discussion gives rise to the question of class versus caste in interlacustrine social formations. Mafeje argues that from the standpoint of political economy, class and caste are relative terms, although the same may not hold true ethnographically. Historically, it seems that caste-based kingdoms appeared much earlier than class-based ones. Mafeje does not offer a proper periodisation of these events to provide clarity on the specific epoch to which earlier caste and later class refer, although analytically and theoretically this is important information. As it is, Mafeje's analysis does not say much about class structure and its evolution. Did this take place during the colonial period or before it? Often, when anthropologists speak of class, all they are referring to is social stratification. Mafeje was not unaware of this and discusses the class versus status question in some detail. However, in this instance, it is important to spell out the period in which class takes root in the interlacustrine social formations. Bernard

Magubane, for example, speaks at length about the anthropological con-fusion between class and social stratification in the colonial situation and refers to social stratification as a descriptive concept that 'implies sets of positions in a hierarchical arrangement'.[14] It simply entails wage or salary differentiation, but not necessarily different class positions. Class, on the other hand, is a much more analytical concept insofar as it relates to divisions in society based on individuals' relationship to the primary means of production. Owing to its antagonistic nature, class division implies political action.

With regard to the question of political centralisation, Mafeje uses genealogical charts of the ruling dynasties and concludes that in the case of Bunyoro this would have taken place somewhere in the fifteenth cen-tury. He says the actual date is ultimately immaterial because the social age of a society is not dependent on chronology. That may well be the case, but in the search for class and state formation in the interlacustrine kingdoms, historical accuracy may be important and to ignore it is to deprive the reader of the nature of class formation in that region. Mafeje mentions Giovanni Arrighi's critique of Andre Gunder Frank:

> His objections to Frank were not only to the fact that he had given a determinate role to exchange instead of production relations in his study of Latin American social formations but also to the fact that in his general analysis *class structure* got subordinated to colonial structure. Arrighi saw this as a form of historicism which militated against dynamic analysis as well as anti-imperialist struggles, since it attributed lack of development in Third World countries to a prior and unchanging cause. He further protested that in this way differences in class-structure in various ex-colonial societies and at different stages of their development could not be grasped. He charged that, instead, in Frank's work one is presented with an over-generalised postulate which lacks specificity both in historical time and in social content.[15]

It would be extremely uncharitable to accuse Mafeje of having made the same mistake. Nevertheless, such specificities as are demanded by Arrighi from Gunder Frank are equally required from Mafeje, particularly with reference to historical time and social content.

In any case, at this point Mafeje is concerned to characterise the nature of the distinction between what he calls the heterogeneous and the homogeneous formations. The former, with observable affinities and resemblances, include Bunyoro, Ankole, Rwanda, Burundi, Buhaya, Buha and Buzinza. The latter include Buganda and Busoga. Mafeje writes that in the Banyoro oral tradition there were three dynasties: the Tembuzi, the Chwezi and the Babito. The big puzzle, according to Mafeje, was that there is no mention of the Bahuma (or Bahima, as they are called elsewhere in the region) dynasty. Anthropologists and historians only make cursory references to a Bahuma aristocracy that purportedly originates from Hamitic people (believed to be so by virtue merely of physical appearance). For Mafeje, the likelihood is that the Bachwezi were chased out of Bunyoro by Babito invaders, possibly in the sixteenth century, the period in which they made their southward movement. Another puzzle relates to the arrival of the Bachwezi in Bunyoro. On this question, the Banyoro oral traditions were, in Mafeje's words, utterly ambiguous.

Mafeje goes on to argue that if the original inhabitants of Bunyoro were agriculturalists, as opposed to pastoralists, it is not clear why and how cattle herding became predominant in Bunyoro. One explanation could be that the cattle came with the invading Babito, but this leaves unexplained the prevalence of Bahuma pastoralists further south in such places as Ankole, Burundi and Rwanda, where there was no Babito invasion. Added to the puzzle is the presence of 'light-brown', purportedly half-Hamitic people in Bunyoro and Toro. For Mafeje, the solution to this puzzle is to discount the likelihood that original agriculturalists ascended to royalty in Bunyoro. He says the idea that pastoralism became an elite pursuit can be explained by pointing to the 'Hamitic' invaders who migrated from south-eastern Ethiopia and southern Somalia, 'with their long-horned cattle'.[16] Mahmood Mamdani considers this account of events in the interlacustrine kingdoms spurious. Against Mafeje, Mamdani argues:

The migration hypothesis was further reinforced by regional myths that predated the colonial period and were recorded by early anthropologists and explorers. They have recently been strung together and framed into a single grand hypothesis by Archie Mafeje in a recent work, *The Theory and Ethnography of African Social Formations*. The central myth concerns the Bachwezi dynasty in the kingdom of Bunyoro in western Uganda. The Bachwezi are said to have 'migrated from south eastern Ethiopia and southern Somalia with their long-horned cattle', but moved on after 'a few generations' when 'chased out by Babito invaders' from the north. Following the myth, Mafeje suggests a migration in 'a south-westerly direction where ecological conditions are ideal for cattle-keeping'. Mafeje thus links the Bachwezi of Bunyoro with the Bahima of Ankole and the Tutsi of the Great Lakes. While many may be reluctant to accept the restatement of myth as historical fact, few would dare dismiss it as outright fiction. At the same time, one needs to beware that public memory – in this case, myth – also changes and that this change is not entirely unrelated to official discourse. A context in which official discourse privileged some because they were said to have migrated from elsewhere was certainly an incentive to those concerned to embellish stories about their having come from elsewhere.[17]

Although Mamdani charitably argues that a myth cannot be dismissed as outright fiction, he nevertheless caricatures Mafeje's argument as 'a single grand hypothesis'. Although Mamdani acknowledges that the said myth is part of the interlacustrine public memory, he nevertheless puts Mafeje in the same camp as the colonial anthropologists and explorers that Mafeje criticised. The genius of Mafeje, which clearly eludes Mamdani, consists in taking his objects of inquiry and intellectual interlocutors on their own terms in order to expose internal inconsistencies in their views, taking the myths he supposedly 'strung together' to be part of the interlacustrine oral traditions. Mafeje's approach of taking his objects of inquiry on their own terms is less condescending than Mamdani's suggestion. In fact, one of the points Mafeje impresses upon the reader is that 'the early recorded accounts by European explorers and ethnologists such as Speke, Baker and Roscoe often substituted fantasy for facts, largely because of [a] lack of respect for indigenous oral historians'.[18] While Mafeje beseeched African scholars to take ethnography seriously, he was not an empiricist because real knowledge making does not reside at the level of facts, but at the level of interpretation. Mafeje's study is meant to be a critique of colonial anthropology, historiography and the ideology it represents and not, as Mamdani takes it to be, an affirmation of the same. What Mafeje intended to do was to furnish the reader with the arguments of colonial anthropologists on the nature of the interlacustrine kingdoms and then show how their arguments are conceptually flawed, and to do this, he did not necessarily need to furnish any facts of his own about the history of the interlacustrine kingdoms.

Mafeje says that the Bachwezi were succeeded by the 'darker-skinned' Luo speakers from north of the Nile. According to Banyoro oral tradition, the Luo speakers were not known for pastoralism. The question then is why both the Hamitic pastoralists and the Luo speakers, neither of whom organised themselves around kingdoms or kingship institutions, decided to establish kingdoms when they settled in Bunyoro. Mafeje posits three basic considerations. First, in order to form a state, there must be a settled population for the purposes of production and generating revenues; in Bunyoro, only the Bairu met this condition. Second, although land was abundant among the agriculturalists, they nevertheless lacked cattle – so much so that they treated cattle as prestige goods associated with royal rituals. Whoever had a large herd of cattle enjoyed a high social status. Thus, the pastoralists had an advantage over the agriculturalists (Mafeje does not spell out how this advantage was secured). Third, the mystique and prestige associated with cattle ensured a position of privilege for the pastoralists. Based on these considerations, Mafeje argues that neither the pastoralists nor the agriculturalists should take credit for the development of kingship in Bunyoro. Instead, this development should be viewed as an outcome of dialectical interaction between the two groups. The Bairu agriculturalists 'provided the agricultural base and services and the pastoralists, relieved of any onerous duties but in control of prestige goods, indulged themselves, turned the latter into mechanism for political control and ritual mystification'.[19] (One might, however, argue that this would not have been feasible without military domination.)

This phenomenon is replicated in at least five other interlacustrine kingdoms in addition to Bunyoro: Ankole, Burundi, Buhaya, Buzinza and Rwanda. Mafeje calls it 'an integration of the economic instance with the instance of political power, despite the co-existence of two distinct modes of existence – pastoralism in the hands of the Bahuma and agriculture in the hands of the Bairu'.[20] Mafeje is quick to caution that this should not be mistaken for a mere division of labour or mixed farming, as is the case with the Bantu speakers of the south. There may have been crossing of political boundaries, but this is far from being an assimilation of one mode of existence into the other. Mafeje reasons that 'the two modes provided a basis for status as well as class distinctions'.

With regard to the occupation of land, the two groups adopted a usufruct rights system, which suited both, so long as they were not encroaching on each other. This is true of all the other segmentary societies. If there was no encroachment, there would be cordial relations and interaction between them. Bunyoro is exemplary because it was a model for and a challenge to other people in the region and its significance lies in the idea that it pioneered the centralisation of political power in the interlacustrine by synthesising diverse elements, in so doing also dispensing with politics of ethnicity – so much so that in the interlacustrine states people of different ethnic backgrounds lived under the same political authority. Far from being what anthropologists called a 'well-integrated empire', Bunyoro actually spawned new kingdoms, and dynasties in the region can trace their genealogy to the founding dynasty in Bunyoro. In instances where original autonomous groups formed what Mafeje terms a 'veritable kingdom', one could not refer to such an entity as a multi-kingdom as other anthropologists did. Suitably understood, this case marks 'a different stage of political development', as Mafeje puts it.

Thus far, the dynasties to which Mafeje refers were descendants of the founders of Bunyoro – the Bahuma and the Babito who originated

from outside the interlacustrine. These dynasties were assimilated lin-
guistically, culturally and to some degree socially. Having argued that
nomadic pastoralists have no known record of establishing kingdoms,
Mafeje attributes the rise of kingdoms in the interlacustrine to the settled
agriculturalists who laid the foundation for exchange of goods and services in the midst of a diverse group of people.

Mafeje takes pains to understand what he calls the heterogeneous
formations (there are also the homogeneous formations of Buganda and
Busoga, both of which are traditionally agriculturalist). First, Mafeje finds
it difficult to credit John Hanning Speke's view that the people of Buganda
were Galla, from Ethiopia, by origin.[21] Mafeje found that neither the Baganda
nor the Basoga had the physical characteristics attributed to the Hamitic
genetic stock and neither boasted of pastoral traditions. Accordingly, they
were not like the dominant pastoralists and subordinate agriculturalists –
both were traditionally agriculturalists, yet they were collectively known
as *bairu* (of lower social status). Mafeje was puzzled that the Baganda and
Basoga, isolated but also occupying a vast territory, were known by the
same name, *bairu*, whereas the concept of a tribe requires that a group be
known by a specific name. He takes the genealogy and the significance of a
collective label to be of some importance and says that the term *bairu* must
be thought of as referring to status or occupational reference, rather than
genetic stock (this is similar to terms such as Mahima/Mahuma/Muhinda/
Mututsi, which are associated with status or political office in such places
as Bunyoro, Buhaya, Buha and Buzinza). He theorises that if that were true,
it would be possible to account for the rise of Buganda and Busoga districts
without isolating the Baganda and Basoga from fellow agriculturalists in
the region. He therefore wanted to know at what point the kings of Buganda
became sovereign authorities, rather than simply *primus inter pares* (first
among equals) in a segmentary society. Ultimately, Mafeje concludes that
the importance of Buganda lay not 'in its chronological but rather in its
social age' and Buganda reached the same level of development as Bunyoro
because of its indigenous agricultural population.[22]

Like Buganda, Busoga had no record of stratification based on dominant pastoralists and servile agriculturalists, and there was a linguistic

affinity between Luganda and Lusoga. There was a huge difference between north-eastern and south-western Busoga. At issue was how this division came about. There were three critical issues for Mafeje. First, Busoga was not a unitary kingdom, but was made up of autonomous political units much like the clan or lineage structure of segmentary societies. Second, ordinary people viewed themselves as Basoga, regardless of the origins of the ruling dynasties and they rejected non-Bantu origins; as far as they were concerned being Bantu or of Bantu origin carried no negative connotations. This not only represents an integration of different peoples, but also of pastoralism and agriculture because of ecological conditions. Third, the kingdom of Busoga was simultaneously founded by agriculturalists and immigrant pastoralists. This created a common culture. The Basoga adopted a model of political organisation created by the Baganda in the eighteenth century – a unitary structure with the king, his senior chiefs and commoners. Although Basoga later dominated Buganda and Bunyoro, British intervention supported the Buganda mode of political organisation that they tried to replicate in southern Uganda. This led to the disruption, though not quite the demise, of pre-existing modes of political organisation. Mafeje was interested in studying the nature of the mode of political organisation prior to this disruption.

Modes of political organisation in the interlacustrine kingdoms

It is important to bear in mind that in Mafeje's view the concept of social formation consisted of the economic instance and the instance of power, and the two found expression (or, more appropriately, articulation) within a recognisable sociocultural context. Unlike social formations, modes of political and economic organisation are more concrete and are variable, even within the same general context. For example, organisational differences between Buganda and Bunyoro were not based on principle as such, but on adaptive responses, even though the mode of political organisation was more or less the same. Mafeje was well aware that for some Marxists and political economists the separation of politics from economics is spurious. Nonetheless, he argued: 'After due consideration based on material evidence we concluded that the relationship between modes of political organisation and modes of economic production is not absolute but relative.'[23] Mafeje distinguishes between a mode of political reproduction in the abstract sense (centralised kingdoms) and modes of political organisation in the sense of operational mechanisms (administrative structures and hierarchies). This then raises the question as to when practical adaptations, cumulatively, lead to qualitative change. Mafeje underlines the question of variability of forms in a socio-historical context, resisting the temptation to turn historical developments into evolutionism.

Bunyoro was the first in the interlacustrine region to adopt political centralisation. This prompted other kingdoms not only to follow suit, but also to try to tailor the Bunyoro model to their own contexts and circumstances. Mafeje says: 'This resulted in variations within broad uniformities of language and culture which overrode ethnic differences in most cases.'[24] Anthropologists classify the resultant modes of political organisation as one-kingdom tribes, multi-kingdom tribes and unitary kingdoms with a tribal caste system. Buganda is the best example of the first category;[25] Busoga, Buhaya, Buzinza and Buha exemplify the second; Ankole, Rwanda and Burundi fit into the third. Mafeje left out Bunyoro and Toro, both of which were single kingdoms, because in each of them the boundaries between Bahima/Bahuma (an upper stratum of pastoralists) and Bairu (a lower stratum of agriculturalists) 'got so attenuated that these terms were virtually emptied of their original connotations'.[26] This suggests grounds for investigating the nature of the relationship between status categories and ethnic nomenclature, which has implications for the entire ethnic classification so typical in conventional anthropological writings. In general, attempts to describe with accuracy the political systems of the interlacustrine region are likely to be spoiled by terminological difficulties such as the awkward concept of 'multi-kingdom tribes'. Tribe, in this sense, has a purely cultural referent and is delimited by a common language. Mafeje argues that in the past the term 'tribe' referred to a particular stage or form of political organisation, rather than a mere reference to culture and language.

Theoretically, tribes entail particular forms of political organisation that are kin-based, the chief's seniority deriving from his being the most senior of the founding clan. He precedes other heads of clans or lineages in his tribe. In segmentary societies, however, the chief is simply *primus inter pares*. The notion of the royal clan and ruling lineage entails hierarchy and differential access to prestige goods; in principle, this is not any different from privileges enjoyed by elders in a lineage structure. Taken together with the distributive function of kin-based groups, this means that tribal communities were 'pre-class' societies – the hierarchy of their structure does not necessarily mean that there were antagonistic relations among members. Contrary to the claims of Marxists and anthropologists such as Claude Meillassoux,[27] elders in African societies did not constitute an exploitative class.

According to Mafeje, while terms such as 'tribe' and 'kingdoms' are used interchangeably, there are observable qualitative differences between the two. Historically, Mafeje contends, kingdoms appear much later than tribes (although my sense is that this is at odds with his claim that tribes are an invention of colonialism). At any rate, kingdoms represent a coming together of pre-existing segmentary or tribal societies to unite or submit to a supreme authority. Sociologically and historically, the rise of kingdoms entails the end of kin-bound forms of political organisation. In turn, this translates into the rise of centralised official bureaucracy. The council of tribal elders or members of a royal lineage in tribal societies do not constitute an official bureaucracy, but simply represent segmentary or particularistic interests. Ultimately, Mafeje argues, the notion of multi-kingdom tribes is an oxymoron.

Anthropologists who speak of 'tiny kingdoms' fail to see the blind spot in their concept in that they mistake a linguistic group for a form of political organisation. It is possible that any number of descendant groups can co-exist under the same cultural or linguistic category. There is a possibility of competition where even defeated sons of the same chief could form new chiefdoms or new ruling lineages. This pro-liferation of political units is possible under the tribal mode of polit-ical organisation yet this does not necessarily mean that it is contingent on linguistic affinities. In South Africa, the case of amaXhosa, who have about 15 chiefdoms, is a good example. Mafeje contends that the case of amaXhosa, amaZulu and amaSwati, all of whom fall under the sociocultural entity Nguni, can be extended to other areas such as the interlacustrine region. Part of the intention of his study is to situate the interlacustrine kingdoms in the wider African context. Modes of political organisation do change, even though the cultural and linguistic context in which they are found may not. To the extent that this is so, the cultural and linguistic context that is shared by a number of societies reveals nothing about their social age. The determining factor in the age of a society is the articulation between the mode of political organisation and the mode of economic production.

The notion of kinship is not contingent upon the size of a social unit. Mafeje hastens to point out that 'centralising tendencies imply incorporation of smaller units by bigger or stronger ones over time, especially if they all occupy contiguous territory',[28] which accounts for the rise of single kingdoms in places where several tribes once existed. Mafeje is not referring to empires but to unitary or integrated structures. In the interlacustrine this took two forms: kingdoms in which the citizenry was composed of more than one group and those that consisted of only one ethnic group. Bunyoro managed to centralise political authority much earlier than others did and it was Bunyoro's dynasties that initiated the same practice in southern kingdoms, creating what became known as multi-ethnic kingdoms. However, there is no evidence to suggest that centralised political authority was established through the efforts of any one particular ethnic group or, for that matter, that ethnic groups persisted throughout history. For Mafeje, the rise of dynasties such as the Bachwezi and the Babito is best understood as a class phenomenon, not an ethnic epiphenomenon. Mafeje adduces no comprehensive argument save to say that the term *banyoro* originally referred to a political rank, not the people of Bunyoro; he argued also that two categories of people were recognised – *bairu* (agriculturalists) and *bahuma* (pastoralists) – and at that time the two categories did not translate, as is assumed, into the ruled and the rulers. Although the pastoralists enjoyed the prestige that came with large herds of cattle, they were still subject to political control by an official bureaucracy.

Political office in Bunyoro, putting aside the royal clan, had little to do with ethnic origin. The mode of political organisation was primarily bureaucratic. Apart from the dynastic Babito, the bureaucracy consisted, in the main, of appointed chiefs, categorised into territorial chiefs (*bakungu*), district chiefs (*batongole*) and the village chiefs (*bataka*). Although there existed the usual patron-client relationship between chiefs and their subordinates, it cannot be said that there was direct exploitation of the tenants as labour. The economic value was extracted in political terms based on the patron-client relationship. This raises the question of whether there was a ruling class in Bunyoro. It can be said, Mafeje reasons, that in Bunyoro the transition from kinship to the bureaucratic mode of political organisation had been completed. Moreover, while this was not formal, land property had developed to 'conversion of official estates into heritable property'.[29]

In Ankole, the Bairu and the Bahima undergirded state power without necessarily being its embodiment. The question then is who controlled the state. Mafeje's response is that 'the government of the kingdom centred on the king, his relatives, his wife's relatives and heads of important clans who acted as the king's power brokers'.[30] The chief minister, known as *nganzi*, and war-band leaders were merely bureaucratic appointments. Leading warriors were entitled to a share of the booty, so that military prowess was closely linked or otherwise translated to wealth in cattle. All officials were entitled to tribute in the form of agricultural products (from the Bairu) and cattle and dairy (from the Bahima). On the question of land, there were never private property rights, but only usufruct rights under the lineage system. Effectively, what this means is that in Ankole, the lines between lineage and bureaucratic mode of political organisation had not been crossed, as they were in Bunyoro, Buganda and Toro. The Bahima and Bairu suffered extraction of surplus value through tributes to those in power. This was a case of social stratification along political and ideological lines, as against class division that turns on exploitation of labour and property relations.

Instead of viewing this as a form of ethnic prejudice – even though in Ankole the system centred on the king, his relatives, wife's relatives and heads of important clans – this region and its mode of political organisation can be termed a pastoral aristocracy. Although tribute was paid to the king, Omugabe, his relatives and a few privileged appointees, there was a 'wider and supplementary stratum of rich cattle-owners who stood in a patron-client relation to the majority of the producers'.[31] Land tenure and utilisation of land was still under the control of heads of lineages. In Ankole, the interplay between kingship and lineage is unresolved. Mafeje argues that tribes, as a result of ethnographic and historical shifts and changes, 'are derived independently of "ethnic" origin' as, in Burundi, the Batutsi were divided into sub-tribes such as the Batare, Bezi, Bataga and Mambutsa.[32] The individual identity of these sub-tribes was much more important than ethnic origin and the population of Burundi consisted of royal and non-royal Batutsi, Bahima and Bahutu. Still, what Mafeje found difficult to establish was whether social stratification (or 'social differentiation', as he puts it) in Burundi, for example, which cut across ethnic lines, was in and of itself indicative of an emergence of a class society. In Burundi, the king, his officers, princes and entourage received tribute and dues from pastoralists and agriculturalists alike – yet in spite of being entitled to tribute and dues, the king and the princes held no property in land. Claims to land resources were determined politically through the general rule of administrative domains. Autonomous local chiefs and ordinary citizens accessed land resources through their patrilineage.

Although property and labour relations could not be used as mitigating factors for the division of Burundi society into classes, the term *banyaruguru* referred to the privileged stratum in society, which consisted of royalty, the princes, bureaucratic chiefs and sub-chiefs. They lived on revenues derived from ordinary citizens, but 'they were not as yet independent of their patrilineages'.[33] In Rwanda, unlike Burundi, there was a highly centralised political structure. At the top of the hierarchy was the king, known as *mwami*, and an official council of chiefs, who played an advisory role. All chiefs were appointed by the king and could be dismissed. The chiefs were divided into the district and hill chiefs and in turn further divided into two categories – land chiefs (Bahutu, who dealt with agriculturalists) and cattle chiefs (Batutsi, who dealt with pastoralists). Chiefs collected tributes and dues from the citizenry (dairy products and cattle from pastoralists and, from agriculturalists, bananas for brewing beer), from lineage or family heads and not from individuals. This was apparently a way of strengthening kin group and family ties insofar as kinship members assisted family heads. The second role of the chiefs was to settle disputes over land and cattle, but it is important that whereas the land chiefs arbitrated in land cases, cattle chiefs did not arbitrate in cattle disputes, which were dealt with by the army. This is because the army was responsible for raiding of cattle and for protecting national herds. In contrast to other interlacustrine kingdoms, Rwanda had a standing army and thus a mixture of lineage and bureaucratic modes of political organisation.

However, as Mafeje notes, only the Batutsi were warriors. The Bahutu were herdsmen who rounded up cattle during raids or carried supplies for the warriors. The booty was shared between political leaders and army chiefs, but only warriors could receive a share. Although everyone paid dues and tribute, only Batutsi had access to cattle, a symbol of prestige and power, because the distribution of the spoils of battle would undermine the Batutsi's position as the ruling elite. Although this may strike many as a case of ethnic division, Mafeje insists that this indicated processes of class differentiation. In Rwanda, as in other pastoral kingdoms in the interlacustrine region, land was not considered property, though it was controlled politically. The king had the right of control over the whole country; Bahutu chiefs acted as representatives of local lineages. The king allocated official estates to chiefs, who in turn collected dues and tributes and were entitled to the labour services of heads of families (clients of the chiefs or the king) for up to two days a week, which signifies some control over the labour process. Still, clients were exploited less as labour than as subjects. Exploitation in this context was not, strictly speaking, extraction of value per se, since labour relations were not crystallised. In addition, the exploiting ruling elite, with the exception of the king, had no formal mechanisms of 'reproducing itself indefinitely as a class'.[34]

Illuminating though this discussion is, Mafeje does not concede that it was a case of ethnicity, instead calling it a case of pastoral aristocracy, rather than a Batutsi aristocracy or a caste, because the Batutsi 'were neither rich nor exempt from exploitation by the state and its bureaucracy'.[35] To prove his point, he appealed to the case of Buganda, which also had a centralised system, but was characterised by one ethnic group. The question then is whether the elite in Buganda was on the verge of consolidation as a class in ways that transcended the limitations of pastoralism in a kingdom such as Rwanda. The qualitative difference between agricultural and pastoral societies seems to lie in the fact that the former has a labour process and possibilities for conversion of value while the latter involves accumulation of cattle by individuals or families.

The social and economic character of the interlacustrine kingdoms

In *The Theory and Ethnography of African Social Formations* Mafeje labours to understand modes of political organisation in the interlacustrine kingdoms. He links the study of modes of political organisation to the study of modes of social production. In the African context, however, the study of the latter is handicapped by lack of data, the result in part of disciplinary divisions of labour and ideological biases. According to Mafeje, Marxists, who champion the notion of modes of production, are newcomers to the continent. The study of Africa until this point had largely been the preserve of liberal researchers who, to all intents and purposes, were reluctant to study Africa from the standpoint of political economy. They focused, in the main, on micro studies, aspects of a given phenomenon, without relating them to the wider sociological and historical context. To be sure, they studied African production processes, but rarely situated such processes in the social and political institutions in which the production processes obtain. Mafeje maintains that they overlooked African land tenure systems. Where they had studied them, they simply dismissed them as communal institutions, a hindrance to Africa's development. This is true of liberals and Marxists alike. For their part, colonial administrators sought to replace land tenure systems with their own, so as to further their ill-gotten gains. Ultimately, according to Mafeje, studies in land tenure and land use have receded to the background. Those who attempt to study these issues, chiefly Marxists and political economists, adopt formalistic approaches with little regard for concrete realities. Significantly, what is missing in all these studies is 'systematic data on the social and technical conditions for material production in traditional societies – something which was so crucial in the understanding of agrarian societies and their transformations in Europe'.[36]

According to Mafeje, social scientists describe the interlacustrine kingdoms as feudal by virtue of their kingships, bureaucracy and fiefdoms or clientage. He argues that some social scientists point out that political centralisation means that the labour force withdraws from primary production into administrative activities, something that translates to extraction of economic value by the political bureaucracy. Mafeje says this is not good enough because the question of tenure, the 'seigniorial mode of estate management and fiscal arrangement', as he puts it, has to be known and studied before one can declare, a priori, that a feudal system exists in the interlacustrine kingdoms.[37] The British social anthropologist Jack Goody referred to this as the economic approach to feudalism, as opposed to the political approach about which Mafeje speaks.[38] Thus, Mafeje's study includes, along with modes of political organisation, other modes of production insofar as they bear on production relations. One cannot study agrarian societies without taking into account land and its use. Not only are concepts used in the study of land tenure by Marxist and liberal social scientists who write about land in sub-Saharan Africa Eurocentric, they also lead to misconceptions. To counter such prejudices, one needs to study 'the specificity of African social systems'. This is the task Mafeje sets for himself.

Dues and tribute were the only recognisable extraction of economic value in Buganda. Both of these measures were meant to raise state revenues and ensure a high standard of living for chiefs. Tribute to chiefs also meant better political relations between patrons and clients. Of theoretical significance here is that what went through the hierarchies as dues were perishable goods such as banana beer, barkcloth, meat and fish, and there was therefore little to no accumulation at the top of the hierarchy. Added to this is the fact that in Buganda chiefs' estates and administrative posts were not inherited, and upon the death or dismissal of a chief, the vacant post reverted to the king to decide on a successor. Under these circumstances it is difficult to sustain the view that there existed in Buganda a ruling aristocracy or a class system with reference to property relations. Nor could one speak of a ruling elite on the basis of recruitment. Just as chiefs who had fallen out of grace could be demoted to peasant status, a politically successful peasant could be promoted or elected to the position of a chief.

In southern Busoga there developed the same pattern as in Buganda. However, apart from Busoga and Buganda, other interlacustrine kingdoms were dominated by the pastoral mode of production, as opposed to being entirely agricultural. Mafeje adds that 'from the point of view of land tenure, most of this was not only nomadic but was combined with agriculture practised by the majority of the population, the so-called Bairu'.[39] In such places as Bunyoro and Toro, evidence suggests that 'the principle of usufruct rights under lineage supervision' was outside of official estates, in other words not under complete control of the king through chiefs and district governors. Even then, it seems that people and cattle, rather than land, were under administrative control. Big cattle owners enjoyed social prestige because cattle were prestige goods. Mafeje reminds us that this was far from being a caste system, as anthropological literature suggests. In Bunyoro and other places in the interlacustrine region, in contrast to Buganda, cattle were a family asset and could be inherited. Further, there was no limit to the number of cattle that a family could accumulate. In addition to dues and tribute, chiefs in Bunyoro and Toro collected succession, marriage, burial and grazing fees. A very large part of Bunyoro had been taken up by private estates, although the king reserved the right to confirm or refuse who might or might not occupy official estates. What this meant is that in Bunyoro there was a property-owning stratum (or 'class', as Mafeje puts it) that could reproduce itself. Mafeje is not sure whether this 'class' constituted a 'landed aristocracy'.

Chiefs and other Bahuma patrons received services and economic value from their clients. This is something that clients did as loyal suppliants.

There was no bondage. Mafeje argues that the clients did not consider themselves a labouring class, but viewed themselves as loyal followers or clients, who provided public or private services to the chief or patron and did so without losing their autonomy as producers. Mafeje seems to have been relying on the subjective conception of labour service by the clients, rather than the more objective focus on labour time performed for the chiefs. Who is to say what each client thought or believed and what would happen to the client who refused to render these services? The autonomy of the clients as producers is constrained, as the labour time expended in the service of the patrons/chiefs is labour time lost to themselves – the equivalent of expropriating the produce of the clients. Although some refer to this stratum as 'peasants', these people had neither an independent tenure nor user rights, unlike producers who operated within the lineage system. Mafeje contends that although property relations in Bunyoro were akin to a feudal system, production relations suggested otherwise. Without quite spelling it out, Mafeje declares that in spite of superstructural differences in favour of Buganda, processes of class formation were much more advanced in Bunyoro. It was mainly at the level of productive forces that Bunyoro had a headstart over Buganda – that was where the first iron smelting in the region occurred (discovery of salt also helped to improve trade in Bunyoro).

In Bunyoro there was a more intensive exploitation of internal labour. The objective was to provide utilities to the chiefs and the Bahuma quite generally – unless, as Mafeje argues, 'cattle are seen as a form of investment in a semi-pastoral economy'.[40] In Ankole, Burundi and Rwanda there were much deeper divisions between pastoralists and agriculturalists than in Bunyoro, Buhaya, Buzinza and Buha, owing to dominant pastoralists who limited the access of agriculturalists to unproductive cattle, reinforced by an ideology that drew invidious distinctions between the Bairu and Bahima. At issue is that the two modes of existence (agriculture and pastoralism) emerged side by side – and that they emerged concurrently does not mean that they were held in the same regard. Agriculture was considered subordinate to pastoralism, and agriculturalists (the Bairu) were considered inferior or otherwise subordinate to the pastoralist Bahima and consequently excluded from power – particularly in Ankole and Rwanda. This does not lend itself to ethnic categorisation or, for that matter, to separate modes of production. Mafeje rejects the view that the distinction between the two strata was ethnic or ideological. For him, to argue in such a way is to provide a justification, rather than an explanation. The real explanation, for Mafeje, lies at the level of production and property relations. This, too, is not self-evident, but an object of inquiry. In all three kingdoms property rights in land did not seem to have been the issue, nor did the Bairu and the Bahima try to stake personal or permanent claims on it. The emphasis on both sides was on usufruct rights. Even kings did not claim land as resource or property. In a strict sense, the king potentially had more rights to land than anyone else, but it was a right he hardly used unless he wished to punish someone guilty of a crime, in which case he would take the land away. In Rwanda, the king had similar rights over cattle. Thus, Mafeje concludes, the question of the king 'owning' land should be seen as a case of 'suzerainty' over the territory and its people, in contrast to Buganda and Bunyoro where the king had substantive control over land and property rights.

Among the Banyankole and Watutsi, the king allowed territorial chiefs and political favourites to administer these duties and the latter were, like the kings, entitled to tribute from their subjects in the form of cattle products, or cattle proper, beer and other agricultural products. Territorial chiefs could also share the dues collected by land and cattle chiefs who fell within their domains. As in Bunyoro, political office was appointive, but could still be handed down or passed on if the king agreed, but unlike in Bunyoro, this had no bearing on ownership of land by the incumbent. The prevailing rule was usufruct rights in order to cultivate and that rested on heads of families. In northern Rwanda, land was considered the right of patrilineages, notwithstanding the suzerainty of the king. In sum, ownership was limited to cattle. Even cattle ownership had a usufruct rights component among pastoralists (this is also true of amaXhosa in South Africa). Such rights fell under the ambit of production relations. Among the herdsmen and the cultivators there existed a symbiotic relationship of exchanging pastoral and agricultural products – this could not involve compulsion or exploitation.

However, the same did not hold for the relations between the rulers and the producers. The king and his members extracted economic value from the producers in the form of tribute and dues: from the pastoralists, cattle and fresh milk and from agriculturalists, fresh produce. Labour dues were required from the Bairu and Bahutu in the form of public works, as in Buganda and Bunyoro. On the other hand, Bahima and Batutsi commoners were required only for military service; this was in line with their social prestige and habitual cattle raids among pastoralists. In Ankole, Burundi and Rwanda, there was, apart from kings and chiefs, a 'non-producing class' of wealthy cattle owners who depended on the services of those who needed cattle or protection. These servants were usually, though not exclusively, cultivators. This is the patron-client relationship of the pastoral kingdoms that had long started in Bunyoro, independent of official bureaucracy. Although this was a relationship of great inequality, it nevertheless gave rise to usufruct rights in cattle. A patron could bestow on his client a cow to milk and to whose male offspring he (the client) had full rights, although the female offspring remained the property of the patron in order to ensure that the client could not accumulate. The patron also provided political protection to the client. Following the death of the client, the patron would look after his family. This paternalistic relationship, Mafeje argues, muffled class contradictions and had an ideological function that reproduced political power. Ultimately, it was a direct exploitation of the labour power of the client, 'but once again not as intensely as could be expected'.[41] In the main, the fiscal policy of the pastoral kingdoms consisted in providing perishable consumer goods and personal services for the royal family, the political bureaucrats and the so-called pastoral aristocracy. Although the Bahima and Batutsi were exempt from certain labour dues and owned modest herds of cattle, they did not constitute an aristocracy. Some of them were in fact nomads who often crossed borders for new pastures.

Mafeje, having analysed these kingdoms, rejects the anthropological notion of feudal aristocracy. In the context of ownership of large cattle herds, prestige and power, and command of services and the loyalty of others, he considered a more appropriate concept to be pastoral aristocracy. Then there is the fact that in pastoral kingdoms accumulation was not dependent on the exploitation of labour but was, at best, a neutral process that afforded political advantage to a few individual members of the communities. Mafeje stresses the view that there were no markets, technology was rudimentary and pastoralists as well as cultivators/agriculturalists constituted a class of producers dominated by a pastoral aristocracy. Agriculture and pastoralism formed a single mode of production in order to meet the needs of this pastoral aristocracy. In Buzinza and Buha, however, where there was a community of Batutsi pastoralists who migrated from Rwanda and Burundi, there existed no pastoral aristocracy, and instead there is evidence of a mixed economy that involved both Batutsi/Bahuma and Bairu – a tribal economy, as Mafeje puts it, dominated by the lineage principle. Chiefs in these regions had dominion over territory and the gifts to which they were entitled could not be called tribute, given how miniscule they were. In this sense, they did not have a patron-client relationship with the citizenry. The chief was merely *primus inter pares* and with the nature of the redistributory tribal system he had to give as much as he received. Failure to do so could mean losing his position.

In Buhaya there was a semblance of feudalism, given the nature of property relations. There was a growing landed aristocracy. As in other parts of the interlacustrine kingdoms, production was dominated by patron-client relations, which were, above all else, political, not economic. Mafeje invokes the distinction between exploitation of subjects and exploitation of labour, with the former seeming to hold true in this case. Additionally, considering this distinction 'might signify different modes of production, and different kinds of value'.[42] Here, then, the term 'economic surplus' is of no use since one cannot tell what is surplus and what is not.

Then there is the question of trade. Mafeje mentions the difficulties of long-distance as well as short-distance trade that resulted in neither capital accumulation nor technological investment, and did not increase production using existing technologies. What it led to was the 'drainage of existing manpower'.[43] Without offering concrete reasons why, Mafeje says this did not lead to any dislocation in terms of maintaining utility value – however, British imperialism intervened by devising methods that would stimulate trade. As can be expected, the interlacustrine societies were becoming a market for British manufacturers long before they had time to discover their own capacity to produce goods and trade. The interlacustrine kingdoms, as on the rest of the continent, were not prepared for this imperial and commercial assault. Militarily and politically, they attempted to resist, but with no success. The fragmented nature of the region made British invasion easy – some capitulated and others turned on one another by assisting Britain.

Unsurprisingly, both pastoralists and agriculturalists suffered under capitalism, not least because they were unable and unwilling to turn their instruments of production into capital. If they were not colonised, they could have had added value, but the logic of colonialism and imperialism is such that the colonies should not reap the benefits of their own produce. This would have affected the interlacustrine producers severely, given their economic uncompetitiveness. Mafeje believed that there was logic behind their conservatism. Of course, this is the logic that capitalism is 'meant to destroy'. Mafeje reminds us that this logic is in line with Amin's thesis that 'capitalism is a necessary stage because it is the only way in which productive forces could be developed further in economies in which utility value predominates'.[44] Yet, ironically, the Chinese experiment with socialism has been superseded by capitalism (underpinned by state capital and private capital). Ideologically, if capitalism is a necessary stage, Mafeje observes, radicals like Amin would be hard-pressed to justify the cruelty visited on peasants by capital – especially in the global South (to be fair, Amin might argue that he was not justifying the attendant cruelty and suffering). For Mafeje, 'the fundamental question, though, was whether the requisite technological conditions for development are inextricably bound with particular modes of production or historical stages'. In the final analysis, modes of production do not have to be complete in order to exist, as the interlacustrine kingdoms demonstrate.

Modes of production in Africa reconsidered

Mafeje declares that the foundations of every society are economic. For people to survive, they have to provide themselves with goods and services. This is axiomatic, yet liberals and Marxists quibble about whether the economy is a determinant of all social existence. Mafeje submits that the reasons for such disagreements are ideological, rather than scientific. Liberal economists have treated economic growth, for more than 200 years, as an 'unexceptionable index of social development', as Mafeje puts it.[45]

Mafeje claims that like their Marxist counterparts, liberal economists put a premium on the economic factor. He argues that the difference is largely conceptual. Liberals or bourgeois theorists argue that economic self-interest is the driving force behind development and pour scorn on notions of altruism, arguing that 'avarice is the driving force behind development'.[46] Marxists, on the other hand, assign development to material forces, which are impersonal in character. This enables Marxists to 'decode social systems' and use abstract principles such as modes of production – a concept with universalistic pretensions. Scholars have, however, questioned the veracity of these universalistic pretensions and the usefulness of the term outside of Europe. In Africa, the initial attempt was to search for an 'African mode of production'.[47] The prefix 'African', though important, was of course insufficient. Africa has its own idiosyncrasies, which not only make the prefix insufficient, but also render the concept of modes of production questionable. Towards an attempt at subjecting this concept to critical scrutiny, Marxists and anthropologists like Meillassoux use concepts such as 'self-sustaining agricultural societies' and the 'lineage mode of production'.[48]

Although seminal, Meillassoux's ideas remained inconclusive until Amin's intervention.[49] Amin argues that to extend either the 'Asiatic mode of production' or even 'feudalism' to Africa is itself a form of imposition of Eurocentric categories that have neither historical nor scientific basis. At the very least, Amin argues, one could speak of feudalism, which was unique to Europe, as an 'incomplete stage' of a more general mode of production, 'the tributary mode of production'. In this way, he displaces both feudalism and the Asiatic mode of production. Mafeje, following

Amin, seeks to comprehend this concept in relation to some parts of the interlacustrine, particularly Buganda and Rwanda. Before undertaking such a study, Mafeje submits that by the 1960s the concept of feudalism had lost currency because of 'dependent land tenure between vassal and lord, territorial autonomy of feudal lords within the state, and the organisation of agricultural production'.[50]

The interlacustrine social formations did not meet any of these three points and in this sense they differed markedly from European feudal societies. In European feudalism, the relationship of people to land determined political and social status and because landlords possessed and disposed of property rights, the relationship between them and their serfs had permanence. The same was not true in the interlacustrine kingdoms, not even in Bunyoro and Buhaya, 'where the nearest thing to fiefdoms existed'. There were no bonds for tenants and office estates could not be inherited. Thus, there were no property relations in land and there was no dispersal of political authority through autonomous landlords, as was the case in feudal Europe. Moreover, Mafeje says: 'Whereas in feudal Europe the seigniorial mode of estate management was an important source of private wealth, in the interlacustrine kingdoms the idea of a lord's demesne cultivated by the corvee labour of bonded tenants did not exist.'[51] Instead, office estate-holders depended on the labour of their wives and domestic slaves for subsistence production.

Most of the above-mentioned studies in Africa were written by anthropologists trying to compare African societies with those of European feudalism. The French anthropologists, on the other hand, as Mafeje observes, could not be accused of the same, but they attempted to extend the 'Asiatic mode of production' thesis to Africa. Ultimately, the specificity of African social structures needs to be investigated, not asserted. For Mafeje, the question that confronts African scholars is whether any generalised mode of production applied to pre-colonial Africa. Here, Mafeje invokes the notion of universals and particulars – or nomothetic versus idiographic inquiry – in the social sciences. This is no mere theoretical issue. It has concrete implications since, as Mafeje correctly points out, Africa's 'knowledge is still incomplete'.

Amin rejects arguments that rely on specificity or 'variety of formations' in order to negate the notion of mode of production, which he considers the 'unifying principle'.[52] Furthermore, he argues that French Marxist anthropologists, in refusing to credit a radical distinction between relations of co-operation and domination and relations of exploitation, ultimately mistook the peasant mode and the domestic mode of production. Mafeje argues that Amin's conception of the dividing line between forms of knowledge and anthropology is surprisingly anachronistic, but nevertheless he does not immediately reject Amin's work. Indeed, part of Mafeje's plan is to appraise Amin's 'tributary mode of production' thesis and to use the interlacustrine kingdoms as a concrete case study to test its validity. Mafeje cautions against studies that seek to prove their case by relying on analogies, a practice he found patently unscientific. Applying such a method in the case of the interlacustrine kingdoms would constitute 'a travesty of facts that can only lead to a theoretical confusion'.[53] Similarly, a search for an 'African mode of production' may amount to chasing shadows. This is where Mafeje credits Amin's work and the notion of the tributary mode of production.

Although Mafeje is sympathetic to Amin, he feels that his concept, while not derivative, is negative. Mafeje is not saying that Amin's proposal had negative connotations – to say a concept is derivative is not to question its substance but to question its novelty, but when Mafeje says Amin's thesis is negative, he is saying that it proceeds from a negative critique. Apart from that, Amin's thesis, unlike the Asiatic mode of production, has a substantive referent (a tributary relationship), which is capable of 'universalisation', of being theoretically extended to, or applicable in, other contexts. The veracity of Amin's concept, Mafeje argues, remained untested in 'black Africa' precisely because the region was historically under-researched and the concept must remain a hypothesis until further comprehensive studies have been conducted. In the meantime, Mafeje proposes, the veracity of the term should be tested in subregional studies, such as the one he pursued in the interlacustrine kingdoms. Studies with universalistic pretensions might lose their theoretical and political relevance if they are not supported by concrete investigations.

Amin's thesis has a 'three-stage' theory: (i) the communal (in relation to land); (ii) the tributary (also in relation to land); and (iii) the capitalist (in relation to means of production 'other than land').[54] Mafeje points out, quite rightly, that Amin's reason for excluding land as a means of production in the capitalist stage is not at all clear – in any case, Amin emphasises the content of property in terms of social control and not in its juridical and ideological forms. Mafeje wants to comprehend the second mode of production, the 'tributary'. He is of the view that in the light of the foregoing schema, the interlacustrine kingdoms can only fit the tributary mode and Amin himself had treated them as such. There are four 'diagnostic features' to Amin's tributary mode of production. Mafeje eloquently summarises these features as follows:

> First, the surplus product is extracted by non-economic means by an exploiting class, as against a dominant group which does the same for purposes of collective use in the communal mode of production … Second, the essential organisation of production is based on use value and not on exchange value. This is a natural economy in which transfers, whatever their nature, do not represent commodity exchange … Third, the tributary mode of production is characterised by the dominance of the superstructure … Samir Amin sees state religion, as against local religions, as an essential feature of tributary social formations. Moreover, class struggle is here muted by the dominance of the ideology of the ruling class. Fourth … one of the attributes of the tributary mode of production is 'its appearance of stability and even of stagnation'. This characteristic is supposed to be true of all tributary formations, including European feudalism, and is considered to be one of the consequences of the dominance of use value.[55]

Mafeje is fully aware that abstract concepts do not always accord with reality, which is why he chose the interlacustrine kingdoms as the prime candidate for Amin's tributary mode of production, in order to 'separate chaff from the grain'. Mafeje reminds us that the institution of tribute is to be found in all of the interlacustrine kingdoms. He agrees with Amin's sub-mission that the extraction of surplus products in the region was through non-economic means. At this point, Mafeje's worry is that in the context of the region, the distinction made by Amin between an 'exploiting class' and a 'dominant group' was not very clear, as they are to be found in both class and classless societies. Specifically, although it is known that there is a relationship between being an office-bearer and extraction of value, it was not self-evident that the beneficiaries of tribute in the interlacustrine kingdoms constituted a class. To get around this puzzle, one has to raise the question of property relations and labour relations that, theoretically, define modes of production. Amin refers to tributary property in land or, in his parlance, 'tributary of the land' versus communal property. For Mafeje, it was a serious misconception to speak of land as property in the social formations of sub-Sahara because in this region people only had use rights and land was used as an instrument of labour, not as property.

Mafeje argues that one could speak of societies in transition from non-property to property relations. Lack of definite property relations makes them similar to 'communal social formations', like the development of cap-italist agriculture in other parts of sub-Sahara that do not necessarily have a system of individual property rights in land. Akin to this is the devel-opment of industry under state capitalism as, Mafeje states, 'it is apparent that control over resources and labour can take forms other than property and that private appropriation of value is not contingent only on private property'.[56] The other side of modes of production is labour relations. In the interlacustrine, the labour process took three clear forms concur-rently. The first was family subsistence production – and this applied to all families, including that of the king, whose wives and domestic servants were responsible for farming, labour being divided along gender lines, with women doing agricultural production while men were pastoralists ('with a few exceptions such as among the Bahutu'). The second form was clientage. The patron-client relationship was a personal and free con-tract in that a man who was not well resourced would offer his services to the wealthy in exchange for political protection and material support. But because the client gave more than he received, one could say there was extraction of economic value without expropriation or bondage. This highlights the importance of political dominance over property relations.

Tribute and dues constitute the third category of the labour process. In all of the interlacustrine kingdoms office-holders treated their vassals as people who owed them tribute that was shared in ascending order. What separates the labour process from dues and tributes is that these two 'were part of the fiscal policy of each kingdom and underwrote a high standard of living among its office-bearers'.[57] However, tribute was typically in the form of perishable goods and the office-estates were not capable of being inherited. Thus, although it cannot be said that there were strict labour relations in the interlacustrine kingdoms, exploitation was rife, if not the norm. What this means is that there was a move away from relations of domination – though they existed in small measure – to relations of exploitation and such relations were not, Mafeje insists, remotely close to Marx's concept of 'generalised slavery'. Not every man had a chance of becoming an officer or an estate-holder and the governing bureaucracy was bound to look for ways to perpetuate its domination. As regards Amin's first postulate, Mafeje acknowledges that in the absence of property relations or defined labour relations, one cannot conclude that tribute recipients constituted an exploiting class. This is true in spite of the fact that there was exploitation in the interlacustrine kingdoms. Extraction was not strictly identifiable in terms of relation, either to property or to labour. There was extraction, Mafeje concedes, but the question as to the sort of exploiters who existed in the interlacustrine kingdoms must be answered 'scientifically' and not 'ideologically'. The biggest asset in the arsenal of exploiters was political control, although it is difficult to credit this as constitutive of class or property relations in the conventional sense of the term. Mafeje agrees with Amin's second postulate that in the tributary formations the organisation of production is based on use value rather than exchange value. Additionally, the majority of the interlacustrine kingdoms were never involved in trade, local or long distance, until the colonial era.

Mafeje partially agrees with Amin's third postulate, conceding that in the interlacustrine kingdoms the tributary mode of production was characterised by the dominance of the superstructure – Christianity and Eastern religion facilitated the extraction of the surplus and cemented relations of exploitation. The real question, however, turns on whether there were state religions. This harks back to the question of political domination versus class exploitation or labour relations. Mafeje says the interlacustrine kingdoms fell short of Amin's criteria of religion. He rejects outright Amin's fourth postulate about stagnation or stability on theoretical and logical grounds. Mafeje is not denying that societies can be described in those terms; the issue is that such characterisations cannot be offered as theoretical and one cannot describe the interlacustrine kingdoms as if there are no discernible differences among them. Yet it should be said that Amin's idea of stagnation or stability was in reference to each of the interlacustrine kingdoms as distinct entities in historical terms. It is on this basis that it can be faulted, not with regard to differences among the kingdoms. Mafeje advises that it is in conducting systematic regional studies – which do not compartmentalise social anthropology and economic historical development – that one may 'establish the necessary rules of exclusion, without relativising theory'.[58] In other words, while one should insist on regional specificity, one should not at the same time insist on taxonomic categories that are only empiricist in character. Generalising must be accompanied by alertness to differences in quality and a search at all times for new concepts or theories from one's research findings. Mafeje's intention was to find a suitable categorisation of the interlacustrine kingdoms.

Mafeje is thus interested in rethinking modes of production in Africa altogether as part of 'a painful struggle to understand the present as history'.[59] The said history is African history as part of a universal history. Mafeje is concerned with understanding this history in a generative way and not in reductionist terms. In so doing, he draws attention to specificities of historical instances. He is the first to admit that not only does this assignment lead to unconventional usage of terms and concepts, but also that it becomes controversial.

With regard to modes of production in Africa, Mafeje begins by stating that household economy was the general feature. There were family herds and fields, an empirical feature that differs sharply with the Asian village economy and integrated tributary social formations. In Africa, social formations were, as is the case today, 'balkanised and combined unevenly'. It is for these reasons that, theoretically, Marxists and liberal economists alike referred to African societies as societies without an economic system. Furthermore, what made this household economy 'communal' is the right of access and not necessarily that of property, as is the case in other parts of the world. As such, the chief-client or patron-client relation was a political, rather than an economic relation. Societies without recognisable property relations in land are hard to explain in classical European theories, Marxist or otherwise.

The temptation to use classical European theories has led to a number of misconceptions and distortions. The concepts of class and property, for example, are hard to credit since African social formations are characterised by the use-right principle. The notion of use right in land does not necessarily lend the land tenure system in these societies to 'communal ownership' of land. The very notion of ownership has a lot to do with fixation with the concept of property. African social formations do not deal with land in terms of ownership, but in terms of *dominium eminens*, a principle that guaranteed use rights and a practice organised along family units. The absence of property rights in these societies does not translate into absence of exploitation and domination. The issue, for Mafeje, turns on how one conceives of the processes of exploitation and domination in societies such as the interlacustrine kingdoms. Communal social formations are characterised by kinship hierarchies that have a redistributive function, not classes. This raises two main questions: (i) Does exploitation imply the existence of classes in society? and (ii) Is the existence of classes dependent on property relations? The next question is about dialectical and historical materialism since, for orthodox Marxists, these are core principles in class analysis. Mafeje points out that dialectical materialism as an epistemology cannot be limited to class societies. The problem is simply that analytical categories in historical materialism presuppose the existence of classes; the case of the interlacustrine kingdoms calls for new thinking about such analytical categories.

In the search for new concepts, Mafeje discards the concept of class in relation to the interlacustrine kingdoms and retreats into the non-Marxist but Weberian concept of status. He was justified in abandoning the concept of class. Concerning the concept of exploitation, Marxists tend to get entangled in logical and conceptual knots, on the one hand denouncing exploitation on political and moral grounds; on the other hand, deeming it a necessary condition for development and the intensification of technological advancement. The upshot of this line of thought is that not only do Marxists 'make a virtue of what they otherwise reject ideologically', but they also 'go out of their way to find "classes" even where none exist'.[60] Elsewhere, Mafeje said in response to Harold Wolpe that one does not have to invent classes in order to conduct class analysis, but one has 'to be alert to possible mediations in the process of class formation'.[61] Important though this is, Mafeje said it at the cost of admitting that there is class analysis to conduct in the first place. In the final analysis, 'exploitation need not be equated with class any more than productive use of economic surplus is correlated with class'.[62] Much more prevalent in the interlacustrine kingdoms than classes were 'hierarchies of dyadic relations' and so 'we cannot infer class simply from extraction of value'.[63] What seems to have been important to Mafeje is how the value, the process of reproduction and production, is realised and used. In the context of the interlacustrine kingdoms, one 'can only think of classes in the process of becoming'. Mafeje was well aware that he was skating on thin ice. For one thing, he admits that exploitation was widespread in the interlacustrine kingdoms, and yet he is disinclined to overgeneralise and categorise the exploiters as a class. This has to be so because the notion of class exploitation presupposes not only the existence of classes, but also the existence of property and labour relations. None of these features was found in the interlacustrine kingdoms.

Mafeje's position on modes of production in Africa concludes that to the extent that in the past 300 years the interlacustrine had dispensed with kinship as a core feature of political organisation, and to the extent that they substituted reciprocal economic relations for 'extractive relations between rulers and the ruled', the concept of tribe was no longer

applicable to them. Furthermore, to the extent that there were no individual property rights over land, and no 'seigniorial relationship between
the lord and vassal or serf for private exploitation of estates', and to the
extent that there were no autonomous landlords to dominate within social
formations, the interlacustrine kingdoms cannot be described as feudal.[64]

Having assessed Amin's four diagnostic features of the tributary mode
of production, Mafeje affirms the view that the interlacustrine had entered
it. First, the organisational principle that defined economic and political
relations in the interlacustrine was that of tribute to the rulers (a way
of extracting economic value from the citizenry and a way of ensuring
relations of political dominance). Second, although there were no property relations and labour relations in the interlacustrine kingdoms, the
tributary method of extracting value was extra-economic. Third, and
consistent with the second point, there was a dominance of use value
that did not altogether 'preclude conversion of utilities from one form to
another by whatever means'.[65] Although Mafeje endorses these features,
he nevertheless argues that the aspects that concern religion, dominance
of the superstructure and the tendency toward stagnation are arbitrary
and redundant.

In the same way that Mafeje rejects the concept of feudalism in
characterising the interlacustrine kingdoms, he argues that it has no
bearing on the concept of the tributary mode of production. The only
thing that the tributary mode of production shares with feudalism is the
dominance of use value. In the interlacustrine kingdoms there was no
private property in land or exploitation in the form of labour relations.
Thus, feudalism cannot be one of the features of the tributary mode of
production.

Mafeje argues that Amin not only subsumed feudalism under the tributary mode of production, but also argued that it was 'incomplete' due to
its 'fragmented political authority'. For Mafeje, this was to privilege the
superstructure at the expense of the economic base. In this regard, Amin
adopted an 'un-Marxist' procedure.

Linked to the above point, Mafeje argues it might be much more
appropriate to think of modes of production as transitional, rather than

incomplete. To the possible question of when modes of production are complete, Mafeje responds by saying that modes of production can be thought of as complete 'when they are able to reproduce themselves indefinitely'.[66] Modes of production, however, do not reach a point of completion because they are 'subject to decay' through internal contradictions. Conceptually, however, Mafeje insists that modes of production have to reach a point of completion because incomplete concepts are decidedly 'ambiguous'.

Instead of adopting the usual Marxian parlance of extraction of economic surplus, or surplus value, the capacity of the dominant group to take more than they have produced, Mafeje uses the concept of economic value. This is because the two concepts cannot hold in an environment with 'determinate production-relations'. In the interlacustrine kingdoms, this situation did not obtain.

Logically and empirically, with regard to Mafeje's proposed usage of the concept of social formation, the instances of political power and of economics are articulated through tributary relations, rather than the co-existence of two modes of production, pastoralism and agriculture. All production in the interlacustrine kingdoms was geared towards subsistence, not trade. Hence, for Mafeje, social formation had nothing to do with modes of production and pastoralism and agriculture were not modes of production, but were 'amenable' to modes of production, such as the tributary and the lineage. In other words, pastoralism and agriculture were subsumed under these modes of production, rather than being modes of production in themselves. Mafeje contends that they were 'modes of existence'.

The concept of articulation of modes of production is misleading because modes of production are not characteristic of all social formations. In addition, the concept could lead to the standpoint that modes of existence are modes of production – as is the case with pastoralism and agriculture. In the interlacustrine kingdoms, pastoralism and agriculture were not two distinct modes of production but a single mode of existence that represents one mode of production – the tributary mode of production.

Finally, one of the most important methodological lessons of Mafeje's study is that ethnographic detail can help to avoid crude and mechanistic interpretations of society. Far from advocating relativism and paro-chialism, this method helps to generate new concepts and theories, as evidenced by his study of the interlacustrine kingdoms. It is important to underline this point because, for Mafeje, there was no negation without affirmation, no deconstruction without reconstruction.

Deconstruction and reconstruction

The quest for non-disciplinarity is not, or will not be easy to achieve since it is fraught with epistemological, theoretical, methodological, psychological and emotional problems. The search for new paradigms is made much more difficult by the fact that epistemology guarantees certainty and is thus intolerant of uncertainty and violation of tenets. Strictly speaking, this refers to paradigms rather than epistemology, yet Mafeje believed that non-disciplinarity might be achievable because the accent has been on 'free styles of thinking and the breaking of dis-ciplinary boundaries'.[67] Mafeje called theory a term that lacks a fixed meaning so that no one adheres to it strictly – but although there may indeed be a lack of adherence to specific theories among academics, that is a different proposition from the idea that theory as such lacks a fixed meaning. At any rate, Mafeje argued, various disciplines have different ideas about what constitutes theory and this surely must be so because not only do disciplines deal with different subject matter (even when they deal with the same subject methodologically, they approach it differently) but the same is also true *within* disciplines – scholars are likely to adopt different theories according to their epistemological and ideological inclinations based on the dictates of their subject matter. There can be no consensus as to what theory scholars should adopt. Lack of consensus on what theory is, contrary to Mafeje's position, should be welcomed and not lamented. One has to make a distinction between the idea of theory as theory and the idea of consensus around specific theories. There is a distinction between what theory is and which theory better explains the issues in question. It is for the very same reasons that diversities of epis-temological approaches to making sense of societies will generate diverse theories of societies.

Mafeje conceded, however, that it is the role of theory to make apparent hidden connections and to explain them. This is why there are many theories within any one discipline, and in abandoning theory a great deal of work within disciplines will be academic without being intellectual or simply empiricist. Mafeje was not against theory, but rejected the idea of a theoretical framework as a presupposition on which field research should be based. Here, Mafeje broached – without being explicit – the distinction between deductive and inductive reasoning. It is clear that, based on his own approach to research, Mafeje arrived at his conclusions through inductive logic. Methodology (a theoretically laden concept) is a term of abuse usually (and wrongly) used as a collective noun for methods/ procedures and techniques. Methodology refers to essential choices in knowledge making; methods, by contrast, are a matter of convenience largely driven by the problems under investigation. In mistaking methodology for methods, the former loses its 'higher theoretical status'.[68] This is true, but the argument raised by Mafeje was conventional. Methodology is a higher-order philosophical evaluation of methods (as techniques of research). Athough some academics might consider emotional and psychological constraints to be extra-curricular, such issues are in fact at the core of the deconstructionist problematic. Disciplinary adherents, although sometimes critical of their disciplines, are still unable or otherwise unwilling to dispense with them not only for intellectual reasons, but also for emotional and psychological ones. Academics have, according to Mafeje, stakes in their disciplines and although some anthropologists might denounce anthropology for its role in colonialism, they would still insist on pursuing anthropological work.

In the spirit of deconstruction, Mafeje adopted non-disciplinarity as opposed to a disciplinary or even interdisciplinary approach, as his work on the interlacustrine kingdoms demonstrates, yet it must be said that he benefited from his anthropological background. Mafeje claimed that had he adopted an interdisciplinary approach in conducting his study he would have been 'bogged down in intractable methodological problems'.[69] To avoid such problems, he simply used the discursive method. In the second instance, he was 'not unduly concerned' about epistemology. He rejected positivism and gravitated towards Marxist thought categories – though he subjected them to critical scrutiny.

It is important to appreciate that this was at the time of Mafeje's flirtation with postmodernism and post-structuralism. All that discursive method means is 'exploration of meaning produced by language use and communication'; an analytical approach, rather than a research technique for generating data.[70] Related to his flirtation with postmodernism is that when Mafeje talks about epistemology, in this instance, he actually means positivism/functionalism. Marxist historical materialism/ dialectical materialism, with which he constructs much of the meaning of the interlacustrine kingdoms, is an epistemology – a theory of knowledge, an approach to how we may know the world. One has to make a distinction between the rejection of particular epistemologies and the claim of rejecting epistemology. Even hardcore postmodernism (for all its rejection of grand narratives, itself is a grand narrative) is an epistemological approach to making sense of the world. It does not claim that the world is unknowable. If the discursive method was Mafeje's way of making sense of the interlacustrine data, then at that very moment it became his epistemological framework. Postmodernists put a lot of stock in deconstruction, but anyone familiar with Marx's *Grundrisse* would recognise the method of abstraction as reconstruction through deconstruction. Mafeje did not, however, commit himself uncritically to any epistemology – Marxist or otherwise. As a Marxist, Mafeje started from Marx, but he did not stop with Marx. In the final analysis, he concedes that 'dispensing with existing epistemologies does not solve methodological problems in the intermediate term and the long-run'. Rather, it 'creates space for the emergence of new styles of thinking. To survive, the so-called emergent styles of thinking must not only be aware of one another but also of new styles of thinking within existing epistemologies.' To test these deconstructionist ideas Mafeje studied the interlacustrine kingdoms. It could have been any other society. As he says: 'I could have used the Nguni or the Sotho in South Africa for exactly the same reasons that I chose the Interlacustrine'.[71] He was engaged in this process as an authentic interlocutor.

Without understanding Mafeje's deconstructionist disposition, one cannot understand his work on land and agrarian issues, or on revolutionary theory and politics. In Mafeje's work these topics are interrelated. His inductive approach in these various clusters of his work is not only a sign of originality, but also of remarkable consistency.

Part II
On Land and Agrarian Issues in Sub-Saharan Africa

4 | The Land and Agrarian Question

Land and agrarian studies are an integral part of Archie Mafeje's *oeuvre*.[1] He acknowledges that Africa is still largely a rural continent and that an agrarian economy is likely to persist for a very long time to come.[2] Because he is writing about the post-independence period there is, he argues, no land question in sub-Saharan Africa: it is an agrarian one. He hastens to point out, however, that southern Africa is an exception, as the subregion has a white settler community. Sam Moyo, who also conducted extensive work on the land and agrarian question in southern Africa, suggests that 'unequal land distribution and land market relations in non-settler Africa had in fact been growing by the late 1990s'.[3] Even in those countries where land is no longer owned by settlers, there is land alienation – the land is still not owned by the black masses. This is what Moyo refers to as the emergence of 'a distributional land question'. Moyo agrees with Mafeje, however, that 'the fundamental land and labour relations of Africa's pre-capitalist modes of economic and political organisation had persisted during and after colonialism and capitalist penetration in the former non-settler territories of Africa'.[4] Mafeje and Moyo reject 'the dominant view that agrarian transformation in Africa was constrained by alleged deficiencies in African land tenure systems'. (I should like to add that rural development is not limited to agricultural activities.) Relying on concrete examples, Mafeje attempts to overthrow Eurocentric paradigms – which is consistent with his search for an epistemological break. In addressing the land and agrarian question, Mafeje took historical sociology seriously.

The problem in its intellectual setting

A problem with the system of foreign aid is that international agencies assume recipient countries have no professionals to advise their own governments. This is an ideological issue. 'The aim is clear,' as Samir Amin writes. '[It is] to create the conditions that would allow modern islands of agribusiness to take possession of the land [non-governmental organisations and donor agencies] need in order to expand.'[5] Mafeje argues that this 'volte-face exposes the cynicism of the epistemology of subject-object in bureaucratically conceived strategies for development'.[6] In this regard, even scientific prescriptions become hard to distinguish from ideological rationalisations of preconceived assumptions. It is always possible to find scientific grounds for co-operation between specialists and ordinary people. However, such co-operation may not always be desirable for those who benefit from currently skewed relations, not only between specialists and ordinary people, but also between the North and the South.

In a 2013 article on the classical agrarian question, Moyo, Praveen Jha and Paris Yeros refer to this as a 'sustained myth of industrialisation as the basic objective of transformation … born in the late nineteenth century among the European vanguard, then consolidated as an axiom during the Cold War, only to be resurrected in the neoliberal period by a professionalised discipline of "agrarian studies"'.[7] Amin observes that 'capitalism, by its nature, cannot solve the global hunger crisis, because it cannot resolve the historical agrarian question of how to mobilise the surplus from peasant agriculture to industry without eliminating that same peasantry from agriculture'.[8] Governments in less developed countries tend, unfortunately, to share the views of international agencies and advisers from the North who, Mafeje argues, promote the superiority of their views and degrade local knowledge systems. At the level of knowledge production, this is evident in what Syed Farid Alatas terms the intellectual division of labour, where Northern scholars collect data from the South and theorise; he refers to it as academic dependency.[9] Paulin Hountondji makes the same point, calling it scientific dependence.[10] Scholars from the North come to dominate scholars from the South and the latter accept the North's ideas without actively insisting on their own views; this, according to Syed Hussein Alatas, is intellectual imperialism.[11]

For Mafeje, however, it is precisely 'in this area [of agrarian studies] that African social scientists are likely to make a distinct contribution. The underlying reason is that their societies are predominantly agrarian [but] contrary to all logic, the agrarian question in them is the least studied'.[12] To this, Moyo, Jha and Yeros add: 'There is an urgent need to think creatively about alternatives in development and, indeed, to rethink the fundamentals of modernity, if we are to save it from its own barbarism. What we cannot do is blind ourselves by established conventions, create myths about the past and illusions as to the future.'[13]

Development theorists tend to defend and rationalise particular modes of production either by extrapolation or by simply making ahistorical assumptions. Eurocentric models divert attention from the needs of would-be objects of development (ordinary African people). Epistemologically, imported models deny any possibility of knowledge systems outside of the mainstream orthodoxies. In taking seriously the uniqueness of sub-Saharan land tenure systems, Mafeje was convinced that African scholars might be on their way to overthrowing deeply held assumptions and, therefore, raising new questions.[14] One of the universalising tendencies in agrarian studies is for the resolution, by industrialisation, of the agrarian question – despite, as Mafeje points out, the fact that a rigorous analysis of African agrarian systems 'shows that there is more than one way to agricultural and rural social development'. Mafeje condemns Eurocentrism in the study of the agrarian question in Africa. He argues that for too long agrarian studies in sub-Saharan Africa relied heavily on categories derived from Europe, Latin America and Asia.

Agrarian revolution and the land question: The case of Buganda

In spite of the agricultural revolution – and subsequently the Industrial Revolution – in Europe, the world is still faced with the old problem of how to earn a living from agricultural activities.[15] Given knowledge, expertise and technological advances, one would expect that there would be solutions, but the situation in underdeveloped countries shows that solutions are still elusive. It is a global capitalist and structural problem, wherein developed countries thwart development in the developing countries. Mafeje observes that 'not only is the way ahead blocked by entrenched vested interests, but also vision is obscured by certain historically determined belief systems and perceptual categories'.[16] To illustrate this point, Mafeje uses the case of the evolution of land policy and development in the Buganda region of Uganda during colonialism.

Buganda is an agrarian society, with land the source of wealth and sustenance. However, land distribution and agricultural produce have gone through a number of changes in the past 100 years. Women were the real cultivators of the soil, yet they relied on men to acquire the plots. In order for the men to acquire the plots, they had to attach themselves to the political elites who had close relations with the king. This was a system of 'tiered dependence', which meant that the Bugandan economy was not limited to the household economy. Having acquired the land, a small producer would have to pay tribute and dues to his overlord and serve him as a craftsman, housebuilder and warrior. The chiefs served the king by supervising the population, collecting taxes and raising armed forces in order to raid neighbouring states, with the spoils usually shared between the elite and the king. This, Mafeje argues, created an 'economy of predation', rather than one of production.

To the extent that small producers were not obliged to work in their masters' fields, they were not serfs in the European sense. The chiefs of Buganda held their estates because of their political appointments, not hereditary rights in land, and they were not feudal lords in the European sense. The chiefs had strict control over the land and the population and had opportunities for primitive accumulation and the consolidation of power. With their powerful positions, the chiefs and other royal appointees mounted a coup in 1888 and expelled the king, establishing themselves as new masters of the state. The British colonialists arriving in Buganda shortly afterwards accepted them as such.

Buganda became a British Protectorate in 1894 and the land policy became an issue in 1900. Mafeje states: 'It was in [1900] that Sir Harry

Johnston, the British Special Commissioner for the Protectorate of Uganda (Buganda), signed the famous Uganda Agreement with the Bugandan new political captains. The terms of the Agreement are a clear indication of the extent to which the chiefs had managed to consolidate their power, at least, against the general population.'[17] The land question was foremost in the chiefs' negotiations with Johnston, precisely because land was a source of political power and access to resources. Johnston had no understanding of the land issue in Buganda. The British had considered Buganda a feudal society and their treatment of it resulted in its actually becoming close to feudalism. Prior to the coup and to British colonialism, land was no longer vested in the hands of the king but in the hands of individuals who held it in perpetuity. Following Johnston's intervention, the land was allotted in square miles. This new system was a double-edged sword, as Mafeje points out: 'It at once complemented the feudalist ambitions of the chiefs in Buganda and, at the same time, created grounds for the emergence of capitalism in the area. Cultivation of cash crops made it possible for the individual landowners to acquire wealth by means other than primitive accumulation or predation.'[18] The Agreement of 10 March 1900 excluded the rest of the population from ownership of land and created three types of land tenure in Buganda: public (crown) land (about 6 800 square miles); land held by the king, chiefs and private landowners, divided into official mailo (about 700 square miles) and private mailo (about 8 000 square miles);[19] and freehold land transferred from the crown to individuals or corporations (104 square miles). This created all sorts of problems insofar as it inaugurated a new type of property relations in which land became a commodity that could be bought and sold at the discretion of the individual. The landowner had no legal obligation to the king or the people who settled on his land. In a very short space of time, 'land became an important commodity for investment and [the] generation of continuous wealth through exploitation of hired labour'.[20]

By this time, Buganda had reached a new economic stage that began with the arrival of cotton from the United States in December of 1903. The people of Buganda were forced to work and increase production for the British imperialists, but in spite of the increase in production, the Bugandan economy proved to be a case of 'growth without *development*'.[21] There was no investment in people. The value of production was shipped to Britain. The landowners and chiefs were the only native beneficiaries. The situation in Buganda began to change when the landowners and chiefs decided not to fulfil their obligations of increasing agricultural production for the British and began to retain dues and tribute from the population for themselves. The imperialists and the chiefs had, in effect, fallen out, for the British imperialists were concerned primarily with production and not with the natives – royalty or not. It is recorded that from 1910 to 1915 production was no longer the preserve of the chiefs but that of the small producers. As a result, by 1916 British administrators effectively sided with the peasants against the landowners.

According to Mafeje, the chiefs were now seen as 'mere parasites' or 'forested plutocracy' growing rich by extorting money and services from the true agricultural producers. But although one may speak of agricultural producers in Buganda, they could not, strictly speaking, be termed 'peasant producers', at least not before 1900. If peasant production existed at all, it came about because of the 'individualisation of rights in land and the introduction of cotton cultivation for the world market'.[22] Small-scale production only became dominant in Buganda from 1916 onwards. Moreover, the ways in which the landowners operated were not markedly different, in technique and scale, from their tenants – in subsequent decades there emerged a sizeable number of small producers who worked on independent plots after original estates became fragmented by inheritance and sales, and tenants became upwardly mobile as they purchased land with money earned from cotton.

Immediately after the introduction of cash crop production and new economic gains by individuals, Bugandan society experienced certain tensions. In order to maximise their gains, landowners began to make excessive demands on the peasants. Measures were taken in 1926 by the Lukiiko (the Bugandan Legislative Assembly) as it 'tried to fix these by legislation at the increased rates of 35 per cent of the cotton cultivated by the tenants, two pounds of coffee for every ten pounds grown and one pound of every ten pounds of any other cash product'.[23] The administration responded sharply to these measures and there are reports of evictions of tenants by landowners and sustained agitation by the king and other minor chiefs and landless persons. This gave the colonial government an excuse to strike at the landowner-chiefs. On 15 October 1926, the government declared that it would pass legislation to secure tenure for small producers and to limit and regulate rents and tribute to landowner-chiefs, and a year later the Busulu and Envujjo Law was passed. It set out to guarantee security of tenure for small producers, as long as they 'met their stipulated obligations of ten shillings dues (*busulu*) per annum and a tithe (*nvujjo*) of four shillings per annum in respect of each acre or part thereof under cotton or coffee'.

The importance of this is that it protected the small producers from being exploited by the landowner-chiefs, but the outcome was another structural problem: the British colonisers had created 'distortions or contrary motions' – to the point of forestalling any agrarian and capitalist revolutions – which appear to have the people of Buganda pay the necessary price of 'progress'. The primary concern of the British was production and they had switched loyalties – from siding with the native administrators to siding with the small farmers – as soon as they realised that the latter, not the landowner-chiefs, the 'mere parasites', were the real producers. Objectively, the British had no loyalty to either. They minimally protected the small producers, primarily on the basis of their being producers and not out of a sense of goodwill or obligation. The British were colonialists and imperialists, after all.

In spite of structural contradictions, production flourished in Buganda. By the end of the 1920s, it had expanded production to coffee. This quantitative background notwithstanding, there are significant qualitative issues. In spite of everything that the British did, there seem to have been some small victories for small producers: they determined not only the pace, but also the volume of production in the Bugandan agricultural economy.

Intellectuals and colonialists referred to the Buganda of the colonial period as 'a firmly established peasant economy',[24] but this appellation is based on the scale or volume of production, not on property and production relations. Very few small producers or peasants owned land, which lay in the hands of those who were privileged by birth or other financial means. The term 'peasant', such as it was used in respect of Buganda, does not necessarily mean the same in other parts of the world. In the early twentieth century, the small producers in Buganda were, in fact, cheap foreign labour; by 1934 wage labour was 'drawn exclusively' from people from other parts of Uganda. In addition, the men of Buganda relied exclusively on the labour of women for subsistence. Thus, while one should remain critical of the colonial state, it is necessary to high-light the process of exploitation internally and how production relations sustained such a process. Mafeje concludes that the Baganda 'benefitted from and were in part responsible for the exploitation of their weaker or less fortunate neighbours' and, moreover, 'have great contempt for farm labour and generally regard themselves as an "employing class"'.[25] Unlike other agricultural communities in Africa or in Europe, the Baganda were indifferent to collective production and were extremely individu-alistic (because of the availability of cheap foreign labour) even when it came to family labour, which is acknowledged as a backbone of peasant production.

The question then is whether reliance on hired labour and individualised production made *kulaks* – progressive farmers or rural capitalists – of the Baganda. Mafeje addresses this question as follows:

> First, let it be stated as a general rule that peasants are isolated producers but who rely more on family labour than anything else. In contrast *kulaks* and agricultural capitalists rely more on hired labour than family labour. Nor is it just a question of the type of labour used. It is also a matter of qualitative difference brought about by a distinct combination of labour-power, tools and capital, i.e. technologically and historically, the two categories represent divergent tendencies. But the surprising thing in Buganda is that increased production at the time in question did not represent a qualitative change *technologically*. Generally speaking, the scale and the techniques of production remained the same for all farmers.[26]

It is thus unwise to conclude that the Bugandan small producers are peasants. Mafeje suggests that entrepreneurship was in any case not a dominant feature of production in Buganda. There were no measures in place to improve the efficiency of labour or would-be entrepreneurs. In other words, the level of 'real capital' (in scientific and technological terms) of rural Buganda stayed the same. In point of fact, the Bugandan economy operated as a 'function' of British industry.

Even when production was at its highest, the people of Buganda were never going to benefit technologically from the British since the division of labour was racially determined. This was the essence of underdevelopment – Buganda was incorporated into capitalist production and world market relations without reaping the benefits. Shortly before the Second World War, attempts to improve African agriculture were limited in Buganda to soil conservation and the introduction of tractors (which did not succeed because of Buganda's broken terrain and dense vegetation). In the post-war period, small production was no longer seen as a viable option and, as in European development, large-scale farming was considered a better substitute – yet, in 'sub-Saharan Africa, large-scale farming connotes something rather different from what is generally understood by the term in more developed parts of the world',[27] and material conditions in Buganda were not sufficiently technologically advanced for such attempts. Nor did the relations between the Baganda and their labour reach any qualitative changes. Workers continued to be labouring tenants and their skills had not changed since the end of the nineteenth century. Mafeje argues that 'what we are confronted with here is an overall level of *real capital* which is too low to justify any *capitalist* expansion'.[28] There were, however, very few individuals engaged in farming at a size above the average. This was made possible by three factors: '*ownership* of sufficient amounts of land (inherited or purchased), favourable crop prices for a prolonged period, and increased labour inputs consequent on good market prices'.[29] They were soon to catch the attention of the colonial administrators who, in turn, treated them with solicitude. These so-called professional farmers were given government aid 'in the form of mechanisation schools, research institutes, training programmes and general extension services'.

In 1953 the professional farmers were thus 'adopted' officially by the government, their potential having been identified by the Agricultural Productivity Committee. In 1956 two farm institutes were established in order to train them and their farmworkers. This was the creation of the farming elite, to correspond with the bureaucratic elite, which had also been established by the colonial government. While the historian Christopher C. Wrigley speaks about the professionalisation of agriculture in Buganda,[30] Mafeje contends that 'it would seem that, from the point of view of underdevelopment or "Jim-Crowed" agricultural revolution, what is more important than the said professionalism is the *differential* treatment of the producers by the government and the emergence of parasitic elitism as part of the colonial heritage'.[31] His hypothesis is that parasitism is an 'aberrant feature' of 'Jim-Crowed' or 'shanghaied' capitalism. Mafeje distinguishes this form of capitalism from 'normal' capitalism in which exploitation is characterised by dynamism that 'leads logically to fuller mobilisation of resources and, above all, to a release of new energies among the exploiters (capitalists) and the exploited (proletarians) alike'.[32]

In the case of Buganda, the preservation of professional farmers in the post-independence period did not yield any qualitative change in agriculture or innovation consistent with 'capitalist revolution', as Mafeje puts it. It was no more than an addition to the existing stratum of parasitic elites. It is therefore unclear whether independence led to any fundamental changes in how production was organised in agriculture. The national government of Uganda and the federal government of Buganda continued with the agricultural policies of the British colonialists, replacing the term 'professional farmers' with 'progressive farmers', who continued to be prized clients of the Department of Agriculture. In order to ensure capital inflow, the government encouraged non-African investors to enter into partnerships with African producers. Public land was leased for the development of private estates – a tacit acknowledgement on the part of the Bugandan government that progressive farmers were unable to achieve development on their own.

In the absence of a sizeable national bourgeoisie, the government proposed state capitalism as a viable alternative. In truth, the government had no clear theory or policy, and offered no support or guidance. Buganda continued to be a victim of pre-capitalist technology. Its production relations remained fundamentally traditional, while land relations were 'neither feudal, peasant nor capitalistic but a peculiar amalgam of all three'.[33] There was no possibility that progressive farmers could bring about a capitalist revolution. Mafeje advises: 'A radical revision of production-relations should be seen as a necessary corollary of changed land relations. Land should be made available for *surplus production* and the people who, historically and politically, can afford neither to be capitalists nor subsistence men must be organised and trained to carry out the task of economic development.'[34]

Buganda not only illustrates a symptomatic and qualitative case of colonial intrusion on agrarian revolution, but also demonstrates how colonial intrusion led to the agricultural crisis and lack of food security in post-independence Africa.

The crisis in African agriculture and its causes

It is generally accepted that African agriculture is experiencing a continuing crisis in food production, but experts do not fully agree on the root causes. The Food and Agriculture Organization (FAO) declares in its 1986 report *African Agriculture: The Next 25 Years* that six trends currently affect African food production: a bias against agriculture in African government policies; a high population rate in Africa; a declining rate at which arable land and harvested areas are being developed; technological advances have stalled and crop yields have dropped; degradation of the environment has speeded up; and most African countries are not sustaining themselves in the global political economy.[35]

Mafeje argues that if one is to make sense of these trends one has to place them in their historical perspective. The agricultural and food crisis in Africa is not a sudden problem that can be reduced primarily to physical factors. Such a view may have appealed to African technocrats, politicians and international agencies, but it was manifestly mistaken. According to Mafeje, for these problems to be addressed, there needs to be a radical change in production relations and the social institutions that shape them. From this perspective, it is clear that the African agricultural crisis came about as a result of socio-economic factors that pre-date the natural causes outlined in the FAO report – history is important.

Although the FAO and African governments emphasise physical factors at the expense of historical ones, they overlook the fact that physical factors are historically manipulated by humans (global warming being an outcome of human negligence and the growth of capitalism and militarism). Mafeje says that this is 'what technological progress and the destruction of the ecological balance is about'.[36] The reference to history is not necessarily a reference to archaeological testimony from the deep distant past, but to what has happened since the 1880s. There is evidence to suggest that when colonial authorities replaced African inter-cropping with monoculture, soil preservation was adversely affected. Colonialists did not replace inter-cropping with monoculture because of a desire to improve the lives of African people; it was to enrich the industrialised states – as the case of Buganda demonstrates.

Attempts to halt nomadic pastoralism (either by force or arbitrary colonial borders) and to limit pastoralists to small portions of land, in order to make space for arable agriculture, led to overgrazing. This was an inevitable outcome. In East and southern Africa the dynamic was slightly different. The issue was not pressure on land as such. Rather, there was a deliberate attempt by white settlers to monopolise land; in so doing, they managed to force African subsistence producers into the slave-like capitalist labour market. In post-independence Africa this pattern continued and was maintained in countries such as Kenya, Malawi, Swaziland and Zimbabwe (until the land expropriation of the late 1990s and early 2000s). The difference between the pre- and post-independence land distribution is that in the post-independence period the plan is not to cheapen black labour, but to modernise agriculture by encouraging estate farming. Mafeje disputes the accuracy of the FAO's claim that there was lack of technological change in Africa and argues that there has been technological advancement, although the process has been highly selective.

In areas where small-scale producers embraced new technologies they were discouraged through official policies – particularly in southern

Africa. Gradually, poverty and deprivation meant that new technologies were inaccessible and the question as to what type of technology should be adopted in Africa has not yet been resolved. Since the advent of colonialism, improvement of African agriculture has come to mean the direct transfer of technologies from Europe and North America – and over and above technological transfer it has come to mean large-scale capitalist farming. From the physical environment, it is doubtful whether what applies to agriculture in the temperate zones applies to tropical regions. Socially and culturally, it is questionable whether it is possible to reproduce European modes of social organisation in Africa where land tenure and family systems are especially important. Mafeje argues that even the so-called progressive farmers had made no progress (technologically and socially) since the 1960s and there is no evidence that they produced more than the small producers. This remains the case despite the fact that progressive farmers are favoured by governments and interested agencies. The extension services given to progressive farmers have not been effective – if they were, says Mafeje, the rate of social reproduction of progressive farmers would have been much higher than the evidence suggests, whereas progressive farmers have not been able to reproduce themselves, as was expected by African governments.

This is not necessarily an indictment of African agriculture in that it is important for African farmers to deal in export crops. The only period in which would-be capitalist farmers did comparatively well was during the 1950s and 1960s, when they received maximum support from African governments. But in the 1970s and 1980s, African farming was collapsing and reverting to subsistence farming. This is ironic, as African governments had always been more sympathetic to capitalist farmers than to small producers. In countries like Kenya, Côte d'Ivoire and Cameroon, commercial or estate farmers received differential treatment from their governments, but this did not avert the agricultural crisis (save for in Cameroon, a country where commercial farmers played a major role in food production). The urban bias thesis the FAO put forward as part of the cause of the crisis carried no argumentative weight for Mafeje, who contends that 'in aggregate terms all the countries in the world are urban-biased and yet all countries in the world have not experienced a deepening agricultural crisis'.[37] Although it is true that there have been net transfers of value from agriculture to urban areas in Africa, in historical terms it is also true of all countries in the transitional phase from agrarian to modern economies. It is difficult to say what is peculiar to Africa.

Not all African farmers became casualties of disproportional transfer of value from rural to urban areas. The advantage of commercial farmers has been that they benefited from government support, whereas small producers did not, and were often given space to market their own produce. Quite often, commercial farmers had political clout, but were not necessarily the most productive farmers. Examples include what came to be known as 'plantocracy' in Côte d'Ivoire, the Gezira Scheme in the Sudan, the tea estate farmers in Malawi and the 'big ranchers' in Botswana. The medium-sized or self-made commercial farmers of the 1950s and 1960s – the migrant cocoa growers in Ghana, the cotton farmers in East Africa and maize growers in southern Africa, particularly in Malawi – had a potentially dynamic role to play. As they did not have a lot of power, they joined the co-operative movement whose role was more political than economic prior to independence. In the post-independence period the co-operative movement lost its relevance and farmers were open to the vagaries of marketing boards and other government agencies despite their being almost the only category of African farmers who were 'go-getters' with a capitalist spirit, and differing from estate farmers who were not only conservative, but also sought to use resources from government. Many of these estate/commercial farmers were government officials or politicians.

If medium-sized farmers did not have it easy, it was worse for small producers, as not only did they lack bargaining power, they were also unorganised and their produce was largely undervalued. In undervaluing the produce of small-scale farmers, the African governments unwittingly committed what Mafeje calls 'the worst strategic mistake since they came to power'.[38] Two major issues emerged as a result. First, small producers took to cash crop production and, because of their numbers and over-taxation, became the biggest generator of national revenue. Second, small producers continued to be the major food producers in spite of unfavourable conditions. They are representative of an underprivileged agricultural subsector. African governments gave them no technical or financial support. It is beyond dispute that the great majority of African rural dwellers have been poverty-stricken since the advent of colonialism.

The question is why they continue to be poor. The FAO refers to 'technological stagnation' yet such an explanation raises more questions than it answers. Why is this mainly in Africa and less in other regions of the South? Mafeje states that one of the reasons could be 'backwardness in the historical sense'. Moyo, Jha and Yeros take issue with the idea of backwardness 'as the main ailment and industrialisation as the prescribed remedy'.[39] However, Mafeje is clear that the idea of backwardness can be raised without accusing Africans of being inherently inferior or primitive. In objective terms, Africa still lags behind other regions technologically. To qualify this observation, however, one has to take into account the fact that 'technologies are not only culture-bound but are also eminently production-function specific' and whereas Africans are said to be backward technologically they have the ability to meet their needs,[40] but they are struggling to do so. The FAO attributes this to mainly physical factors – demography, ecology, weather, infrastructure – as well as to economic factors.

All are legitimate concerns that are nevertheless 'soft options whose prescriptive value is questionable'.[41] Mafeje puts forward that the problem lies in the production function of the African agricultural economy in which the production units have been unable to reproduce themselves consistently and progressively. For Mafeje, this inability has been historically determined. The FAO takes it as established that there is thriving capitalist production in Africa – the recommendations of the FAO are based on this assumption – yet they miss the link between the development of capitalist agriculture and continued landlessness among poor rural dwellers. The FAO misses, too, the declining rural incomes or very low agricultural wages and scarcity of labour in agriculture. Mafeje's argument is that African agriculture need not develop along capitalist lines; the reason capitalist development succeeded in developed countries

117

is precisely because 'it was consistent with itself' whereas in Africa there are noted inconsistencies between property, production and exchange relations. In addition, as Mafeje points out, 'more than in any other region, a major disarticulation [exists] in the production function of the agricultural economies'.[42]

Prior to colonialism, production and catering to the needs of the population were closely linked. However, since the advent of colonial capitalism there continues to be a widening gap between the use of resources or production and popular needs, including both subsistence and the production of raw materials for nascent industries. What colonial capital did was to create external demand, not only for production for estate and medium farmers, but also among small producers. The upshot is that when the African agricultural economy flourished in the 1960s, it did so not because of growth of domestic markets, but because of external (primarily Euro-American and advanced Asian) markets. Similarly, when external markets/economies collapsed or fluctuated, they led to the worst crisis in African agricultural economies. What most advanced agricultural economies did was to subsidise their farmers and dump the surplus in developing economies, reducing their revenues even further. It should be noted that advanced agricultural economies already suffer from chronic structural surpluses; African agricultural economies, on the other hand, suffer from structural deficits.

Mafeje suggests there are two structural issues at play. The agricultural sector needs the urban area as its market; equally, the urban area needs to be supplied by the agricultural sector. The main problem preventing the potential of this economic dialectic from being realised is that the farmers are uncompetitive and their production cost is comparatively high. Yet urban wages are comparatively low. Both sides are unable to realise their livelihoods. Mafeje submits three solutions: government subsidies for certain food crops, cheap food imports, or wage increases, but notes that 'government subsidies are always accompanied by price controls that often prove to be a disincentive to the majority of producers'.[43]

An important question then arises about the nature and future of African agricultural economies. The capitalist mode of production has not hitherto yielded any fruits in sub-Saharan Africa and there are a number of structural issues to be resolved in this regard. The land question is still central to the way African people live, combining subsistence farming with labour migrancy. Mafeje adds that rights do not always connote access to land but, rather, sustainable kinship claims to land. Access to land or land tenure systems in Africa are not organised along the lines of individual property in land and the collective use of land, therefore, is quite compatible with the commercialisation of agriculture.

At a theoretical level, it is important to emphasise this point so that one is not led to conclude that development of a market in agriculture or commodity relations necessarily entails the emergence of the capitalist mode of production. That the majority of African agricultural producers participate in the capitalist market does not necessarily make capitalists of them. Radical African scholars like Amin and Moyo argue that African agriculture need not follow the Euro-American capitalist path.[44] Amin observes that 'within historical Marxism, only Maoism understood the size of the challenge. Therefore, those who charge Maoism with a so-called "peasant deviation" show by this very criticism that they do not have the analytical capacity for an understanding of what is actually existing imperialist capitalism.[45]

Although there exists general exploitation of the small producers through bureaucracy, there is no prevalent or systematic exploitation of hired labour in the sub-Saharan region. It is mainly commercial. There are estate farmers (though very few) who enlist the services of hired labour. Small producers rely on household labour.[46] Even in the case of estate/ commercial farmers, labour is never hired on a permanent basis, but tends to be migratory or seasonal. In addition, the relationship between the labour force and the employer might also take a non-capitalist path. An observable feature of sub-Saharan Africa is that the region has not seen 'a progressive division of labour in agriculture'.[47] Far from capitalist development in agriculture, sub-Sahara is characterised by what Mafeje calls the household economy. Not only has this been mischaracterised by Marxist theorists, it has also been mislabelled as 'family farming', 'peasant production', 'subsistence production' and so on. What family farming, peasant production and subsistence production have in common are small-scale production geared towards subsistence needs, the prevalence of joint family rights in land and kinship-based division of labour. According Amin, 'on family farms, labour supply is reduced to one or two individuals (the farming couple), sometimes helped by one, two or three family members, associates or permanent labourers'.[48] Insofar as this is true, family farming is not capitalist. Production and the social reproduction of labour in African agricultural communities take place within, or are governed by, these parameters.

In this context, 'household' connotes 'that unit which has effective control over its allotted means of production (land and/cattle), allocation of labour and redistribution of the product'.[49] Unlike Amin, Mafeje maintains that this unit does not necessarily denote a family, but the household has a common budget, regardless of its actual kinship composition. In answer to the response that the same holds true for a family, Mafeje says that family members may 'live variously' – a family unit need not have a strict and effective control over its means of production in the manner of the household. This is not, however, a particularly convincing argument. Two external factors have undermined the self-sufficiency of households in Africa; they relate to migrant labour and the capitalist market. Mafeje elaborates: 'They share labour with commercial farmers and urban employers but bear the cost of the social reproduction of all such shared labour. The persistence of labour migration is a clear indication that even under these very unfavourable conditions most households cannot do without wages from outside.'

With regard to the national economy of sub-Saharan countries, there exists a 'schizophrenic situation'. Not only is there a failure in agriculture to specialise in order to support itself, but also industry does not expand in such a manner that it 'absorbs permanently the migrant workers and their families' and structural transformation is required for African economies to grow and realise their potential.[50] Additionally, given that the African agricultural sector is unspecialised, to develop a capitalist market in its current state may be imprudent because it presents a conflict between the needs of rural households and external demand. It is true that households need cash income to procure consumer goods and other services, but that should not divert attention from the fact that African economies are distorted in how they function. Mafeje argues that 'there is no running away from the fact that in economies such as the African ones the relationship between use and exchange value is not self-regulatory'.

This is an important policy issue that supersedes any possible technical solutions. It is not a simple question of subsistence and surplus production because to maximise utility value is not to discard the generation of surplus in growing economies. The two are not mutually exclusive. The problem resides in the one-sided development strategies adopted by African governments under the influence of donor agencies and structural adjustment programmes (SAPs). Production on the African continent should be directed towards catering for local needs, rather than external markets, and for this to happen effectively local producers must be afforded opportunities to reproduce themselves progressively and consistently. This could, potentially, intensify surplus generation and technological development, but it depends, of course, on the availability of land and livestock: medium-sized plots and reliance on family labour. This is the current practice among and within households, but there is a lack of support from African governments whose primary preoccupation is large-scale farming. Similarly, industry needs to have an established and skilled workforce, so that it earns enough to be able to reproduce itself. In both cases, there is a need to dispense with migrant labour in order to bring about stability.

The dynamics of African land tenure systems

Mafeje contends that most African governments have no land policy but an agrarian one – Ethiopia being one of the exceptions, following the 1974 'revolution'.[51] Yet Moyo argues that 'in recent times Africa's land question has received growing research and policy attention largely because of concern over persistent food insecurity and rural poverty'.[52] In contrast, Mafeje's conclusion follows from the premise that there is no land question to speak of in sub-Saharan Africa, except for in the white settler societies of southern Africa. Mafeje and Moyo were not fully agreed on whether there was a land question in Africa and the related question of whether there were peasants on the continent.[53]

Land allocation in most sub-Saharan countries was meant in part to boost agricultural production among a handful of farmers who were beneficiaries of certain development schemes. In southern Africa, except for Zimbabwe, tinkering with the allocation of land is to appease landless black people 'confronted with intransigent white landowners'.[54]

The 1989 FAO report *The Dynamics of Land Tenure and Agrarian Systems in Africa* shows that over 90 per cent of the land rights enjoyed by African agriculturalists and pastoralists came through customary land tenure.[55] But Mafeje argues that allocation of land is still determined by membership in given lineages or clans; this is not to deny that there exists an exchange of land across lineage boundaries but, rather, it is to say that the belief in the inalienability of land persists. In the past, use of land could be granted to the needy in exchange for a portion of the produce. This led to the phenomenon of migrant farmers in West Africa and in southern Uganda, 'made possible by the separation in African customary law between the *solum* and its manifestations'.[56] It also gave rise to the process whereby access to land could be made available to more users through the introduction of cash crops – without putting at risk the security of lineages. These issues led to conflicting views from development theorists. According to Mafeje, some scholars blame rural dwellers and small producers for their insistence on corporate rights and the inalienability of land, which hinders investment in land because its users fear that their plots might be taken or given to other claimants. A contrary view is that individualisation of land rights would, in all likelihood, lead to the monopolisation of land by a few to the detriment of the majority of the rural population. Both arguments have merit, but they fall short because they do not grapple with the dynamics of African land tenure systems.

Mafeje objects that there is no evidence to suggest that African agriculturalists are worse off because of lack of access to arable land or because of 'insecurity of tenure under customary tenure regimes'.[57] He contends that evidence suggests that agricultural production in sub-Saharan Africa expanded greatly in the 1950s and 1960s. Moreover, the first argument, that there is no access to arable land, does not explain the growth of the expanded petty mode of production in a number of African countries with customary land tenure systems. The second argument, about insecurity of tenure under customary tenure regimes, is mainly a theoretical construct, with no concrete basis. For example, in the post-independence era, over 90 per cent of rights in land are generated through customary channels, in spite of the preferred individual land tenure systems by African government and policy advisers. In those countries where individual land tenure was introduced, there have been attempts by ordinary citizens to regain corporate rights over land given to individual owners. In Kenya, this was taken to unprecedented proportions by the *majimbo* (regions) movement when residents who were not the original inhabitants were evicted by force. To make matters worse, politicians took advantage of the situation and created for themselves conditions to grab land for their own benefit.

This is an extreme, or even perverted, version of what Mafeje calls 'reversionary rights'. In places such as the Central Province and the Rift Valley in Kenya the situation was different in that landless people elected to occupy land previously owned by clans or lineages or simply established organisations, or 'companies', to repurchase their ancestral land. This goes to show different forms of resistance against individualisation of rights in land. Mafeje sees these actions not only as forms of vetoing govern-ment policies, but also as an assertion of 'African cultural values toward land and its use',[58] which militates against the idea of individual rights in land in Africa and highlights instead the extent of popular resistance to individualisation. Mafeje points out that the mistake made by left-leaning critics has been to assume that commercialisation of agriculture translates to individualisation of production (whereas individualisation is not neces-sary for the commercialisation of agriculture). To see this, one need only take into account that in sub-Saharan Africa commercial agriculture has taken place on family plots. Furthermore, although the educated elites insist on title deeds, such deeds are for the whole family and not neces-sarily the educated individuals who insist on them – which is in contrast to the Eurocentric view that assumes title deeds entail absolute property.

What makes all of this possible – and unintelligible to West-centric scholars – is precisely the lineage mode of social organisation in sub-Saharan Africa, which departs radically from the conventional Western unit of a nuclear family. What has changed, Mafeje contends, is manipulation of user rights more than the generation of land rights.

In the former colonies land is allotted in two ways. First, there is customary tenure wherein chiefs or heads of lineages distribute land within a local community bound together by agnatic ties. These do not, of course, hold true for every member of the community, but it demonstrates how strong founding lineages are and the way in which land is passed down from generation to generation. Although the system is designed along the lines of equity, certain individuals who have been allotted land may still wish to maximise their benefits. The second manner of allotment, particularly after independence, is through government. With the intention of improving agricultural production, several African governments have sought to modify existing customary systems of tenure through legislation and administrative measures. Because of the mistaken idea that 'communal ownership' hinders investment in land, governments in such countries as Kenya, Lesotho, Nigeria and Zambia attempted to introduce individual land tenure by granting title deeds to certain plot-holders or leaseholds for up to 99 years. Appropriation was left to market forces, following the introduction of individual titles. This strategy was never comprehensive, as Mafeje realises, 'because it was limited to government-sponsored consolidation, resettlement, irrigation schemes and a limited number of estate farms that were inherited from departing white settlers'.[59]

When sub-Saharan governments speak of land reform, they are not referring to redistribution of land, but to 'limited land and technical reforms in selected areas, usually "released" land or public land'.[60] For Mafeje, this vindicates the view that there is no need for land reform in sub-Saharan Africa. Mafeje could not, obviously, have foreseen the extensive 'land grabs' – land expropriation and leasing to multinationals (and countries) – on the continent in the aftermath of the 2007/2008 global food crisis. Prior to this point, African governments attempting to implement land reform were mindful that they would be met with resistance by, in Mafeje's words, 'the custodians and adherents of customary tenure'. As a result, the generation of land rights is still up to the people, as that is their prerogative. 'This,' Mafeje argues, 'is not found anywhere else in the modern world and might point to alternative modes of social organisation that had been ruled out by Eurocentrics.' Significantly, although the concept of communal land tenure is frequently used, it fails to explain how land rights are generated in sub-Saharan Africa and is incapable of making a distinction between different kinds of rights in land. While grazing grounds (*amadlelo*) and firewood trees (*iinkuni*) are used communally, plots of arable land (*amasimi*) are not communally shared. They are restricted to certain production units that are represented by minimal lineages, or 'extended families' in popular idiom. Maximum security of tenure depends on cultivation and production, unless the allottees are 'excommunicated by their kin or banished by the territorial authority under whose jurisdiction they fall'. However, given that this rarely happens, minimal lineages tend to keep their allotted land in perpetuity. Under conditions of land scarcity, allotments may be revised and sub-divided among more holders, particularly members of the same family.

Mafeje stresses that this is not a communal arrangement, as the sharing of land takes place 'among those who already have certain common rights in movable or immovable property and are bound together by exclusive ties of mutual obligation'.[61] 'Therefore,' Mafeje continues, 'it can be concluded that sub-Saharan African customary tenure rights are vindicated by membership in recognised corporate groups and by continued use of the land by recipient productive units.'

What prompted the introduction of individual land tenure was a belief by African governments that it would offer greater security of tenure than customary systems and would encourage investment in land. It is ironic that a Marxist theorist like Amin argues that private property in land is a necessary condition for agricultural development in Africa.[62] Mafeje objects to this view because it is premised on European historical experience – in Asia, agricultural revolution occurred without the introduction of private ownership of land. In fact, it was collective production that inaugurated large-scale agricultural projects such as irrigation schemes and economies of scale in agriculture in Mesopotamia, Egypt and India. In sub-Saharan Africa, as Mafeje points out, it is not yet proven that investment in privately owned land is higher than in equivalent plots that are held under customary tenure.

In sub-Saharan Africa, rights in land are closely associated with membership of particular descent groups and are governed by customary prescripts, even in countries where governments initiated individual land tenure systems. The question of agrarian reform leads to some confusion and lack of direction, which may spell conflict between government and small producers – and this also points to a negative reflection on the agrarian policies adopted by some African governments. Except for Ethiopia, and more recently Zimbabwe, land reform programmes in sub-Saharan Africa were not intended to redistribute land, but to improve 'what was thought to be insecurity of tenure under customary tenure'.[63] Thus, the land reform programmes were linked to individual land tenure because of the impact of colonialism. In the post-independence period, African governments implemented various schemes of land distribution that did not entail eviction or the expropriation of cultivators. The schemes were implemented on vacant land (which was largely considered public land) or even on occupied land with the consent of current occupants who wished to secure title deeds to the plots (Kenya is an example). In some cases this applied to planters who wanted to secure ownership of their trees by securing rights over the land itself. The estate farms of colonial settlers who were leaving Africa were sold mainly to privileged individuals through government loans.

Overall, individual land tenure systems in African countries are few and far between. In Kenya, Côte d'Ivoire and Malawi such tenure systems make up less than 20 per cent of the land available.[64] Mafeje states that 'in spite of the existence of individual titles, surveys carried out as far back as 1986 showed progressive fragmentation of African estates, illegal squatting, labour tenancies, borrowing and lending of private land to kinsmen and friends, and sharecropping'.[65] Such transactions, illegal in some countries, played a part in preventing sub-Saharan governments from implementing individual land tenure. Those who opted for land titles were not necessarily interested in being capitalist farmers in the sense intended by their governments. By signing up for individual land tenure, they were not necessarily forsaking their membership of descent groups but, rather, trying to 'enhance their personal status within the corporate group and in the wider society'.

Government responses to the agrarian question

Mafeje argues that most estate farmers in sub-Saharan Africa are 'absentee farmers'. This is due in part to the fact that they have other occupations, as civil servants or as politicians, and engage the services of family members or close friends to run their farms. Some estate farmers use their land titles to get loans to finance business ventures that have nothing to do with agriculture. Once they have accumulated some riches, a portion is invested in family members and the community, guaranteeing them the services and labour of poor relatives and clients. The elites become rich not necessarily because they exploit the land, 'but rather through its direct control'. They are not landlords in any meaningful sense, but 'big men' who are in turn appreciated and respected by kinsmen and small producers in the villages. This situation does not easily lend itself to class analysis (the same practice is to be found among smaller landowners and commercial farmers, albeit on a smaller scale).

Smaller landowners and commercial farmers generate their revenues through cash crop production and focus on direct exploitation of their land. Once they have accumulated enough revenue from the land, they branch off, like the estate farmers, and explore other business initiatives. The question of individual land tenure, usually propounded by African governments, has minimal benefits and is not an improvement over customary land tenure. One of the most important reasons for this, according to Mafeje, is that 'a significant portion of the value derived from privatisation of land went into circulation and consumption. Thus, by the end of the 1960s, agricultural production in sub-Saharan Africa had reached a plateau, while a few speculators continued to prosper.'[66] Another problem with African land reform programmes is that they have encouraged exploitation and parasitism between big and small farmers.

The land reforms have failed to 'develop a self-producing class of agricultural capitalists, relying on full-time labour divested of any means of production, as predicated by the classical European model'. The notion of individual land tenure is strongly associated with the introduction of new technologies and technical expertise – consequently, the farmers with title deeds not only secured bank and government loans, they also received technical advice from government technocrats. In Malawi, these farmers were called *achikumbe*; in Zambia and Uganda they were known as progressive farmers; in Tanzania they were known as *kulaks*. In the late 1970s, Kenya's medium-sized farmers were also called capitalist farmers, but the label did not stick because these farmers could not be distinguished from the country's so-called middle peasants, who were credited with Kenya's 'success story'. The volume of production does not necessarily translate into property and production relations. Hence it is difficult to label Kenyan middle peasants as capitalist farmers.

Although these developments advanced agricultural production, it is not clear whether this translates into technological revolution in agriculture. Mafeje suggests that there did not seem to be any significant difference 'between those African farmers who are on freehold plots and those who have only usufructuary rights under customary tenure but have enough resources of their own to engage in expanded petty commodity production'.[67] He points out that the FAO attributes the agricultural crisis in sub-Sahara to 'technological stagnation'. Whether valid or not, this supposition calls into question the claim that individual tenure would open many more development opportunities than customary tenure – a claim that mistakenly led African governments to allocate more resources to private landholders. At the conceptual level, African governments mistook private landholders for capitalist farmers in the classical sense of the term. The socio-economic cost of the measures was the complete neglect of the vast majority of agricultural producers and of food production. While governments are important players in the development process of their countries, it is equally important to note that they do not necessarily have a monopoly on innovation and initiative when such opportunities are available and pursued vigorously by small producers and peasants.

According to Mafeje, small producers in sub-Saharan Africa have proved to be responsive to the capitalist market, as evidenced by large quantities of maize production in southern Africa and Kenya. In Uganda and Tanzania there were the cotton growers, and groundnut and rice production in West Africa. Following the long agriculture crisis in sub-Sahara, especially in Kenya, Tanzania, Zimbabwe and Senegal, small producers abandoned traditional crops and opted for hybrid maize, horticulture, paddy rice, poultry and dairy farming – all of these adaptations within the context of customary tenure. Individuals involved in these endeavours have basic education and have lived in urban areas as migrant workers; they have been able to mobilise kin group resources and labour in order to meet the requirements of changing market conditions. Mafeje reasons that under the circumstances the number of people engaged in these activities is likely to rise in that under customary tenure participation was open to potential participants. In fact, it was in their interests to ensure that participation remained open, which was both possible and desirable because those successful individuals depended on their descent groups or relatives for support and labour. Equally, the principle of customary tenure relies on reciprocity.

What altered this system was the individual tenure championed by governments in favour of progressive farmers who were meant to rely on hired labour rather than family obligations, support and labour. In some cases, individual tenure was rejected by communities who preferred customary tenure (the Luoland region of Kenya is an example) and the government of Ghana encountered the same problem when it tried to protect the rights of migrant workers. This kind of kin or group solidarity among the small producers does not, of course, mean that there is no exploitation from within. Those individuals who have become successful tend to take advantage of the less successful members, although the more successful cannot discard the less successful and in order to retain their loyalty the farmers have to invest socially. Under these circumstances, hunger can be kept at bay and the livelihood of the less successful can improve – which is not the case in the context of 'modernising' and individual tenure systems that were advocated by governments and policymakers from the

West. Under the system of individualised agricultural production, the less fortunate become even worse off. Ironically, this is something that has happened in the West as well.

There are several arguments against customary land tenure. First, there is generally underinvestment in such a system. Second, a kinship-based system such as customary tenure does not yield greater capital and labour returns. Third, in a system where there is no competition for land, labour and capital, there is likely to be an unproductive use of scarce resources. With regard to the first argument, there is evidence to suggest that over the past 50 years or more, African cultivators with access to the latest technology have been able to take advantage of and participate in the capitalist market. This reached a crescendo in the 1960s. What is germane to the present argument is the fact that much of this success can be attributed to the emergence of the middle peasants and cannot be attributed to the so-called capitalist farmers, of whom there are very few (and whose technological competence was no better than that of the middle peasants). It is said that African agriculture became technologically stagnant by the end of the 1960s; however, a study conducted by Nikos Alexandratos found that 'land use intensity actually estimated to prevail implies that African agriculture uses land at cropping intensities close to those compatible with the intermediate level of technology of the PSC [potential population-supporting capacity] study ... However, the yields actually prevailing are decidedly closer to those of the low technology of PSC study.'[68]

Whatever the problems of agriculture in sub-Saharan Africa, they are not customary land tenure or technological stagnation. It is notable that the crisis in African agriculture pervades all sizes and descriptions of farmers and their farms. In reality, small farmers fare well compared to capitalist farmers. Mafeje concludes: 'Their survival strategies, such as developing parallel markets, bartering agricultural commodities with producers in neighbouring countries, and switching to high-value crops, though on a modest scale, seem to have paid off. Thus, the question of technological innovation or its opposite, technological stagnation, needs to be studied afresh, as does the question of who should "mobilise" whom.'[69]

It is known that small producers or rural dwellers in sub-Saharan Africa have been oscillating between town and country as migrant labourers and 'petty cash producers' who were in one way or another embedded in the capitalist market. The problem, however, has been their structural relationship with their governments. Equally, although the markets grow concurrently with capitalist development, the two do not grow or develop evenly everywhere. In sub-Saharan Africa this issue is more acute and in promoting capitalist or commercial farming in the post-independence period African governments knew very well that they had to provide all the requisite marketing facilities. They opted for marketing boards. This approach promised better coordination and regulation of prices as well as opportunities for generating revenues. The failure on the part of marketing boards was their inability to transcend cash crops such as they were understood or conceived by colonial governments. Capitalist or commercial farmers were also amenable to cash production. The upshot was the failure to grow domestic markets for food crops, which led to the neglect of the so-called subsistence farmers. The long-term effects have only been felt in recent years, particularly in the wake of the sub-Saharan agricultural crisis. Although the marketing boards were meant to be institutions to facilitate the agricultural markets, they eventually became what Mafeje terms 'powerful instruments for extracting surplus' from small producers under customary tenure and from commercial farmers.[70] According to Mafeje, this is to the point that small producers were in some countries taxed 'as much as 70 per cent of the world market value of their produce'.

But that would be taking extreme cases to hang a perfectly good idea. Marketing boards were, at their inception, intended to protect farmers against the volatility of international commodity prices and to facilitate income for farmers. In theory, they reduce the transaction costs that small-producer farmers face, they create economies of scale in providing inputs to farmers and they help to ensure product quality for farmers. These are only a few of the things that marketing boards, properly organised, can do and have done. In most countries, the elimination of marketing boards was one of the conditionalities imposed by the Bretton Woods institutions under their SAPs. (It is interesting that left-leaning arguments of expropriation of farmers by marketing boards were initially used by the right wing in order to enforce a market-centric regime for agricultural produce; the result in several countries was a collapse in agricultural output.) The issue is about reforming marketing boards to fulfil their core objectives, not to demonise the idea itself.

Owing to commercial farmers being 'well-represented in the government bureaucracy', they were exempted and could sell their produce 'on floor shows'. Small and middle producers responded to these policies by 'withdrawing from the regular market and by engaging in what is officially called "smuggling" or by cutting down production'.[71] The 'liberalisation policies' of the World Bank in the 1980s were of no use. This continues to be an unresolved problem between African governments and the small producers; the former have to be responsive to the needs of the latter and not the other way round – and whereas the classical peasantry are said to be land-rooted, the same is not true for the African peasantry. For Mafeje, the African peasantry were usually migrants who dealt in petty commodity production, migrant labour and petty trading in agricultural commodities – yet, this is not an idea that travels very well in every part of Africa (in West Africa, for instance, the migrant labour idea is not sustainable). Much of Mafeje's analysis tended to be biased towards southern and East Africa.

Neoliberal theories and resultant policy proposals have led to disastrous outcomes in sub-Saharan economies generally and the agrarian economies particularly. What exacerbated the problem were SAPs, whose effects are still being felt. The political and ideological timing of the SAPs is that they came shortly after the adoption of the Lagos Plan of Action in 1980, an acknowledgement on the part of African governments that there was a need for a social and political way out of the economic impasse. It was the World Bank that advocated the intensification and diversification of export production among those farmers with the necessary resources; the elimination of price controls on agricultural commodities; the removal of government subsidies to farmers of all sizes; the withdrawal of food subsidies by governments; cutbacks of social services and withdrawal of the state from production.[72]

One might add to this list the closing of marketing boards. These recommendations were not only consistent with the Berg Report,[73] but were also part of the loan conditions of the World Bank and the International Monetary Fund (IMF). Noteworthy is the fact that not only were they incompatible with the Lagos Plan of Action, but also that they came right after its adoption. Equally important is the fact that the African Council of Ministers in Tripoli in 1981 had rejected the prescriptions of the Berg Report, although 34 African governments backtracked and gave in to the demands of the World Bank and the IMF. The SAPs, as is known today, were disastrous and led to high rates of poverty and huge debts on the part of those African countries that adopted World Bank and IMF recommendations. The SAPs led to what became known as the 'lost decade' of the 1980s in Africa. Well-considered criticisms of the SAPs are to be found in the 1990 report of the Economic Commission for Africa, *African Alternative Framework to Structural Adjustment Programmes for Socio-Economic Recovery and Transformation* and then, a decade later, in the book *Our Continent, Our Future* by Thandika Mkandawire and Charles Soludo, which marked a radical break with the neoliberal paradigm of the Washington Consensus, but did not give clear direction to the agrarian question, which is said to be the cornerstone of African economies.[74]

5 | Peasants, Food Security and Poverty Eradication

In 'Peasant Organisations in Africa: A Potential Dialogue between Economists and Sociologists – Some Theoretical/Methodological Observations' Archie Mafeje argues that the socio-historical category of peasants in Africa was not as self-evident as is often assumed, and that given the history of sub-Saharan Africa one cannot use the category without some qualification.[1] The ongoing agricultural crisis in Africa, and the acknowledged role of small producers in agricultural development and poverty eradication in rural areas, necessitates that African scholars be clear about who they are referring to when they speak of small producers and whether they can be defined as peasants. This raises theoretical and empirical questions that have implications for social mobilisation and strategies for future development. Mafeje contends that in order for one to speak meaningfully about peasants there are methodological conditions that should be met – one has to theorise the concept in relation to the state and to history. To speak of the role of peasants in social development, Mafeje says, one has to systematise 'the dividing principles between different spheres of activity in which peasants feature as such or as members of given solidarity groups in different agrarian social settings' and one ought also to review the few specific studies on the subject from different parts of the continent.[2]

Writing in the early 1990s, Mafeje noted that in the last 15 to 20 years a fair number of studies had been conducted on the African peasantry, particularly in South Africa, Tanzania, Kenya, the Sudan, Ethiopia,

Nigeria and Uganda, but he immediately added that sub-Saharan Africa had no recognisable tradition of peasant studies. The Ethiopian sociologist Dessalegn Rahmato agrees: 'I agree with Mafeje that the tradition of peasant studies in Africa is woefully underdeveloped, but that, it seems to me, is mainly because of the failings of African social scientists.'[3] Sam Moyo argues that not only has there been a paucity of peasant studies, but also that dominant urban-biased research perspectives tend to minimise the role of the peasantry.[4]

As a start, Mafeje states that a distinction ought to be made between 'peasant organisation' or 'organisation of peasant societies' and 'peasant organisations'. The former refers to a generic mode of existence and production associated with peasants while the latter connotes social groups formed by peasants. In classical theory, the growth of peasant societies is associated with the incorporation of a society that was previously autonomous but became a centralised state dominated by classes other than the peasantry. Unlike serfs or slaves, however, peasants are an independent category of producers who are generally subject to an impersonal political authority – the state – rather than a master. Another point to note is that peasant organisations occur in specific agrarian settings and do not necessarily constitute a peasant society.

Small producers or peasants?

Mafeje's 1985 article 'Peasants in Sub-Saharan Africa' is, of all his works, the most focused on peasant studies, the resurgence of which, particularly in Asia and Latin America, in the late 1960s, coincided with the demise of modernisation theories, the failure of bourgeois development strategies in less developed countries and the rise of the dependency school.[5] Prior to the rise of peasant studies, conventional social science set considerable store by the 'modern sector' in African societies, supposedly the only sector with the potential for economic growth. By the late 1960s and early 1970s it became clear that this understanding was headed in the wrong direction; that the overemphasis on the modern sector or the 'formal sector' neither acted as a catalyst nor promoted development. Instead, the modern sector was so unevenly integrated with the imperialist economies that it created underdevelopment in the 'backward' or 'informal' sectors of the African economies. The urban or formal sector in the African economy is too small to cater for or compensate for small producers in the rural or informal sector.

When economists were concerned with development and growth in the modern sector, sociologists with the notion of urbanisation, and political scientists with nation building, social anthropologists were still grappling with the notion of 'tribes' in the rural areas. In spite of their studies of the rural areas, anthropologists treated tribesmen and peasants as separate categories, focusing on the former and omitting the latter. Mafeje considers this not only justified, but also perfectly logical because in order to conduct studies on peasants in sub-Saharan Africa one should establish whether small producers are to be known as peasants and also study the 'objective nature of the African social formations'. Epistemologically, Mafeje argues, one needs to study the 'state of the arts in the social sciences'. As regards the study of African social formations, his point is that one cannot make universal claims or statements about Africa, particularly if such claims are based on experiences from elsewhere.

In 1971, the anthropologist Monica Wilson revisited the rise of the peasantry in South Africa.[6] Wilson links its emergence more to missionaries and less to colonialism. She states that peasant communities, 'in the sense in which the term is used in the book, began in 1738 with the foundation of the first mission station in South Africa'.[7] She continues: 'Families were urged to settle; the hunters were pressed to become herders; the herders were taught to cultivate; the cultivators were taught to use a plough and irrigate, and all came into much closer relationship with the outside world.'[8] In other words, the peasantry in South Africa did not develop organically.

According to Mafeje, the South African peasantry was created by colonialists and missionaries. Prior to the 1960s and 1970s, 'the approach to the peasant question was generally cultural'.[9] The values and cultures of African people were stripped of their content and reduced to a caricature as a result of the European civilising mission and of colonialism. At all times, colonialism entailed an expansive capitalist mode of production, which was considered by colonialists not only valid, but also justified and desirable. In an essay titled 'African Peasantries', John Saul and Roger Woods attempt to give an overview of the African peasantry. They argue that 'despite the existence of some prefigurings of a peasant class in earlier periods, it is more fruitful to view ... the creation of an African peasantry ... as being primarily the result of the international capitalist economic system and traditional socio-economic systems'.[10] Deploying the criterion of a household economy, Saul and Woods maintain that there is no point in distinguishing between African agriculturalists and pastoralists: at the political level both are subject to the same higher authority. The problem, however, is that Saul and Woods were unable to grapple with the dynamics of land tenure in sub-Saharan Africa, which is characterised by lineage land tenure systems – or what in popular parlance is called 'communal land tenure'.

Saul and Woods casually talk about 'certain rights in land', but they do not explain or define the phrase. In 'Peasantisation in Western Africa', Ken Post attempts to address the question of property versus usufruct rights in land in Africa by arguing that 'in both the pre-colonial and colonial periods it would seem that, from the point of view of the individual, land *use* rights must be treated as more important than property rights'.[11] Although this is a fairly theoretically sophisticated formulation, in trying to determine 'threshold between the communal cultivator and the peasant', Post might, Mafeje surmises, 'have created opposed categories where none existed'.[12] Mafeje argues that what binds the studies by Post and Saul and Woods is that both 'represented a conscious focus on class analysis'. Moreover, they evaluate the impact of Western capitalism on African societies. In contrast to the liberal study by Wilson, with its emphasis on culture, these studies emphasise structural analysis.

Mafeje is quick to point out that points of convergence and divergence between Wilson, Post, and Saul and Woods are not characteristic of the usual division between scholars of liberal and Marxist persuasion because when peasant studies gained currency in Africa most scholars (liberals and Marxists alike) 'espoused "political economy" almost as a fad'. South Africa was one of the first countries to be put under the spotlight in peasant studies.[13] These studies were historical in character, with political economy as the object of investigation, and focused mainly on the nineteenth and early twentieth centuries. Studies on the Orange Free State and the Transvaal (both Boer republics) and the Cape and Natal (two British colonies) determined that the black peasantry emerged around the mid-nineteenth century. In the Boer republics, the black peasantry formed out of squatters and sharecroppers on 'white-owned' land, which meant that white 'landowners' had a supply of labour. Although black small producers were producing for the market and were under the authority of the white state, they were denied property rights in land.

Although some producers were able to generate enough income from this set-up, a good majority of them resorted to working on other farms as well, or simply migrated to towns, during off-season, for employment. In this way, they were able to supplement their meagre income from agriculture. In the British colonies of Natal and the Cape, as Mafeje says, 'participation in a market economy got associated with missionary establishments and colonial imposition of taxes of all sorts'.[14] In his book *The Rise and Fall of the South African Peasantry* Colin Bundy points out, however, that the rise of peasants was not limited to mission stations and production was widespread even among those who were not Christians. What seems to have mattered is the introduction of a market economy, tax imposition and the demand for industrial goods, which would have been much more pronounced among Christian converts who were compelled by missionaries to participate in the market economy. Post argues that this did not depend on property rights in land because access to communal land, tenancies and sharecropping on white farms was sufficient. What created the impression that the black producers had property rights in land was the quit-rent system.[15]

The quit-rent system and the non-freehold system of tenure in the black reserves made the status of black subsistence producers even more 'ambiguous', according to Mafeje. He believed that South African peasant studies paid insufficient attention to the question of property rights among black producers. The tendency was to write about the peasant mode of production as cash crop production for the market, the use of new production techniques and the use of family labour, with the emphasis on usufruct rather than property rights – which presented a theoretical conundrum in that while it 'might be empirically justified, it detracts in no mean way from the classical definition of "peasants". A peasant mode of production which is not founded on petty bourgeois rights in land is unknown to classical theory.'[16] Mafeje argues that in Tanzania, specifically through *Ujamaa* policies,[17] intellectuals set out to understand the role of the small producers in the development of the country – yet the question of whether there were peasants in Tanzania to begin with is never addressed and it is taken for granted that small producers were peasants. Small producers in Tanzania were linked to an external market, were taxed and were subject to state authority. They never owned land, although their access to it was determined by the customary land tenure system, which continued in Tanzania even after land had been nationalised. As in colonial South Africa, individual families treated allotted land as if they owned it. The system in Tanzania was such that there was no limit to the amount of land that each family could cultivate and well-off families could grab more land for themselves. The Tanzanian government sought to put an end to this by banning hired labour, but could not prevent the emergence of the so-called capitalist farmers, or *kulaks*. Ownership of land or of the means of production was not the issue, since none owned the land, but simply used it. The issue, instead, turned on the instruments of production. Mafeje's reluctance to use the category 'peasants' (since this refers to petty landholders) in relation to African small producers makes a lot of sense, but I believe that it flies in the face of his strong claim that there is no land question in sub-Saharan Africa – the question is an agrarian one. If African small producers do not own the land but simply use it, then the land question in sub-Saharan Africa is far from settled. One could argue, however, that my concerns only reinforce Mafeje's argument in that, historically, land tenure systems in sub-Saharan Africa turn on the usufruct principle, rather than ownership of land as property.

The Kenyan context raises similar theoretical problems. While capitalism developed within the agricultural sector in Kenya, Mafeje maintains that it was not clear whether this entailed the existence of classes – 'an indigenous rural bourgeoisie, a rural proletariat, and an independent peasantry'.[18] With regard to property relations, he says: 'The introduction of individual land tenure under the 1-million acre scheme and the transfer of the white highlands estate farms to Africans after independence established private property in land.' Ownership of land in and of itself did not necessarily mean that an African rural bourgeoisie existed in Kenya. In order for the bourgeoisie to realise itself, the essential condition of ownership of capital was necessary, and ownership of capital was not available to landowners in Kenya – denied by the multinational corporations that controlled agricultural capital. Production relations were seen as between international corporations and local labour, primarily, and not between Kenyan landowners and rural workers. Part of what this meant was that rural workers were proletarianised, although there was no development of an agricultural capitalist class. In this regard, Kenya was similar to South Africa, where displaced black people were turned into cheap labour as part of the settler agricultural economy. Cheap labour came about as a result of private property in land – and not only did it mean landlessness, it also meant that those who were economically weak became smallholders and therefore even weaker. Mafeje argues that there was in Kenya a class of small private landowners who could be categorised as peasants in the classical sense of the term. These landowners are called, variously, middle, small, rich or poor peasants (depending on the size of the units of operation). Rich peasants depend on hired as well as on family labour. Poor peasants, who sell their labour either in towns or on plantations in order to supplement their income, are akin to the propertyless proletariat. In this sense, they have no independent economic status, but are directly exploited by capital. Mafeje reasons that the Kenyan peasantry was either in the process of proletarianisation or being transformed into *kulaks* who were employing labour.

While Post and Polly Hill credit individual development and private appropriation, respectively, under the communal land tenure system, Samir Amin and Catherine Coquery-Vidrovitch each independently trace the lack of progress in African agriculture to the absence of privately owned land.[19] Amin's and Coquery-Vidrovitch's claims are not entirely accurate because a lack of formal or juridical rights in land does not prevent accumulation once individual families use land in a sustained way. Furthermore, under the customary system, security of tenure was guaranteed socially but not legally. There is no evidence to suggest that families were evicted because of absence of legal rights to land – they were usually expelled on political grounds such as disloyalty to the king or chiefs. Therefore, the idea that customary land tenure gives rise to insecurity is not historically founded. African families have always held their allotted plots in perpetuity as long as there was sustained use of the land. For Mafeje, the materialist point of view dictated that it is use that gives value to property, and vice versa.

If there is an African peasantry, it exists notwithstanding a lack of property rights in land. Under the social conditions discussed, African societies do not easily lend themselves to neat class categorisations. Mafeje argues that liberal theorists tend to deploy stratification theories and use income differences, land holdings and farm equipment as indices, while Marxists propound theories about alliances between peasants and workers. Yet these refer to two entirely different things – what the liberals say concerns social stratification among agrarian elements and what the Marxists say concerns political alliances. Mafeje elaborates: 'True enough, on the ground it has proved too difficult to say who is a peasant and who is a worker in Africa. However, there is a noticeable ideological inclination on the part of the majority of Marxists who are concerned with this problem to derive as many proletarians out of the so-called peasants as possible on largely mechanistic grounds. In some cases this verges on crude proletariat Messianism.'[20] A deeper sociological appreciation of African societies would not lead theorists to contrive class categories where none exist. Mafeje goes on to argue that African small producers had links with urban workers because of labour migration, while at the same time urban workers protected their usufruct rights in the rural areas through family members or relatives. Historically, neither urban workers nor small producers had property rights in land. Mafeje claims that regardless of whether they were in town or in the rural areas, the workers and the small producers were exploited by international capital; yet the proposition assumes that the two were involved in the same production relations. That is not entirely true because, as Mafeje points out, 'whereas the urban worker depends entirely on wages for the social reproduction of his labour, the migrant worker depends partly on the labour of his family for the social reproduction of his labour'.

The question is whether the African small producers are proletariat living in the countryside or industrialised peasantry. Mafeje insists that they were both, for both had a rural referent. Similarly, both notions, industrialised peasantry and proletariat, have worker or urban undertones and this connotes 'both continuity and ambiguity – peasant-worker'. This ambiguity occurs at the level of social reproduction of labour, rather than at the level of property relations. The migrant worker traverses both ends of the spectrum. Far from being permanent labour, the mode of existence of the migrant worker is unpredictable. If the market economy in Africa created the peasantry, it equally destroyed them through the demand for cheap labour. Having been stripped of their land, Africans became itinerant wage earners – especially in southern Africa. Because African economies are largely agrarian, there will be people whose mode of existence is agricultural production. Mafeje concludes that it is difficult to tell what form the agrarian revolution will take in African countries. It is notable that the introduction of capitalism in Africa has not led to a capitalist agricultural revolution, except in South Africa and Zimbabwe – particularly in sectors controlled by white settler farmers.

The agrarian question, food production and food security issues

The food crisis in Africa must be viewed as a failure of current agricultural systems. Food security is one of the major peace and security conditions in any country or region. As Sam Moyo, Praveen Jha and Paris Yeros argue: 'There is no country today that can ensure the food security of its people into the future; no major investor that has not bet on agriculture and natural resources; no international organisation that is not concerned with its consequences; and no serious social or political movement that is not considering the peasant path as a modern solution to the multiple crises of our times, the economic, climate, energy and food.'[21]

In the southern African region this has been the case for over three decades. According to Mafeje, food security has been deteriorating since the 1970s as a result of a combination of natural and social factors.[22] Since the 1970s and 1980s, Africa has had some of the highest population growth rates in the world, at a time when the economic crisis has been at its most severe. Politically, it does not help that African countries are lethargic about the regional co-operation or integration that would go a long way towards improving the continent's negotiating position against Western countries – and also the lives of African people. The problem appears to be the inability of individual countries to strike a balance between national and regional interests. Mafeje argues that regional bodies such as the Southern African Development Community (SADC) ought to develop regional strategies and a common negotiating position. If regional co-operation is to succeed, it requires not only complex negotiations, but also an equitable distribution of costs and benefits in joint projects. This has been a thorny issue and a major obstacle among member states of regional bodies such as SADC and the continental African Union (AU).[23]

Having pointed out the objective conditions facing the sub-Saharan region, Mafeje addresses epistemological and methodological issues in order to understand the African continent. His argument is that in studying Africa, one should keep two perspectives in mind, the broad and the local. In the past, there were two tendencies in studying Africa: the liberal empiricist tradition of the British and Americans, and the Marxist tradition pursued mainly by the French historians and sociologists.[24] The liberal empiricists focused primarily on the English-speaking southern, eastern and western African countries. Among the liberal empiricists, the social anthropologists produced particularistic studies of tribes. Agricultural economists among them, while not affected by particularism, gravitated towards regional studies with less focus on tribes. What held anthropologists and agricultural economists together, however, were generalisations about Africa. They were, Mafeje claims, 'guilty of generalisations by extrapolation'.[25]

At the level of theory and method, anthropologists and agricultural economists conducted comparative studies, which were meant to guard against individual bias and overgeneralisation. These studies, Mafeje argues, lead to taxonomic categorisations. The tighter the taxonomic categorisations become, the more they become static, and when that happens they are incapable of accounting for dynamic processes: for example, in anthropological literature tribes are frozen and categorised as pristine.

Agricultural economists espouse the notion of communal land tenure systems in Africa, which are said to be an obstacle to development. The classification of African land tenure systems as communal is premised on a comparison with the European model of individual land tenure. Marxists like Amin, Coquery-Vidrovitch and Claude Meillassoux, on the other hand, are interested in thematic studies in order to generate theory. They are most interested in those western and central African countries colonised by the French.[26] Their mistake, says Mafeje, is falling into the same trap of generalising by extrapolation about black Africa. The Marxists maintain, for example, that the rise of African kingdoms is traceable to long-distance trade. In the 1970s and 1980s, this line of thought gained currency, as evidenced by the works of Amin and Coquery-Vidrovitch, although the history and ethnography of the interlacustrine kingdoms and southern Africa seem to suggest otherwise. Amin had what Mafeje called a 'more differentiated view' of black Africa, which he, Amin, divided into four socio-historical zones: colonial economy, concessionaries, labour reserves and pseudo-feudal systems.[27]

What Mafeje considers the greatest contribution to African Marxist studies is the importance of lineage organisation, even in areas with tributary formations – a view shared by Meillassoux and Coquery-Vidrovitch. One thing that makes this idea a unique contribution is that it is informed by concrete African socio-historical realities and is not derivative with an over-reliance on European analogies and textbook knowledge. Mafeje notes that in agrarian studies, 'classical concepts such as "feudalism", "tribalism", "capitalism", "Prussian path", "peasants", "communal land tenure", etc., etc. are used uncritically'.[28] Subjecting these inherited concepts to critical scrutiny would throw into relief some of the specificities of the African agrarian question. In so doing, African social scientists stand to make a lasting contribution to the agrarian question. Particular reference has to be paid to small producers since they are the 'foundation of African agrarian social formations'. In this regard, Mafeje counsels that African scholars have to go back to the roots and not limit themselves to inherited classical texts. For this to be realised, one has to be informed by the 'specificity of African local history'.

Mafeje concedes that, although it has had a negative impact, colonialism forms part of African history and in order for Africans to transcend its negations, and be fully liberated, they ought to 'abandon colonial modes of thinking and doing'. The fundamental contradiction between decolonisation and neocolonialism turns primarily on this issue. In agriculture, colonialism found expression in the binary between export crops and subsistence crops. What this means is that African economies cater to the needs of the industrialised countries as suppliers of primary agricultural communities and the subsistence needs of Africans fade into the background. The monetary language adopted, cash versus subsistence crops, to rationalise this practice does not hold because in a monetised economy all crops are cash crops. In structural and functional terms, the main difference is at the level of modern and traditional sectors. Insofar as the modern appropriates and subverts the traditional sector, this is a dialectical process within a single economy, rather than a dual economy. The so-called modern sector 'appropriated the best soils, the best labour and received the best technical inputs, services and scientific support from the colonial governments at the expense of the traditional sector'.[29] This was done for the benefit of the metropolitan countries. Simply put, while the local modern sector benefited by underdeveloping the traditional sector, the former was itself being underdeveloped by colonialists and imperialists and the local modern sector could not reproduce itself, at least not progressively, to transform the agricultural economy into its own image. This whole process has irreparably damaged national food production and security and has led to a food crisis in Africa. African governments, despite colonial distortions, have added to the crisis by continuing with colonial policies. In this sense, they 'instituted colonialism in their own countries'.[30] They worsened the problem by seeking to accumulate wealth long before they learned how to produce it. The waste of resources is accompanied by super-exploitation of primary producers. Unlike the bourgeoisie in Europe, the African petit bourgeoisie has no viable economic or political project. Nor do they have an alternative source of wealth in the form of colonies, as is the case with their European counterparts.

The response from small producers has been to withdraw themselves once they are disillusioned. Although it is acknowledged that the problem of the agricultural food crisis in Africa is traceable to colonial structures and neocolonial policies adopted by African governments, there are varying degrees to the 'impoverishing dialectic'. They vary from region to region. For example, Mafeje says: 'West Africa never had the white settler problem, whereas southern Africa is the epitome of precisely that.'[31] It remains the case that both areas have the modern/traditional sector contradiction; the fundamental difference is that in West Africa the indigenous population always effectively occupied the land. According to Mafeje, the remainder of the problem is not race but class, with clan and lineage affiliations as mediating factors.

Mafeje's primary focus is southern Africa, with the hope of explaining the main difference between settler economies and the colonial mode of production in Africa more broadly. However, in speaking of southern Africa, he is not only referring to the region in geographical and political terms – he also uses socio-historical indices characteristic of the region. The most enduring legacy of southern Africa is the alienation of land to the white settler population, divesting African people of their means of production. This was the surest way of making black people available to white capital as labour. This made logical sense to the white settler. In spite of the logic of this colonial strategy, southern Africa 'ended up with a schizophrenic situation', as Mafeje puts it. For white settlers, land distribution was organised along capitalist lines with laws that only accepted individual land tenure. Conversely, the African migrant worker maintained the customary land tenure with the service of lineages and the guardianship of chiefs.

This social 'schizophrenia' found expression in the labour process as well. This is so because white 'landowners' with estates measuring hundreds and thousands of acres, assumed the role of feudal lords instead of capitalists and, in turn, treated black workers as bonded labour paid in kind by rations and squatting rights. In exchange, black workers supplied labour available for 24 hours a day that extended to the worker's family members. It does strike me as rather odd that Mafeje saw this situation as schizophrenic. The implication of such a concept is that this situation was anomalous and therefore something apart from the logic of conquest and colonialism. Yet, all the schizophrenic examples he enumerates seem consistent with the logic of colonial dispossession. The South African Masters and Servants Act of 1845, along with the Tangatha system in Malawi, held that 'bonded workers had no right to withdraw from the contract'.[32] These were slave-like conditions. What is not entirely clear, however, is Mafeje's characterisation. The idea that this was a schizophrenic situation, as if it were a by-product, rather than the primary motivating factor, gives the impression that the colonialists could have been much more benevolent or conciliatory than they were.

South African agriculture remained backward until the 1930s. This was the time when it had to be modified because of the government's policies that had been biased towards Afrikaner farmers. This was the period when the effects of the Great Depression were still felt acutely and poor white farmers were flocking to the cities, compounding the problem of unemployment. In the case of Malawi, white estate farmers were slacking until the 1960s when the government threatened them with eviction if they did not improve. It is not clear why the government only issued a threat instead of expropriating underperforming farms and giving them to black people. In Rhodesia, and some parts of Natal and the Western Cape in South Africa, white-owned farms were successful through cheap black labour. In Swaziland, farms remained idle, even though black small producers were begging to cultivate the land.

The 'racially-inspired stereotype', as Mafeje puts it, which gained currency a long time ago was that black people have always engaged in primitive agriculture for subsistence. Yet evidence points to the contrary. By the mid-nineteenth century, black people throughout southern Africa had demonstrated that they were as capable of innovation in agriculture as white farmers. In fact, by 1840, they had begun to use 'the European plough' and maize had become a staple crop. Those who were successful among them had also adopted 'the iron planter, the mechanical weeder and the harrow'.[33] They had also started using manure. In this way, the black small producers became attractive to exploitative white landlords who turned them into labour-tenants or sharecroppers, particularly in such places as the Orange Free State, the Transvaal and the northern part of Natal. The black sharecroppers were expected to use their own tools, oxen and seeds. This was a practice known as 'farming on the half' or 'kaffir farming' by racist white farmers and landlords who wanted black people to be reduced merely to farm labour and, in turn, for whites to be labour-employing capitalists. The 1913 Land Act halted this practice. Mafeje observes that 'it took the 1913 Land Act to stifle any further development of the share-cropping system and labour-tenancies. Otherwise, both land-hungry blacks and work-shy whites found it convenient'. What is important to note is that 'between 1860 and 1900, the Africans, barring the Western Cape sheep and fruit farmers and the sugar plantations in Natal, were the most dynamic agricultural producers in South Africa'. During that period, the volume of food production by black small producers was much higher than that of white farmers, who depended on black people for their food.[34]

The agricultural production of the black small producers fell after 1913 when black people were not allowed, by law, to buy or own land. They were also not allowed to sharecrop with white landowners. In general, these measures were extra-economic and the point was to cheapen black labour in order to benefit white employers and to protect uncompetitive white farmers. White farmers, who were protected by law, particularly in the two Boer republics and northern Natal, 'complained that they could not compete with the "kaffirs" who relied on their extended families rather than employed labour'.[35] This is not unique to South Africa, as Mafeje points out. The same happened in Rhodesia where, in African purchase areas, black farmers were quite competitive, and it is also true of black farmers in post-independence Malawi, where 'they accounted for what is considered to be one of the four success stories in Africa (the other three being Kenya, Ivory Coast and Cameroun)'. This historical detail is of great significance in current South African narratives on land repossession when, in everyday conversation, its proponents are typically asked, 'What are you going to do with the land once you get it?' or told: 'Black people will need to be trained on how to farm.' The successes or failures of black people in agriculture and in food production must be understood in the historical context of the objective conditions that shaped their lives. Other constraints to black agriculture included overcrowding in the native reserves, absolute poverty and state neglect, outdated production techniques and unfavourable physical and ecological conditions.

What is not talked about is the cost of labour and its social reproduction. Labour migration to urban areas among black people is an index of poverty. It also marks diminishing returns on agriculture. This was the whole point of the social design of colonialism – to disable the social fabric and economic architecture in the rural areas so that black people were forced to sell their labour to the demands of capital in urban areas. The inescapable problem was that colonial capital was not prepared to pay the cost for 'the social reproduction of the African labour', as Mafeje argues.[36] Far from being a place that guaranteed subsistence for black people, the native reserves became a dumping site for unserviceable black labour. The reserves had to bear the cost of social reproduction of black labour whose services were needed in urban areas. Meant to supplement the low wages that black people received from their employers, the reserves could not develop or sustain subsistence agriculture – if they had succeeded, colonial capitalism would not have been a success for colonialists, for if the black small producer were content with conditions in the rural areas, he would not have to make himself available as labour to colonial capital. In fact, the 1913 dispossession was designed to enforce such dependency because until that point black small producers were thriving in the countryside.

After independence, such countries as Swaziland, Botswana and Zimbabwe did not do away with the colonial model, but instead continued with it. The reserves became a colonial remnant, which continued to undermine the economic self-sufficiency of black people whose subsistence needs could not be guaranteed, even under the most benevolent of African governments. Thus, the point was to dismantle them entirely as part of an attempt to transform radically the agrarian structures in southern Africa. There is a lot that must be done in order to fulfil such a radical promise. Mafeje proposes three solutions. The first concerns redistribution of land according to the needs of small producers in the rural areas. The second relates to land reform in line with the requirements of the national economy (land reform should also include self-sufficiency in food production). The third solution relates to the revision of current land tenure systems relative to racial, class and gender discrimination. Taken together, Mafeje argues, the three solutions constitute the agrarian question in southern Africa.

By the 1980s even the apartheid government of South Africa had come to accept that the reserves were politically unsustainable and attempted to dissolve them. In Zimbabwe, the Zanu-PF Executive Committee had, as far back as 1976, taken the decision to do away with the reserves. It is markedly different in Swaziland and Botswana, where post-independence governments felt that it was best to preserve the system of reserves in order to protect the rural small producers from capitalists. The difficulty in Swaziland was that the government sought to buy back the land from white 'landowners' in order to supplement the overcrowded National (tribal) Lands. This became a burden financially and politically, and the status quo continued. The consequence is that prospects for land reform became so slim that the possibility of enabling black small producers to be self-sufficient in food production seemed remote; still, policymakers in Swaziland contended that theirs was one of the few self-sufficient countries in Africa. This is correct because food production increased through white capitalist farmers, but the problem is that it flies in the face of the independence of black people.

In Botswana, all land belonged to the 'national patrimony'. If it were not for white dominance, Swaziland could be compared to Malawi, where only 17 per cent of arable land belonged to white estate farmers, although small producers accounted for about 70 per cent of the food production.

The problem with Malawi is that estate farms (white or black) were given primacy over small producers. This bias needs to be understood historically and holistically. During European industrialisation, land became commercialised and was accompanied by migration from the countryside to the cities. Agricultural production became the preserve of a few farmers. Owing to the demand for food in the cities, production increased exponentially. In sub-Saharan Africa, under the impact of colonial capitalism, neither industrialisation nor agricultural revolution took place. Furthermore, since the turn of the twentieth century food production has been steadily on the decline. What made the so-called African capitalist farmers irrelevant is the fact that they specialised in growing crops for export. In southern Africa, black small producers were confined to the reserves and significant agricultural production became the preserve of white settlers.

Not only did food production by white farmers keep up with the demand, but those farmers also became responsible for all export crops. The general indifference of the white government to the plight and needs of black people, compounded by the strong political lobby of the white farmers in southern Africa, meant that the question of intervention to address the plight and needs of black people never surfaced. Mafeje arrives at the conclusion that 'the racial question overlays a number of basic issues which otherwise centre on class relations. The white farmers in Southern Africa exploited and dominated Africans as a capitalist class, supported by a capitalist state.'[37] In South Africa, whites prevented – by legal means – any development of a capitalist class among black agricultural producers. The black peasantry that had emerged in the nineteenth century was crushed swiftly and mercilessly. When their labour was not needed in the urban areas, they were confined to the reserves on plots that were around four acres and for which they had to pay quit-rent to the colonial government. The same methods and policies were to be replicated in other British protectorates in southern Africa. These other British protectorates also served as labour reserves for the South African white settler state. Unlike in Rhodesia and South Africa, where the emergence of a black agricultural class was forestalled by legal means, in Malawi and Zambia it was achieved through racial discrimination and the manipulation of credit and marketing facilities.

Mafeje argues that 'Southern Africa boasted of no African capitalist class prior to independence but rather a dispossessed or depressed peasantry, which could hardly feed itself'.[38] Post-independence African governments did not remedy the situation. There emerged a black petit bourgeois elite, which used state revenues and projected itself as a capitalist class. This class took shortcuts to wealth. They chose to buy farms. Yet few of them actually engaged in farming. Far from being sites for investment and production, their farms became weekend resorts and family holiday homes or simply 'insurance against old-age' as Mafeje says. Where capitalist or productive black farmers existed, they were so few that their existence had no appreciable impact.

In Swaziland and South Africa, where white farmers were always the main producers, they never concerned themselves with food security for black people – despite the fact that white farmers monopolised the best land. In this context, the term 'agrarian revolution' entails not only radical change in class structure, production relations and social institutions in the rural areas, but also requires technological or scientific revolution. Mafeje argues that liberal scholars tend to reduce this question merely to formal issues such as land tenure (a shift from communal to individual land tenure). Marxists, on the other hand, tend to accentuate class and production relations while leaving behind technical questions. Yet, methodologically, any process of social transformation must encompass both the formal and the substantive. The black small producers in southern Africa have fallen behind on a number of fronts, especially with regard to technology. There are also environmental factors that militate against productivity, particularly in food crops, and there are agronomic issues that continue to elude small producers – lack of technological advances and financial constraints. These are important issues to highlight in order to avoid revolutionary romanticism and the capabilities of the small producers. At the level of science, the soil in southern Africa is said to be low in plant nutrients and too acidic, with certain toxicities.

When unattended, these issues combine to thwart crop production and lead to compaction and soil erosion. The southern African region is known for soil erosion and what has worsened the problem is lack of soil preservation methods. Added to this is the problem of monocropping in maize and overstocking. There is also drought and near-drought, as well as the problem of water wastage and the poor water retention capacity of the soils. Mafeje reasons that prospects for agrarian revolution seemed unlikely – African governments (with a few exceptions) committed themselves to neocolonial agricultural policies and programmes, mainly at the behest of international agencies and experts. Additionally, African small producers, as a stratum, 'are, unlike their counterparts in Asia and Latin America, not organised and conscious enough to be agents of revolutionary agrarian transformation in Africa'.[39]

Mafeje argues that the biggest aspiration of the nationalists was to entrench a bourgeois society in 'which individual appropriation of value would be the rule'. Consistent with this logic, and colonial bourgeois economics, the agricultural sector was associated with individual land tenure. The so-called success stories of Kenya, Côte d'Ivoire, Malawi and Cameroon seemed to vindicate liberal scholars who were partial to this model. Although these countries showed some of the highest growth rates in Africa, the outcome came at a cost: landlessness and poverty among the small producers. In Côte d'Ivoire and Cameroon, although there is no conclusive evidence, there seems to be a stagnation of peasant agriculture, rising unemployment and widespread poverty in the subsistence sector in the countryside. In Kenya, following the food crisis, peasant squatters sought to dismantle big estate farms in favour of the original usufructuary rights. This shows the deep-seated nature of the lineage principle in Africa. The conclusion, therefore, 'is that petit-bourgeois agricultural policies and programmes have, even in the best examples, failed to bring about a genuine agrarian transformation in Africa. Consequently, everywhere they are faced with reserves and deepening agricultural crisis.[40]

In southern Africa, land remains a major obstacle because of the white settler community. In South Africa, the post-1994 land reform programme was forestalled by the property clause or section 25 of the

1996 Constitution of South Africa, which ensured that white-owned property is protected. Zimbabwe has become an exception, with its land expropriation programme. For Mafeje, the best way to address the agrarian question in southern Africa is to adopt a regional approach in which 'it would not make sense to rationalise production at the level of households and not at the level of governments'.[41] Collective self-reliance (depending on the 'elimination of class deprivation and exploitation' that in the southern African context is overlaid by racism) rather than 'myopic nationalism' needs to filter down to the level of the people. According to Mafeje, 'people in Southern Africa might still starve in the midst of plenty. This is a problem, not of petty reformism or charitable ameliorations, but of the Southern African agrarian revolution in which South Africa is the kingpin.'

Prospects for agrarian reform in sub-Saharan Africa

The supposition that there is no land question in sub-Saharan Africa has led African governments, policymakers and intellectuals to suppose that there is no agrarian question either. The fallacious nature of this supposition is exposed by the extended agricultural and food crisis. This indicates that the agrarian question needs careful attention. There is still a dearth of literature on this issue. Mafeje puts forward at least three propositions. First, there is a need to examine current land tenure systems and modes of social organisation in order to meet the needs of agricultural producers. Second, the relationship between the state and small rural producers should be revised; at the moment, Mafeje argues, African governments treat the agricultural sector as one that raises revenue for developing urban areas while neglecting the rural areas. Third, there needs to be a probe on the lack of development strategy based on large-scale farming. These propositions are not only about maximising output, but also about justice, protection of the environment and sustainable agriculture.

In order for these aims to be met, African governments, policymakers and intellectuals must do away with Eurocentric models. While failures of the structural adjustment programmes (SAPs) are widely known, the World Bank and some African governments are still convinced that the free market is the solution to problems facing sub-Saharan Africa and to advancing bourgeois Western individualism through individual land tenure systems. In dealing with the agrarian question in Africa, Mafeje adopts a historical approach and takes the colonial division of labour in agriculture as a point of departure. This division was a determining factor, not only of gender roles between men and women in production – it also shaped the economic structure generally. Agriculture was divided into the subsistence and the modern sectors, something that widened the divide between rural and urban. The latter developed because of the former because there was urbanisation without industrialisation (South Africa being a noticeable exception). Colonialism and capitalism undermined rural households and Mafeje argues that this was the 'underlying contradiction' that was the cause of disagreement between bourgeois liberal and Marxist scholars.

Mafeje denigrates 'bourgeois' theorists such as Arthur Lewis for suggesting that the subsistence sector would be absorbed by the modern sector or capitalist agriculture.[42] Mafeje says this suggestion is akin to the trickle-down economic theory – but Lewis is not actually arguing about trickle-down in the conventional neoliberal/libertarian economic fashion; he suggests that for a government 'to tax its developed sectors and subsidise its under-developed sectors is one of the most powerful ways that a government can use to ensure that the benefits of development trickle-down'.[43] This is widely at variance with the conventional understanding of trickle-down in neoliberal economics, which will not countenance such redistributive fiscal policy. Mafeje uses the bourgeois label a bit carelessly here. Lewis was actually a Fabian socialist. However, unlike in Europe where this sort of capitalist development took shape, it has not occurred in sub-Saharan Africa and there are no indications that it will. Although institutions such as the World Bank and the International Monetary Fund maintain that Africa must follow the Western growth path, they have done nothing but keep Africa in debt, denying Africa any socialist or endogenous alternatives. The historical Western dominance of the African continent remains intact. Mafeje posits that left-leaning intellectuals believe this system is by design, inbuilt in global capitalism, and radical theories such as 'development of underdevelopment', 'unequal exchange' and 'articulation of modes of production' are meant to capture this precisely. The theory of articulation of modes of production is meant to counter the dual theories of the neoclassical theorists. Unlike neoclassical economic assumptions, capitalism in Africa did not take the same pattern as in Europe or North America. Colonialism thwarted African modes of production and modified them in order to subsidise the colonialists and African small producers could not accumulate enough to become capitalists in their own right.

Mafeje goes on to argue that although he earlier rejected the dissolution and preservation theory as functionalist and undialectical, it was still able to account for instances where policies were extra-economic, as was the case in countries such as Kenya and Malawi. Mafeje contends that taking this view seriously one would be able to appreciate its theoretical implications because it allowed for the 'catalytic effect of voluntarism' that was often undermined in classical Marxism in favour of structural arguments. Voluntarism does not always suffice because it is limited by objective conditions and yet 'even under the most coercive and discriminatory regimes the so-called subsistence producers engaged in a variety of other activities out of necessity so as to meet their consumer needs or to supplement their falling subsistence incomes'.[44]

This was more pronounced in southern Africa where the system of reserves was brought to its logical conclusion – subsistence production was no longer guaranteed and the people who lived in the rural areas depended on remittances by migrant workers (remittances accounted for 80 per cent of rural income). The irony is that what seemed to be a confirmation of dissolution or preservation theory ultimately disproved it. Dissolution became an unintended trend and the rural areas became slums and a dumping ground for unwanted or discharged labour in the urban areas, particularly after the implementation of influx control. In other parts of the continent, small producers were not limited to subsistence production, as they were able to accumulate through other means.

Theoretically, it is not entirely clear whether this entailed a shift from what Mafeje terms 'the simple to the expanded petty mode of production'.

Since the 1970s, the underdevelopment thesis raised two key issues. First, it argued that this was a case of 'proletarianisation' of the peasantry because of the transition from subsistence to migrant labour and labour employment. Second, it spoke of 'differentiation of the peasantry' as a result of 'accumulation from below'. Mafeje argues that while the two may appear to be in conflict, they are in reality 'dynamically linked'.[45]

As Bundy indicates, the supposed staple crops, maize being one of them, had already become cash crops by the end of the nineteenth century, with white traders dominant.[46] It goes without saying that the small producers' prices, when dealing with white traders, are comparatively lower than those between farmers and the urban areas – which reduces chances of accumulation from below and forces small producers to subsist at much lower levels than their actual productivity. In spite of the relative technological advances in southern Africa (animal traction, iron plough, the iron planter, harrow, mechanical weeder, manure and fertilisers) none of these improved the productivity of the black producers, especially under apartheid, or had an effect on the declining levels of subsistence. The question of incompetence should not arise here because up to 80 per cent of white farms are managed by black migrant workers.

Technology (or lack of it) cannot be used as an explanation for the failures of agricultural production in southern Africa. The problem turns on unfavourable socio-economic conditions rather than mere presence or absence of technologies. To see this, one should analyse the agrarian question in Central Africa where producers do not use the plough (because of the unfavourable landscape) and discover that Central Africa is not worse off than southern Africa. Mafeje suggests that regions where technology is less used might even be more efficient because the people are able to retain effective control over the land and determine their own conditions of livelihood. This raises questions about the prospects and conditions for the notion of accumulation from below. In the 1993 booklet *The Agrarian Question in Southern Africa and 'Accumulation from Below'*, Michael Neocosmos argues that the theorists of proletarianisation of the peasantry in Africa do not take seriously the liberating effect and importance of accumulation from below.[47] While it is true that the process of proletarianisation in Africa is non-linear, since migrant workers tend to oscillate between the urban and the rural, the process of accumulation from below also cannot be taken as universally valid under all socio-economic conditions. Equally, its liberating effect cannot be asserted a priori. Mafeje considers Neocosmos guilty on both counts, one of the reasons being his heavy reliance on the case of Russia documented by Lenin in *The Development of Capitalism in Russia*. Mafeje warns that 'in social analysis analogies can be very misleading, especially when drawn across continents'.[48] In the case of Russia, Lenin wanted to overthrow the feudal aristocracy and therefore considered the rise of independent capitalists from below to be a negation of feudal bondage. For Mafeje, 'Lenin also surmised that the disappearance of the commune (*mir*) was the price paid for the development of capitalism in Russia and for the unleashing of progressive forces as a prelude to a socialist revolution.' In his work, Lenin considered displaced peasants as one of the progressive forces, and in so doing became the first Marxist theoretician to take seriously the alliance of peasants and workers in the revolutionary struggle. Mafeje's argument, therefore, is that the Russian analogy could not be applied to sub-Saharan Africa, which had no feudal aristocracy, as was the case in Russia, from which the capitalists would want to liberate themselves and thus help to forge a democracy. In addition, the emergent capitalist farmers in sub-Sahara (except in southern Africa) have not displaced small producers, but have turned them into rural proletariat without the means of production.

Part of what has led to the proletarianisation of African small producers is migration from rural to urban areas. Theoretically, this would have made Lenin's task much easier, since he saw a revolutionary potential between workers and peasants. Concretely, however, this purported alliance is yet to be proved and there continue to be qualitative differences between fully urbanised workers and migrant workers. Unlike pre-revolution Russia under the tsar, capitalist farmers in Africa are subsidised by the state and the peasant-state relationship is fraught and antagonistic. Both the colonial and post-independence states used extractive policies in dealing with the peasants and have used violent and repressive methods to make sure that they complied with state policies – and the state was seen as the enemy of the people. Ironically, while the capitalist farmers, or *kulaks*, were favoured by the state, they were not viewed as the enemy, save in southern Africa where capitalist farmers were white.

In this context, mechanistic class analysis is likely to encounter some difficulties. In 'Extreme but Not Exceptional: Towards an Analysis of the Agrarian Question in Uganda', Mahmood Mamdani falls into this trap.[49] Although Mamdani also advocates accumulation from below, he seems to have parted with Neocosmos's conception of it. While Neocosmos posits that accumulation from below leads to, or has potential for, democracy, Mamdani believes that this would lead to more exploitation and political domination of the poor peasants by local capitalists who were, in the African context, not only supported by the state, but also by members of the bureaucracy. Mamdani is additionally of the view that repressive African governments and the absence of popular democracy combine to hinder accumulation from below. This is in contrast to Neocosmos's view that accumulation from below obtains in spite of repressive regimes. Mamdani enumerates examples to show that local capitalists are as bad as government bureaucrats in their dealings with poor peasants. Mafeje suggests that the veracity of Mamdani's claim is in doubt 'if the sociology of these two relations is taken into consideration'.[50] Mafeje questions Mamdani's conception of village capitalists who 'are characterised not by production relations but largely by exchange relations, including traditional forms of labour exchange'. Whereas Mamdani argues that transactions between the two entail 'unequal exchange between rich and poor peasants', Mafeje's conviction is that the Ugandan peasantry, for example, is poor not because of unequal exchange, but because there was no development in the region to begin with. The local capitalists are too few and isolated for their exchange with poor peasants to lead to inequality on a large scale. Mafeje invokes social stratification, rather than class analysis, and argues that differences in income do not necessarily entail class differences.

It is worth repeating that in sub-Saharan Africa the most prevalent mode of social organisation is kinship, 'by which is meant affiliation by descent or consanguinity'.[51] Social reproduction and production centre on descent groups or lineage, the arrangement typically regulated by senior men known traditionally and historically as elders, who are considered 'the representatives of the constituent units of the lineage (minimal lineages)'. The elders not only determine how resources and labour are allocated, but also represent their respective units in political and legal public affairs – and the relationship between them, their juniors and women is necessarily hierarchical. This means that the elders control both the means of subsistence and the means of social reproduction, which has theoretical implications in that (contrary to Marxist universalism) sub-Saharan Africa is said to exhibit an 'African mode of production' (different from the Asiatic mode of production) and/or 'lineage mode of production'.[52]

The African mode of production and the lineage mode of production are not credited by orthodox Marxists, who say that talking about these modes of production will lead to infinite regression and particularism if each country or region has to be judged according to its own mode of production and historical specificity. Mafeje wants to recentre the uniqueness of the African mode of social organisation, which is kinship-based and 'characterised by relations of domination and not of production'. For him it is not, theoretically, a mode of production precisely on those bases, in contrast to what he calls (following Amin) the tributary mode of production. Because of 'corporation existence' in the lineage mode of organisation, community members, when entering into transactions with others, do so as representatives of their groups and not as individuals. While this system of kinship may entail relations of domination, it also has an important welfare function such as assisting others materially. Even educated Africans are a product of this system and continue to be part of it.

In saying that relations of domination are not relations of exploitation, Mafeje does not necessarily discount the notion of accumulation from below. His argument is that 'if by accumulation from below is meant class differentiation, then not all forms of social exchange lead to class formation'.[53] To see this, one need only look at African lineages and their redistributive system that is wrongly said to be responsible for lack of accumulation. Mafeje argues that such a claim can only be valid when approached from the perspective of 'bourgeois individualism'. African producers accumulated income through cash crops and by trading animals in the capitalist market; if they had not, one would be unable to explain the success of the African peasants in the 1950s and 1960s when prices of commodities had risen. The exponential rate of the middle peasants meant that there was a rise of the expanded petty mode of production throughout sub-Saharan Africa – save for southern Africa.

Although African peasants accepted the commercialisation of production with the customary tenure system, they nevertheless resisted individualism of production (individual tenure systems). The customary tenure system prevents the individual sale of land in that when the situation dictates, if the current owner had made arrangements for permanent investment the original owners of the land could invoke reversionary rights and buy the land back with compensation. Mafeje cites Kenya as a place where this had happened frequently. The most successful mode of accumulation from below is one in which peasants take advantage of customary tenure because it allows its owners to use it perpetually. Contrary to Mamdani's supposition, Mafeje assumes that this tenure system need not be exploitative and predatory; for example, in eastern and southern Africa agriculture is aided by remittances from urban areas. In financing production from remittances, the urban-based petit bourgeoisie are able to rely on household labour for production purposes. On the question of household labour, Mafeje cautions: 'The term "household labour" is used here advisedly because in Africa, contrary to the common European usage, households are the production units, not families, whose composition is determined by descent (filiation) and are the repositories of lineage assets and accumulated value. In contrast, in households the primary relation is marriage (affinity) and the primary purpose is reproduction and production.'[54]

In this sense, unmarried individuals do not benefit from allocation of land because of their marital status; they are not entitled to land, regardless of their gender or age. The structural rationale for this is that, traditionally, women had the responsibility of cultivating for their husbands and children, so it would not make sense to allocate land to an unmarried man. In matrilineal societies, the reverse is true – however, this is not simply for the benefit of the wife, but for her family, 'since [the husband] was subject to the authority of her sister's son or his brother-in-law as long as he lived in their compound'.[55]

Even in matrilineal societies, however, men remain legal representatives and assets are passed down through them and not necessarily through women. The son of the wife's sister, not children of the labouring husband, is the heir. Women from either side of the marriage do not have inheritance rights or political and jural authority in the matrilineages to which they belong by descent. The introduction of cash crops has been a source of conflict between wives and husbands in patrilineal societies, as it has allowed husbands to appropriate what is produced by women. This is both domination and exploitation and it is one of the disadvantages of descent or customary tenure. For Mafeje, a possible solution would be to give usufructuary rights to both men and women, married or not. This would not tamper with the question of reversionary rights because the (usufructuary) allottees are not entitled to the land, but only to its produce. The only discernible problem, Mafeje surmises, is that this would restructure the process of social reproduction of the lineages.

Notwithstanding the contradictions and domination in lineages in sub-Saharan Africa, Mafeje does not see a full-scale revolution as feasible. Kinship ties are valuable to individuals who struggle with their livelihoods and in areas where the state has no meaningful welfare system (this is not a problem of the poor alone because even the professional class is affected). But it does not mean that the situation is static. Mafeje argues that in agriculture a sizeable number of households have moved from the petty to the expanded mode of production. While they are not on equal terms, both men and women have been involved in the process, which was achieved through cash crops sold at the capitalist market and aided by the use of household labour, kin and hired labour. Technological intensification of production is also a contributing factor. Thus, Mafeje concludes, the land question or land tenure systems (apart from southern Africa) cannot be counted as a problem in African agriculture. Countries such as the Seychelles and Mauritius, though small in size, managed to solve their land question by dividing the colonial estates into medium-sized farms and expanding the non-agricultural sectors of their economies, which enabled them to absorb the surplus population from agriculture into other sectors. An important part of their strategy was rural development through non-agricultural activities.

The agrarian question entails social and economic reform of technological factors, all of them varying, depending on historical specificities. Women have to be liberated, socially and economically, from male domination, and this could spell major changes in the agricultural sector more broadly, as women agricultural producers account for 70 per cent of small producers in sub-Saharan agriculture, but their full potential is yet to be realised because the male-dominated mode of organisation restricts them. This is a historical reality that has endured every disruption, from the bourgeois individualism of the missionaries and colonialism to the World Bank and similar institutions. Bourgeois individualism, such as advocated by Western or Eurocentric scholars, could in fact work to the advantage of men. Individualism is neither necessary nor sufficient for development. Men already have the upper hand and individualisation could worsen the situation. What would be important therefore is not simply the objective of transformation, but also the method of transformation. Mafeje advocates an all-encompassing approach of equal land rights for both men and women, and that they should equally participate in the labour process. Furthermore, African governments should ensure that both men and women have an equal say in the distribution of agricultural products; this has the potential to transform the lineage mode of organisation. Mafeje is aware that this would be possible only if African governments are democratic and gender sensitive and that women would attain their legitimate rights as part of a broader political struggle for social democracy. If their struggle is not located within these broader struggles, Mafeje maintains, African women could fall into the trap of 'liberal petty reformism'.[56]

Currently, Mafeje argues, although numerous, women in the agricultural sector can be considered poor peasants. In the final analysis, this is one of the issues that needs to be transformed in the agricultural sector, where the challenges faced by women producers include extractive state policies, poor infrastructure and exploitative intermediaries – all of which combine to undermine accumulation from below. Large-scale farming, such as African governments advocate at the behest of the West, has failed. In southern Africa, it created poverty and chronic rates of unemployment and starved the landless rural dwellers. On the other hand, African small producers have shown great resilience, even under crisis conditions. The middle peasants have been able to accumulate more than the rest.

It needs to be said, however, that under certain conditions, accumulation from below has its own limitations. 'For instance, it could be unrealisable under conditions of super-exploitation of the peasantry, political repression or extra-economic coercion, as in southern and, increasingly, in the rest of Africa,' as Mafeje concedes.[57] What is important is that the revenues derived are pre-capitalist to the extent that they have to be turned into capital. When such forms of accumulation have passed the primitive stage they enter into what Mafeje calls 'primary accumulation'. He considers that the middle peasants are capable of both primary and expanded accumulation; their mode of production is the expanded mode of production. Poor peasants, on the other hand, can attain neither primary nor expanded accumulation and operate mainly at the level of meeting subsistence needs. That is not to suggest that they do not attempt to rise above subsistence, but they have had little success and thus their mode of social existence is called 'petty' – they sell their labour to those who are economically better off. For Mafeje, 'the immediate task for African planners and policy makers is to make sure that agriculture can in the foreseeable future feed the rapidly growing African population'.[58]

From poverty alleviation to poverty eradication

Mafeje was generally concerned to understand the concept of poverty alleviation in the context of economic and political conditions as they obtain in Africa.[59] In so doing, he set out first to contextualise the concept and place it in its historical setting, tracing the evolution of development policies within the context of global economy and seeking to identify the target groups of such policies. For him, this provided a background from which one could measure the successes and failures of the notion of poverty alleviation. What is important is that the concept came about because of disillusionment with theories of trickle-down economics in the 1960s, the failures of which meant that in the 1970s the notion of poverty alleviation became, as Mafeje puts it, 'a development objective in itself'.[60]

The notion of poverty alleviation as a development objective was first put forward by United Nations agencies. The World Employment Programme of the International Labour Organisation, which was established in 1976, gave concrete meaning to poverty alleviation by stressing the productive capacity of the poorest. In 1977 the International Fund for Agricultural Development (IFAD) was tasked to increase food production, reduce under-nutrition and alleviate rural poverty.[61] The Food and Agriculture Organization (FAO) produced the 'Peasants Charter' in 1981, which sought to promote equity and advance popular participation in the process of development. In general, those policy proposals fell under the United Nations mandate, but it is notable that they coincided with the World Bank's policy proposals that advocated equal rights for small producers in the 1970s. By the end of the 1970s there was some consensus between the agencies of the United Nations and the World Bank, but divisions emerged as economic and agricultural crises worsened on the African continent in the 1980s, in large measure as a result of SAPs, which diminished emphasis on people and put a premium on market forces. This was a reversal of previous positions that had put the concerns of the poor at the centre of programmes and policies. These changes were rationalised in the World Bank report by Elliot Berg, *Accelerated Development in Sub-Saharan Africa: An Agenda for Africa*, widely known as the Berg Report.

In this way, the World Bank was not only siding with the economically strong, but also punishing small producers and the poor in favour of the old trickle-down theories. This report also came hot on the heels of the Lagos Plan of Action, which advanced policy objectives put forward by African governments themselves. Although aware of the implications of the Berg Report, some African governments went ahead and adopted SAPs. The Economic Commission for Africa (ECA) censored the SAPs in its *African Alternative Framework to Structural Adjustment Programmes for Socio-Economic Recovery and Transformation*.[62] The report is an intellectual response to and political confrontation with the World Bank. Not only did it serve as a reminder to African governments that they should not have abandoned the Lagos Plan of Action, but it also beseeched them to pursue development with equity on the African continent. Although the 1980s are generally referred to as a lost decade in Africa, the ECA discovered that in actuality the failures of African governments were not the result of flawed policy choices on their part, but rather because of the SAPs, and that, had African governments stuck to the objectives of the Lagos Plan of Action, things could have turned out differently. The World Bank could not discredit or refute the findings.

The ECA recentred two things: what African governments sought to implement prior to the SAPs and the question of growth with equity (which it put back on the table) whereas the World Bank sought to relieve the pain of the African continent without dealing with the root cause of the condition. The World Bank's *Poverty, Adjustment, and Growth in Africa* does not settle the central question of whether the SAPs (which failed in Africa because they did not yield any tangible economic growth or eradicate poverty) could be done away with in the 1990s.[63] Although there is consensus on the failures of the SAPs to apply Euro-American economic and developmental models in Africa, there is no agreement on the underlying causes. This case is more acute both with regard to the role of the state in development and in the case of agricultural or agrarian policies, which led to the recognition among African scholars that scholars ought to guard against 'individualisation of land rights and of agricultural production under African social conditions'.[64]

In his 2001 chapter on 'Conceptual and Philosophical Predispositions', Mafeje states that the concept of poverty alleviation was a product of 'social imperatives in *developed* countries and a culmination of the rise of the welfare state, especially in Western Europe'.[65] While this may be so, the concept and its social and philosophical foundations have their genesis in the 'reaction against the great depression of the 1930s and the large-scale deprivation caused by the Second World War'. Mafeje is of the view that its foundations were linked to the notion of a welfare state. If that is the case, then poverty alleviation is a product of affluent societies designed to guarantee 'a decent livelihood for the lowest 20 per cent of the population'. Understood this way, poverty alleviation is at best a product of welfare economics and at worst charitable neoliberalism. In the case of the latter, Mafeje's submission is logically justified insofar as the term 'alleviate' means to lessen or otherwise to make suffering less severe. But the term also assumes the existence of resources to alleviate pain and suffering, which then calls into question the notion of balanced economic development universally. The adoption of ameliorative policies or the notion of poverty alleviation is designed precisely to mask the continued plundering of countries of the global South by the global North.

The decision to speak of poverty alleviation is informed by the predispositions of those who enjoy hegemonic power, both nationally and internationally, towards petty reformism rather than radical change, because radical change entails instability and insecurity. While intellectuals in the West typically eschew any talk of radical changes, history suggests that it is because of radical changes from within that Western countries became what they are today. Typically, Marxists put forward the view that the agent of change is a combination of an impersonal dialectic between a range of social, political and economic factors, yet in reality the agents of change are typically those who are 'frustrated by present social existence or are its objects'.[66] This means that policies are a mirror image of underlying social struggles and 'shifts in intellectual paradigms are neither accidental nor due to factors which are internal to them'. By 1997, the United Nations Development Programme had, after 20 years, shifted from the paradigm of poverty alleviation to poverty eradication. IFAD's *The State of World Rural Poverty* states that throughout the Third World there was never any success in poverty alleviation through the programmes conceived by Western developmental agencies.[67] What happened, instead, is that poverty in the rural areas increased – except in industrialising countries of south-east Asia. In fact, the World Bank has acknowledged that poverty has increased in the global South.[68]

The paradigm shift from poverty alleviation to poverty eradication was a result of a robust discussion within international agencies and the notion of poverty eradication became a catchphrase in the late 1990s and 2000s. However, like the earlier concept of poverty alleviation, poverty eradication did not yield any observable changes in Africa. The question is: who will bring about poverty eradication and how will it be brought about in Africa? This question leads to what Mafeje calls the difficult and treacherous terrain of class interests because the interests of those in power and those of other social classes do not coincide. Mafeje grapples with the question of how the state deals with poverty in Africa. For the purposes of his analysis, he shies away from the question (much loved by political scientists) about whether or not there *is* a state in Africa. He assumes that states already exist and are generally said to be responsible for the well-being and welfare of their citizens through social services. In the welfare state such services are broadened to include employment creation; in contrast, under classical capitalism, providing for the poor is the job of entrepreneurs, through job creation and charitable organisations such as churches.

Mafeje argues that charitable measures such as poverty allowances, as in the case of Botswana, may be successful in the short term, but in the long run they present no lasting solution. This is an important point because of underdevelopment and increasing rural poverty across the continent. In Botswana's case, this was inevitable as there was no real investment in agriculture, but an overdependence on minerals, with the added problem of unfavourable climate and ecological conditions. There is little evidence to suggest that other sub-Saharan states have any sustained poverty alleviation or eradication programmes. What some governments (including Tanzania, Uganda and Burkina Faso – the latter under Thomas Sankara's short-lived leadership) have done is to adopt egalitarian policies combining growth with equality. The irony is that the policies condemned by international agencies in order to justify the SAPs are now implicit in the concept of poverty eradication.

In spite of external factors such as Western imperialism or internal factors such as corruption and the plundering of resources by African leaders, Mafeje still believes that Africa is best placed to eradicate its poverty. What is at issue for him is the conception of new developmental alternatives. The continent is well resourced to see itself through some of its challenges; small producers have control of their means of production or livelihood and are only affected by extractive national governments, which are relatively remote compared to feudal landlordism. Controversially, Mafeje argues that African people have greater chances of overthrowing their dictatorial governments than the peoples of other countries of the global South and that 'African agricultural producers, who constitute the vast majority in any single African country (except in South Africa and Zimbabwe), are not as backward technologically as is often supposed'.[69]

Mafeje claims that 'there is no evidence that big farmers in black Africa are more efficient than smaller ones ... if large-scale farmers were bigger foreign exchange earners until recently, the small female cultivators in Africa were and still are the biggest food producer'.[70] One cannot object to the second point by arguing that food deficits are on the rise in Africa – it would not hold, simply because it provides more of a reason for preferential treatment for small producers than for marginalising them. Equally, there is no evidence to suggest that, overall, big farmers in Africa are more responsive to technology than small producers. If anything, responsiveness to technology has more to do with the cost of innovation than the size of the farms. Mafeje posits that the way forward is not poverty alleviation, but trickle-up strategies for development that would eliminate poverty. He wants to deal with poverty elimination as 'basically development from below'. In sub-Saharan Africa, this is justified in that the vast majority of the people are poor, even though they have access to land. Thus, as Mafeje concludes: 'In situations where the poor predominate it is more efficient to invest in them than in the non-poor who are prone to absorb more resources than can be economically justified. In other words, not only is it cheaper in terms of capital outlay (including foreign exchange) to invest in the undercapitalised majority but also it helps to mobilise their only form of wealth: labour.'[71]

6 | Neocolonialism, State Capitalism and Underdevelopment

Archie Mafeje wrote on revolutionary theory and politics as a politically engaged exiled South African intellectual. In the 1960s and 1970s, South Africans were engaged in the liberation struggle while the rest of the African continent was also decolonising rapidly. Mafeje was not content with repeating buzzwords and slogans in Marxist theory. His intellectual integrity inclined him to interrogate theory and concepts before using them to make sense of the world.

I divide Mafeje's work on revolutionary theory and politics into two parts, his early work and his later work.[1] Except for the paper 'Soweto and Its Aftermath', his earlier contribution to revolutionary theory and politics is much broader in scope and focus insofar as it centres on the African continent specifically, but also on the global South generally. Mafeje was engaged in a sustained conversation not only with African revolutionary scholars, but also with radical scholars from other parts of the world.

The demarcation between Mafeje's earlier and later contributions to revolutionary theory and politics may give the false impression that there is no connection between the two – far from it. There is in fact a strong connection and consistency in his work. The only difference between earlier and later is that the latter focuses on South Africa specifically and southern Africa generally. His attention was on issues in the post-independence state: neocolonialism, underdevelopment, state capitalism and the evaluation of the notion of dual theories of economic growth.

Neocolonialism and underdevelopment

To the extent that international capitalism appropriates surplus in under-developed countries, and the desire by underdeveloped countries to put in place 'an independent base for internal appropriation and reproduction',[2] Mafeje considers nationalist struggles to be justified. He observes that the distinction between such terms as 'neocolonialism' and 'revolution' remains elusive in social scientific studies; the terms have assumed the status of antonyms. Yet neocolonialism admits both continuity and change. I believe that what Mafeje means is that in underdeveloped countries remnants of colonialism linger on, post-independence, after the liberation struggle has ended. Although there is a difference between the two terms, it is often missed because of the overemphasis on continuity. Mafeje concedes that neocolonialism hinges on various forms and methods of control to continue the old relations, yet it is well within the competence of African governments to change these adverse relations between African and Western countries. He makes an important distinction between colonialism proper and neocolonialism; the former an external imposition, the latter 'a *contractual relationship* even if accompanied by very severe constraints'. As a continuation of the old colonial relations, even when a country has gained its independence, if it is economically fragile, it could be manipulated by international capital and turned into a neocolony. One need only look at the United States' foreign policy towards some under-developed countries. The United States had, and still has, territories that are colonial possessions, among them Puerto Rico (1989 to the present); Cuba (1899–1902); Marshall Islands, American Samoa, Guam, Panama Canal Zone (1903–1979) and the Philippines (1898–1946). What seems to matter to Mafeje is not so much a colonial past, but what he calls 'a dependency social formation', which is formed of basic structures that go beyond colonialism as such. Independence does not necessarily mean an end to 'surplus appropriation at the centre and its negative dialectic at the periphery'.[3] Mafeje was writing at the height of the liberation struggles in Africa and during the period of the Cold War. This was the period of capitalism versus socialism as two dominant modes, globally, of production. The Marxists Ernesto Laclau and Andre Gunder Frank speak about an admixture of modes of production in underdeveloped countries.[4] Yet they never quite spell out satisfactorily what that amounts to.

Mafeje argues that the existence of two opposing camps (the capitalist West and the socialist East) made it possible for social democrats to advocate for underdeveloped countries to find their own development paths. Concepts such as non-alignment or positive neutrality gained currency in the 1970s, precisely because of a search for a 'third way' to development. Imperialism, as an international system of capitalist domination, has led to uneven development and this has resulted in relations of dependency in which underdeveloped countries, even when they try to emulate their developed counterparts, go deeper and deeper into economic crises. Logically and politically, this has to be so because relations of dependency mean that underdeveloped countries must remain poor while their developed counterparts flourish. Mafeje observes that 'in the first instance, dependency implies inability to compete with patron countries and, in the second instance, patron status means a basic unwillingness to be equal'.[5] Essentially, imperialism would not be imperialism if it eliminated inequality. Similarly, if it were defeated, internal contradictions in underdeveloped countries would improve – assuming that these countries were free of neocolonialism.

Internal contradictions are informed by external structural contradictions. Thus, Mafeje says that 'advanced capitalism cannot be defeated on its own terms'.[6] Countries that have tried to deviate from the internal logic of capitalism have been severely punished by leading capitalist countries. This has led to further underdevelopment and heightened internal contradictions. The comprador class becomes even more brutal as a form of self-defence: Latin America witnessed this in the 1970s.[7] The same is true of such African countries as Côte d'Ivoire, Kenya, Liberia, Sierra Leone and Gabon, whereas Japan, Thailand, the Philippines and South Korea may be used as counter-examples of countries that tried to tailor capitalism to their own needs. Japan seems to be 'neither an exception nor a contrary case' – it never suffered severe colonial incorporation or underdevelopment of its economy and society. On the contrary, Japan acted as an imperialist force in Asia and 'had full opportunities for internal accumulation and uniform social division of labour'. Japan, therefore, 'was favoured by internal as well as external conditions which are not repeated anywhere else in present-day underdeveloped countries'.[8] Thailand, the Philippines and South Korea are not quite like Japan. Their relative success was a direct outcome of the United States' foreign policy in south-east Asia, although that alone does not explain their development success. In addition, there are significant differences between Thailand, the Philippines and South Korea in terms of development outcomes. These countries were meant to be 'a counter-weight to communist countries in the area'; they depended on the United States, which weakened their ability to pursue independent domestic policies. It became increasingly impossible to resolve the contradiction 'between the capitalist mode of production at the centre and its distorting social formations at the periphery'. Imperialist countries such as the United States succeeded in creating what Mafeje calls 'better off underdeveloped states' in carefully chosen geographical areas – these countries acted as bulwarks against communism in the age of the Cold War. But 40 years later one cannot claim that these countries are still in the service of the United States.

On the African continent, Kenya was positioned to play a similar role in eastern Africa. It was meant to be a buffer between developed and underdeveloped countries or to give credibility to capitalism within the context of underdevelopment. Mafeje's point is that capitalism is not a feasible alternative for underdeveloped countries. Capitalism not only complements neocolonialism, it also deepens dependent relations until it becomes impossible to close the gap between developed and developing countries. Internally, it further perverts relations between the rich and the poor in underdeveloped countries. To address this, underdeveloped countries have to revise their production relations – which is impossible without addressing foreign capital. Revising production relations and combating the interests of foreign capital would provide fertile grounds for revolutionary changes. For Mafeje, this is the only 'alternative to neo-colonialism or dependency'. The idea that combating the interests of foreign capital is an antidote to dependency relations and neocolonialism was a conventional argument within the left in the 1970s, but this radical posture does not say much about the central question of the revolutionary transformation that is to be carried out. Mafeje himself concedes that the idea of a revolution could mean 'any number of things'.

For the purposes of his analysis of neocolonialism and underdevelopment, Mafeje proposes to limit himself to value and labour, or production relations and social formations. Poorer regions are deprived of 'the right to determine the allocation and utilisation of capital on their own behalf';[9] governments of underdeveloped countries are usually unable, or sometimes reluctant, to do anything about the allocation and utilisation of capital, even though they are fully aware of the underlying contradictions. In the post-independence period, governments of underdeveloped countries spoke of 'state intervention' or 'a planned economy'. To varying degrees, state intervention is recognised in both capitalist and socialist-orientated economies as, usually, an attempt to secure what Mafeje calls 'discretionary power'. In left-leaning economies this entails land redistribution or other forms of redistribution of resources. In this way, the state becomes a provider of capital and, through loans and national revenue, it becomes the biggest investor in the national economy. This is imperative in underdeveloped economies. It is what has been called 'state capitalism'.

State capitalism is a historical necessity in African underdeveloped economies. Only national governments have the capacity to protect and boost the economy – and this remains the case in spite of the rhetoric of free market adherents. History shows that leading economies that today advocate a free market economy developed through economic protectionism and state interventionism. Although they may not address some of the underlying internal contradictions, governments 'can eliminate the contradiction between distorted local social formations and distorting central capital by introducing a new social division of labour, whereby adequate employment opportunities and security are created for the now abused migrant workers in the rural economy itself which, contrary to prevailing dogmas, need not be dissociated from *industrialisation*'.[10]

This necessitates that national governments make resources – land and capital – available. Although Mafeje denies classical capitalism as a feasible option for development in Africa, he nonetheless gives primacy to state capitalism as a transient phase of capitalism, which leads to socialism. The state in underdeveloped countries cannot maintain its legitimacy if it does not provide for all citizens; thus, if the bureaucratic elite does not ensure that this is carried out, state capitalism leads to the same contradictions that it seeks to do away with.

Mafeje says that state capitalism ought to intervene on behalf of the producing underprivileged classes – which would lead to conflict between the state and the middle classes and foreign patrons who would no longer have access to surplus. Importantly, however, it cannot be assumed that the underprivileged are inherently progressive and for state capitalism to succeed, the state would need the support of the small producers and the workers. Political mobilisation is key in this regard – but it is equally important to note that some segments of the middle class are quite cap-able of transcending their class interests and equally capable of 'engaging in radical or revolutionary political action', as Mafeje argues. For Mafeje, underdeveloped countries typically have very low levels of real capital among ordinary citizens; moreover, the proletariat (unlike their peasant counterparts) tends to constitute a small segment of the population and, perhaps counter-intuitively, tends to be sympathetic to urban middle classes and their ideologies. Mafeje hastens to point out that the prole-tariat are not immune to exploitation and are fully aware of their class enemies. 'However, in Africa where competition is fairly low both in agri-culture and in commerce, petty-bourgeois aspirations among blue and white-collar workers still hold sway.'[11]

Small producers/peasants, on the other hand, constitute the vast majority of the population and are usually excluded from education and from the technological skills made available to other classes. Workers engage in strikes and industrial action, but no one takes notice of the revolts of the peasants, which indicate the peasants' awareness that they are being exploited. In addition, small producers/peasants tend to be migratory labourers and are not always land-fixed. Mafeje points out that the small producers have shown their revolutionary capacity in China, Vietnam, Cuba, Algeria, Mexico and other countries. In Africa, Guinea

Bissau, Angola and Mozambique are working examples. The peasants' revolt in Mpondoland, South Africa, may also be cited as an example.[12] In order to discuss the revolutionary capacity of the peasants, Mafeje believes, one ought first to study their objective conditions and social quality.

He makes it clear that 'the so-called peasants in underdeveloped countries are, historically, not only contemporaries of the workers in the developed countries but are also their identical objects i.e. they are objects of exploitation by the same international finance-capital'.[13] This is an important theoretical insight in revolutionary theory and politics. In underdeveloped countries, small producers are not only exploited in the market as petty producers, but are also exploited by capital as migrant workers. In this way, small producers are also able to become 'semi-proletarians', but precisely because they are itinerant, small producers become available for labour without being completely industrialised or urbanised. As Mafeje puts it, the old theoretical question arising from this is: 'Are they an industrial proletariat domiciled in the countryside or are they proletarianised peasants?'[14] Regardless of how one may wish to answer the question, what seems to matter to Mafeje is that the 'proletarian part-quality' remains.

In underdeveloped countries there are also categories of workers other than unskilled migrants: white-collar and blue-collar workers. Although they may have different occupations, the tie that binds them is that they earn comparatively high salaries. Marxists refer to them variously as labour aristocrats, salariat, sub-elites or petit bourgeoisie. These categories are often confusing. 'The simplest fact,' writes Mafeje, 'is that all workers who receive high salaries do not represent the same phenomenon any more than all people who enjoy the same standard of living constitute a class. What is diagnostic is the way income is derived.'[15] For example, insofar as all industrial workers exchange their labour power with capital or produce surplus value, they are exploited. Furthermore, to the extent that they produce added value for the benefit of capital, 'in no way can they be said to be benefitting by the exploitation of the peasants'. This is so because both strata are exploited, albeit in different ways.

Another category of workers that Mafeje finds difficult to characterise are those who earn their income by exchanging their labour power not with capital, but with revenue – government employees. As is known, the state is one of the biggest employers in underdeveloped countries, yet government workers do not produce added value. Similarly, such services as education, health (medical facilities) and public transport may produce value, albeit indirectly, but what is important is that they are characterised by consumption, rather than production. This holds true only if production is understood purely in terms of goods or commodities. According to Mafeje, insofar as up to 85 per cent of the national revenue in underdeveloped countries comes from agriculture, the bureaucratic and menial workers benefit by exploiting the peasants and industrial workers. Mafeje espouses an odd claim here because exploitation would suggest that bureaucratic and menial workers are in a production relationship with peasants and industrial workers. What exactly is that relation of production? Bureaucratic and menial workers do not even function in the same circuit of capital as peasants and industrial workers. According to Mafeje, the level of wages of bureaucratic and menial workers can have a negative influence on other workers. Strictly speaking, Mafeje argues, the bureaucratic worker should be characterised as petit bourgeois – and because the petit bourgeois is an intermediate and dependent class, salary differentials not only matter very much, but also are 'arbitrarily determined'. Most importantly, however, incomes determine political allegiance. One might object to this and argue that it confuses the economic sphere with the political. The issue of exploitation – expropriation of surplus value – takes place within the economic sphere; struggles around it happen at the level of the political (even within the factory). Status is being confused for class. It would be a bit strange, however, to separate the economic sphere from the political in revolutionary theory. In the African context, promotion in the bureaucratic sector is not only fast, but also comes with a 'disproportionate amount of political power'. Furthermore, the bureaucracy tends to be antagonistic towards peasants and industrial workers.

Mafeje's theoretical view is that in order to appreciate the behaviour of the bureaucracy, one has to relate it to the behaviour of both the producing and the owning classes. This not only puts class theory into perspective, but also calls into question some of the conceptual blind spots of stratification theory. For the greater part of the African continent, there is not much of a difference between industrial workers and their migratory counterparts. Quite often they are the same people. 'Even in those cases where workers can be described unambiguously as rural or urban, it is well to remember that, ontologically, contrasts are not necessarily contradictions.'[16] Mafeje continues, 'in reply to the usual Trotskyite heresy about peasants and the revolution in underdeveloped countries, I would suggest that the rural and the industrial producers be treated as a continuum which is constantly re-enforced by the intermittence of a high proportion of their number.' So when Mafeje refers to these two allies, he does so based on this objective reality and not out of ideological expediency. As he observes: 'As in any movement, members of a class are at different stages of becoming: there are advanced workers and there are less advanced workers. The fully industrialised workers represent the former but, without the less advanced rural workers, they are like a head without a body.'

Issues in state capitalism

The notion of state capitalism is not free of controversy. Both positive and negative roles have been attributed to it. Mafeje points to eastern Europe and the global South as having set a precedent for controversies associated with this socio-economic system. Yet analyses of state capitalism remain 'necessarily incomplete'. Two positions result. A Marxist position holds that state capitalism is a transitional phase towards socialism (this is not borne out by history). The other view is that state capitalism not only leads to bureaucratic entrenchment, but also to economic stagnation. Mafeje sees these two positions as a good opportunity for him to advance 'further enquiry, refinement and, possibly, formulation of entirely new hypotheses'.[17] Characteristically, in undertaking this task Mafeje starts from the concrete in order to avoid extrapolation or superimposing theory on data. He points out, for example, that the historical development of eastern European countries is not analogous to that of the underdeveloped countries. This view is entirely consistent with his warning that transcontinental analogies in social analysis are misleading.

In the 1960s and 1970s, state capitalism was, in underdeveloped countries, an 'objective fact', which could not be reduced to 'subjective exigencies'. It is not entirely clear what Mafeje means by this, but he goes on to argue that before anything can be said about whether state capitalism is desirable in underdeveloped countries, one needs to study the 'objective determinate conditions'. Given that state capitalism was widespread in underdeveloped countries, it could not have been a historical accident. In considering the historical circumstances leading up to the emergence of the so-called Third World countries, a few discernible facts may be enumerated: these countries were politically subordinate; they were economically exploited; they depended on a capitalist world market largely dominated by a few rich countries. Anti-colonialist and anti-imperialist struggles were waged precisely to fight these problems. The Marxist historian Vijay Prashad observes:

> The Third World was not a place. It was a project. During the seemingly interminable battles against colonialism, the peoples of Africa, Asia, and Latin America dreamed of a new world. They longed for dignity above all else, but also the basic necessities of life (land, peace, and freedom) ... Thrown between these two major formations, the darker nations amassed as the Third World. Determined people struck out against colonialism to win their freedom. They demanded political equality on the world level.[18]

Yet the excitement of independence meant that the leaders of the day failed to study the substantive power of monopoly capital. The decision to adopt the strategy to nationalise the means of production at independence in several countries was part of a response to foreign economic domination and exploitation. It was 'a strategy for self-defence', as Mafeje puts it. The decision to embark on nationalisation policies in underdeveloped countries was not necessarily informed by a socialist ideology. Nationalisation was, rather, 'seized upon by nationalist governments out of sheer expediency'.[19]

In eastern Europe, by contrast, nationalisation was part of the communist ideology and revolutionary strategy that had gained currency at the time.

Mafeje was writing not only at the time of the liberation struggle and in the wake of independence in Africa, but also at the height of the Cold War between the United States/Western countries (the First World) and USSR/eastern European socialist countries (the Second World). Underdeveloped countries were then known as the Third World, which was not characterised by any consistent political and economic forms. The political identity of the Third World, as Mafeje puts it, 'derives from a negative condition – underdevelopment and ex-colonial status'.[20] At independence, Third World countries earned the historical characteristics of being in the 'national democratic stage'. For Mafeje, this was an apt categorisation in that it designated the content and form of the anti-imperialist struggles in which they were engaged. All classes of society formed a united front. He writes: 'This is what constituted the kernel of the notion of the "New Democracy" among communist theoreticians in the aftermath of the First World War and the first socialist revolution in Russia in 1917.' The new democracy referred to the substance or content of the struggle itself, rather than formal freedoms such as freedom of speech or freedom of the press. Mafeje maintains that the ensuing class struggle in the post-independence dispensation emptied the term 'anti-imperialism' of its original meaning. The decline of revolutionary struggle is marked by subsequent proliferation of military oligarchs in Latin America and the petit bourgeois elites who consolidated bureaucratic power in Africa and Asia – to the exclusion of the masses.

There is in underdeveloped countries the question of technological backwardness and financial poverty of the state, which translates into dependency on the leading countries of the West to supply capital and technology. Because the share of capital and technology is smaller for underdeveloped countries, the possibility of internal accumulation and take-off is necessarily low. As Mafeje says: 'It is also true that investment by its very selective nature influences not only imports but also exports insofar as it determines the domestic resource use.'[21] The use of resources, in turn, determines the structure of production and thus shapes the course of economic development. On this dialectic depend a number of contradictions, 'which are the objective ground for a variety of subjective choices by national governments in underdeveloped countries'.

There are three main issues. First, all underdeveloped countries, whatever their ideological orientation, wish to retain their revenue and avoid capital flight. Second, they desire to develop technologically (since technological backwardness is part of the reason they are underdeveloped). Although they supply developed countries with raw materials, underdeveloped countries are characterised by low levels of technology and unskilled labour. Third, underdeveloped countries desire to be in full control of their national resources and seek to nationalise, partially or wholly, the means of production and land, which accounts for quite a chunk of the national revenue. Mafeje notes that as important as nationalisation or seizure of resources may be, this says little about how national governments will utilise the resources. One should, though, be careful not to 'reduce the history of underdeveloped countries to imperial history'. Underdeveloped countries are not mere victims of imperialism, 'which can only be judged by the most minimal standards – an attitude which is shared by both Western European liberals and eastern European communists'.[22] What is important to note is that the underdeveloped state does not neatly fit into classical categories and the question of the role of state capitalism is not posed merely on grounds of expediency. It is informed by historical, political and economic conditions.

In underdeveloped countries, state capitalism has taken two forms. First, it protects the economy and compensates the economic vulnerability of what Mafeje terms the 'nascent national bourgeoisie' – although it does not necessarily liquidate this national bourgeoisie as a class. Second, in some cases it takes the same form, but with the intention of liquidating the national bourgeoisie. To understand the nature of the process involved in the two cases, Mafeje adopts a step-by-step analysis, rather than taxonomic categorisations. He reminds the reader that most underdeveloped countries went through the national democratic stage (which remained the case regardless of the country's ideological orientation). The national democratic stage is characterised by four diagnostic features: anti-colonialism;

anti-imperialism; a united front of classes led by petit bourgeois elements; and a commitment to the re-building of the economy (these features are quite consistent with the principles of the 'New Democracy'). Of the four features, it is the fourth that has given grounds for positive action. It is the same feature that has proved to be the primary point of divergence among different regimes in underdeveloped countries. The centrality or the dominance of the state in underdeveloped countries 'has become a source of severe contradictions and acrimonious theoretical exchange'.[23]

Practically, this had to be so because there are social and economic priorities involved. Theoretically, the issue is so complex and unusual that it does not conform to analogous cases of development in China or Russia. Although it is arguable that the reflexes of the state in Africa or the global South are 'attributable to subjective manipulations by the ruling elite, the state itself is a historical product of objective conditions and so is its dominance'.[24] The emergence of the post-independence state meant that it had to fill a political vacuum left behind by colonial powers. Social classes were, during that period, still inchoate. In the absence of alternatives, the state became the only viable vehicle to carry the huge burden of national and economic unity.

The African state is better understood as not merely a 'colonial over-growth', but as a product of the historical sequence – which in turn means that it had to put a premium on politics over economics. Instead of viewing the African state purely in negative terms, a mere remnant of colonialism, this is the more positive way in which Mafeje aims to understand the post-independence state. It may be that in its organic form, it is a continuation of colonialism. Yet, in its historic form, it became the negation of colonialism, 'insofar as it represents a new division of political power'. It is the use of this power that became the problem of development in post-independence African states. In advancing this argument, Mafeje allows, in his own words, for 'a dynamic marriage between voluntarism and determinism and avoids the idealistic one-sidedness which has become so rampant in revolutionary rhetoric'.[25]

Although post-independence underdeveloped countries had similar material conditions to each other, the discretionary power conferred on their rulers meant that these countries took 'divergent subjective choices'. In his attempt at marrying voluntarism and determinism, Mafeje wishes to understand the political and economic choices made by underdeveloped countries. This makes it possible 'to distinguish between progressive and retrograde strategies, or between what is generally known as "neocolonialist" and "socialist-orientated" regimes'.[26] It is important to note, as Mafeje does, that these issues are shaped by global dynamics. Yet, Mafeje believes that it is still valuable to study some of the choices made at the national level. According to him, 'a single theory of revolution is an absurdity in a world so grossly uneven in its development'. In the post-independence period, some countries pandered to foreign capitalist interests and, in so doing, they chose to 'negotiate for better terms of economic interaction and distribution of surplus-value'. This came to be known as a neocolonialist strategy for development. It gained currency in Latin America – Cuba and short-lived regimes in Chile and Peru being notable exceptions.

African countries differed a lot from one another in terms of policies and strategic approach. Asia, on the other hand, became polarised – between neocolonialist and socialist states. The neocolonial state is willing to collaborate with foreign capitalist countries and relies on them for capital, credit, supplies and technology, which leads to the state acting as a broker between foreign capital and the emerging national bourgeoisie. This, according to Mafeje, leads to at least five 'insoluble contradictions', which are both external and internal. The first relates to the domination of the economy of African countries by foreign monopolies and a loss of domestic income. Second, there is a misalignment between the use of resources and domestic demand because foreign capital focuses on extractive industries like mining and export agriculture, both of which produce commodities consumed locally. Third, technological dependence on foreign suppliers retards domestic capability. Fourth, the local market is monopolised by what Mafeje calls 'import substitution industries and further losses of added value'.[27] Finally, there remains an imbalance of income between the so-called modern (mainly capital-intensive) and informal sectors. The latter sector is usually technologically backward and caters for the majority of the population.

It is notable that these contradictions lead to antagonistic relations within the dominating classes. What tended to happen was that the former national liberation movement became politically divided between those who sided with foreign capital, the comprador, and those who opposed them on the grounds of national interests, the progressive patriots (it is not clear whether Mafeje includes the national bourgeoisie). Those outside of this class, the masses of the people, begin to agitate. In this scenario, those on the right – with the backing of foreign allies – invariably win the battle. 'Thus,' Mafeje concludes, 'the national democratic movement, which started off as a united front of all classes comes to its ultimate contradiction, suffers a complete collapse, and is superseded by bitter class struggles.'[28] The post-independence state played the role of a mediator between contending classes. This is so because at the time of its birth, no particular class enjoyed general hegemony. Yet when reactionary forces consolidate with the help of foreign allies, the state becomes a tool for class oppression and ceases to mediate for the masses.

Without the participation of the masses, the state ceases to be an instrument of development. There develops among the masses anti-capitalist feelings – but these need not be confused with socialism as, politically and ideologically, the two can easily be confused. Although subjective responses are typically an outcome of objective conditions, subjective responses may not always be useful in indicating a viable dialectical alternative. Conditions in underdeveloped countries have shown that these countries cannot be easily described with classical categories. What tends to happen is that state capitalism in underdeveloped countries means that the state does not assume the historical position of capital – it 'intervenes against capital'.[29] This is what Mao Tse-Tung means by 'the regulation of capital by the state so that private capital cannot dominate the livelihood of the people'.[30] Furthermore: 'In the new democratic republic under the leadership of the proletariat, the state enterprises will be of a socialist character and will constitute the leading force in the whole national economy, but the republic neither confiscate capitalist private property nor forbid the development of such capitalist production as does not "dominate the livelihood of the people".'

This uncompromising and nationalistic stance has been much more appealing to revolutionaries of the global South. The choice of strategy, however, is determined by changing world perspectives and objective factors – the great era of American and European capitalist expansionism, for example, was met with anti-colonialist and anti-imperialist struggles in the Third World.

In spite of the view that state capitalism is a transitory phase towards socialism, Mafeje still maintains, following Lenin and Mao, that regulation of capital by the state is not exempt from 'the alienating logic of capital accumulation and, therefore, to social and economic counter-revolution'.[31] For Lenin, state capitalism was a form of class struggle, while Mao saw 'a contradiction between the state and the people'.[32] For Mafeje, this highlights that 'there is no "state capitalism" or "regulation of capital by the state" (whatever we wish to call it) that is immune to the alienating logic of capital accumulation and, therefore, to social and economic counter-revolution'. The fact that this is much more prevalent in 'cases where the social character is still largely petty-bourgeois' does not render the argument invalid – it reinforces the idea that socialism is fluid and transient in nature.

The question of the transition to socialism was the subject of lively debates between Charles Bettelheim and Paul Sweezy in the early 1970s.[33] Although he had argued earlier that state capitalism is a transition to socialism, Mafeje later submits that such a view is an oxymoron because in classical Marxism, socialism 'is *not a mode of production*'.[34] Rather, it is itself a transitional stage between capitalism and communism. The important issue, it appears, is that he wants state capitalism, as 'one of the phases in the socialist transition', to be reviewed constantly in order to see whether it is still progressive. This is to prevent it from succumbing to the 'corrupting logic of capital accumulation' to which it is susceptible. Ultimately, this would allow for unity of theory and do away with geographical divisions. In saying this, Mafeje is not claiming that differences in historical experience are irrelevant or otherwise unimportant. Indeed, he could not make such a claim when he had already argued against transcontinental analogies.

The issue seems to be that if theory is to make sense at all, or if it is to have some semblance of universality, it must be able to account for or explain different social formations (this is, of course, to be done after studying social formations on their own terms). Mafeje attempts to capture something of that when he says it is quite easy to make conceptual categorisations such as 'neocolonialist' and 'socialist-orientated', yet in practice such a priori judgements could mislead because anti-capitalist struggles occur even in neocolonialist regimes and pro-capitalist struggles take place in socialist-orientated states. Mafeje is always keen on a careful examination of cases on their own terms in order to avoid overgeneralisations.

Unlike other developing regions, Africa was incorporated into the capitalist system only in the last quarter of the nineteenth century. By the time colonialism was defeated, African countries had 'distorted economic structures'. The response to these distorted economic structures varied widely. There is an important question about whether the differences in Africa are the result of endogenous or exogenous factors.

Although a lot has been said about the 'African mode of production' and 'traditional and feudal elements', there were varied forms of production at the time of colonial contact.[35] For example, in the colonial period West African markets were characterised by what Mafeje calls 'primitive communalism' and 'pastoral aristocracies'. In the Sudan and Ethiopia, on the other hand, there was feudalism with an admixture of 'mercantilism', 'primitive communalism' and 'pastoralism'. Egalitarian pastoralism characterised Somalia. The same mode of production was to be found in Kenya, Tanganyika and the northern parts of Uganda. Much like West Africa, south-western Uganda, Burundi and Rwanda were more aristocratic. Similar pastoralism was to be found in Angola and in some parts of the Congo. In southern Africa, there prevailed 'primitive communalism' and 'pastoralism' and there were no 'commercial institutions' such as were found in West Africa. On the basis of these examples, Mafeje concludes that feudalism, or landlordism, was not so prevalent in sub-Saharan Africa. Nor was it a general problem. That notwithstanding, when endogenous capitalism developed, those who assumed state power at independence did not focus on production and trade in order to develop their economies. For Mafeje, this is important if one is to understand what he calls 'a basic anomaly in the African development'. The petit bourgeoisie who assumed state power were not necessarily familiar with economic production, but were recruited because of their formal education and bureaucratic skills, which presupposes that they are incapable of production activities. Mafeje maintains that the economy was relegated to a lower or secondary status – the petit bourgeoisie, usurped by colonial capital, supplemented its role 'by mobilising the peasantry for primary production'.

The so-called progressive farmers emerged in the 1950s as a result of colonial governments whose hope was to create a buffer class against the petit bourgeois nationalists. There were no Africans in industrial pro-duction. To the extent that any Africans existed in industrial production, says Mafeje, they were there as exploited labour. It seems here that Mafeje reduces Africa to his field experience of Uganda and Tanzania. Following his line of thought, it becomes clear that 'at independence African coun-tries lacked a national bourgeoisie of any sort, unless concepts are used in a loose and meaningless way'.[36] In any case, in order to ensure that there was rapid accumulation in Uganda and Tanzania, state capitalism became necessary at independence. Although there was some production among Africans during colonialism, it was largely small-scale and family-based. Taking this seriously and putting it in its proper perspective, it becomes clear that lineages and clans remain a 'mediating dialectic' in Africa. Epistemologically, such an insight should caution against any search for pure class categories in Africa. As regards the question of state capitalism, it was an outcome of and a response to colonial underdevelopment. State intervention against capital in Africa was justified 'because foreign cap-ital was causing intolerable contradictions for their leaders'.[37] This was an anti-imperialist ideology. Yet, although some African states espoused Marxist rhetoric, as well as undertaking nationalisation and expropri-ation programmes, they did not necessarily have communist political parties nor were they dominated by the workers. Although it has been stated that state capitalism is a historical necessity in response to inter-national capital, this says very little about whether the state will intervene in a progressive way. Mafeje points out that state intervention is 'a double-edged sword' insofar as it can be used by reactionary ruling classes against the general populace.

Mafeje goes on to point out that state capitalism is a 'contradictory and unstable social form'. He reaches this conclusion after having consulted Sweezy, who says: 'I conclude that "socialism" defined as society characterised by state ownership of the means of production and comprehensive planning is not *necessarily* a way station on the journey from capitalism to communism, and that reliance on the theory that such a society must automatically develop toward communism, can lead to movement in the exact opposite direction i.e. reconstitution of class rule.'[38]

For Mafeje, state capitalism 'carries within it the fruits of bourgeois rule and the seeds of proletarian insurrection'.[39] He summarises this 'basic ambiguity' in six points. Not only did the petit bourgeoisie tend to monopolise power, there was also a tendency to put an emphasis on technical skills (which were the preserve of the technical and administrative staff). State resources were left to the politico-bureaucratic elite, who appropriated state surpluses for themselves. This was compounded by a tendency to undermine the market principle through central planning, while keeping intact other elements of the capitalist system of production (labour as a commodity, private appropriation in the form of wages and extraction of surplus labour). The overemphasis on an economic approach tended to neglect political and social solutions – and, moreover, there was a tendency to mimic advanced capitalist countries 'and thus interpret economic development and modernity in the bourgeois sense'.[40]

The upshot of these elements is that they lead to a political system that undermines democracy and entrenches political rule by bureaucratic means. In such a system, a neocolonialist production structure (an export-orientated economy with little domestic demand) is accompanied by technological stagnation as a result of dependency on foreign technical expertise and equipment to the detriment of the 'backward sector' of the economy. State interference and inefficient bureaucracy lead to a slow rate of growth. Collectively, these issues precipitate 'a crisis of foreign reserves, chronic shortages and political malaise'.[41]

For Mafeje, whatever the problems are with state capitalism, it was a historical necessity in response to imperialism. Although imperialism represents a mature capitalist stage, in underdeveloped countries it had to contend with inchoate social classes. This is true both of the bourgeoisie and the proletariat. The nature of colonial administration was such that there would be an expansion of the petit bourgeois, who were meant to take over at independence, but proved to be incapable of playing 'the historical role of either the bourgeoisie or that of the proletariat and simultaneously of their greater social maturity'.[42] This notwithstanding, the problems associated with state capitalism must be seen as linked to what Mafeje calls 'uneven development of classes' in underdeveloped countries, rather than petit bourgeois lapses and pervasions. The uneven development of classes is historically determined. That the working class and peasants are weak in underdeveloped countries is a great source of hindrance to socialist transformation – yet, in spite of this, without state capitalism at independence no real progress could be made. Whatever problems may have been associated with it, 'the most useful way of contending with the problem under the given constraints is not to wish to by-pass state capitalism in underdeveloped countries but to *transcend it*'.[43] In spite of Nikolai Bukharin's contention that 'the system of state capitalism is the most absolute of all forms of exploitation of the masses by a handful of oligarchs', in underdeveloped countries state capitalism could not have been bypassed.[44] It was meant to be a catalyst for rapid accumulation in order to address the backward economy and to counter global capitalism.

Apart from the weakness of the working class and peasants in underdeveloped countries, one of the greatest constraints to development is a 'lack of self-reliance'. This results in two things. First, underdeveloped countries are unable to process raw materials and turn them into finished products. Second, they cannot 'produce capital goods to supply potential consumer goods, manufacture, agriculture and, ultimately, heavy industry'.[45] Both of these factors mean external dependence and this undermines progressive ideological impulses on the part of underdeveloped countries.

Mafeje sees the alliance between peasants and workers as 'the ultimate antithesis to petty-bourgeois hegemony and contradictions of state capitalism'.[46] In theory, the alliance between peasants and workers seems natural, but in practice there is uneven development between the two classes, something that may make their alliance difficult. Part of the reason is that workers constitute an insignificant number of the population in Africa. And, for that matter, workers tend to align themselves more with urban classes and their values than with the peasants. On the other hand, peasants, who constitute the vast majority of the population, are excluded from 'the benefits of modern life' and are typically 'deprived of education and scientific knowledge and often lack organisational and political skills on a national scale'.[47] Although the peasants hardly side with their 'urban class enemies' and the state, they are nevertheless susceptible to 'rustic ideologies' and 'hierarchies'. Their working-class counterparts, on the other hand, are less predisposed to conservative ideologies and hierarchies. The progressive nature of the peasants cannot be assumed. Although Mafeje seems to ascribe a level of progressiveness to the workers, the same rule applies to them. As he says about the peasants, 'their quality has to be ascertained before any presuppositions can be made about their potential role in the revolution'; the same must be said about the workers – especially in the context of underdeveloped countries where industrial workers 'constitute an insignificant portion of the population'. Yet Mafeje is quick to point out that case studies show peasants to be fully aware that they are no longer exploited in the old colonial way and that their own governments are guilty of exploiting them through marketing boards, the hierarchy of co-operatives and other brokers. Peasants are equally aware that they are abused as 'cheap, unskilled, migrant labour on the plantations and in the towns, as is shown by their songs and utterances'.[48] Mafeje sees the alliance between peasants and workers as 'the ultimate antithesis to petty-bourgeois hegemony and the contradictions of state capitalism'.

The peasants' mobility and their willingness to sell labour power, shows, contrary to classical theory, that they are not as land-rooted as the European peasantry. In countries such as China, Korea, Vietnam, Mexico, Cuba, Algeria, Guinea-Bissau, Mozambique, Angola, and in South Africa with the peasants' revolts, 'it is hard not to ascribe a certain proletariat quality to modern peasantries in the Third World'.[49] Thus, although peasants in underdeveloped countries are not similar to their worker counterparts in developed countries, they resemble them in some respects. Both are exploited by the same international finance-capital. Peasants in underdeveloped countries are exploited in the market as small producers and also, as migrant workers, by capital.

A critique of 'dual theories' of economic growth

As Mafeje states, 'societies in transition are often a source of controversy, as they characteristically abound in ambiguities of both form and content'.[50] At the level of historical sociology, studying societies in transition speaks to the question of continuity and change. This, of course, is as much a question in historical sociology as it is a question in epistemology. At the level of epistemology, Mafeje invokes the question of historical determinism. He argues that the outcomes of historical events are 'not only conditioned but are also conditioning'. This should lead to the underlying theoretical tension in dialectics between determinism and voluntarism.

Mafeje is here discussing the question of historical determinism as it emerges in Marxist theory, yet he concedes that the question of determinism is not unique to Marxist theory since it appears in liberal bourgeois discourses as well – particularly in development theory. The kind of liberal determinism that appears in development theory, Mafeje maintains, assumes that underdeveloped countries will have to travel the same path as Western societies in order to develop. It sounds like something of an oxymoron to say such a view represents 'ahistorical determinism' (since to say something is determined is in part to say that it follows from what came before it or that it has antecedents). But, strictly speaking, what is more problematic about ahistorical determinism in development theory is that, in the notion of 'dual theories', it represents a partial and ideological view of development. Dual theories are not only problematic for the substantive reasons to be discussed below, but also for the formal reason that the idea of 'dual theories' is tautologous.

Mafeje sets out to demonstrate that the kind of determinism that obtains in liberal development theory is biased and 'inherently conservative'. To expose these weaknesses, he contrasts liberal determinism with Marxist determinism. Mafeje, however, is not content merely to replicate what the Marxist theory says. He wants to evaluate, too, its 'peculiarly European presuppositions', which are usually applied to underdeveloped countries. To achieve this, he confronts theory with concrete historical experience of the countries of eastern, central and southern Africa. According to him, 'underdeveloped countries are in a position to make a contribution by reflecting more closely on their experience which is already raising some important question marks about the logic of history'.[51]

The main assumption of dual theories turns on the existence of different economic laws in underdeveloped countries referring to traditional/subsistence and modern/capitalist sectors. The notion of dual theories is the object of analysis in Luthando Funani's Master's thesis, 'State, Democracy and Development: An Exploration of the Scholarship of Professor Archie Monwabisi Mafeje'. In the thesis, Funani criticises not only Thabo Mbeki's perpetuation of this spurious concept, but also Patrick Bond and his colleagues who dedicated a special issue in *Africanus: Journal of Development Studies* to a critical assessment of Mbeki's conception of dual economies.[52] Funani opines that, unlike Mafeje's analysis of dual economies, the arguments raised by contributors to the *Africanus* special issue were not theoretically grounded. In Funani's evaluation of dual theories, Peter Ekeh's widely cited paper, 'Colonialism and the Two Publics in Africa: A Theoretical Statement', comes in for critical treatment for having fallen into the same trap as dualists like Mbeki. Significantly, however, Funani's engagement with Mafeje's assessment of dual economies fulfils a triple objective. First, he finds fault with the notion of dual economies for creating a false dichotomy. Second, given that neither Mbeki nor his critics in the *Africanus* special issue consider Mafeje's opinion of dual economies, Funani raises a crucial issue about the ignorance or erasure of Mafeje's work in South African intellectual discourse. Third, in raising these issues at all Funani succeeds in recentring Mafeje's work.

On the one hand, the so-called traditional/subsistence sector is said to have surplus labour, stagnant production technologies and deficient net savings. On the other hand, the so-called modern/capitalist sector is said to be characterised by efficient labour utilisation and a high rate of savings. Dualists argue that growth occurs when there is a shift from the traditional to the modern – the former is said to be the supplier of labour to the latter because it purportedly creates employment. These assumptions are valid, however, only if one accepts that the traditional sector is dependent on the modern sector. They are valid if structural transformation and the process of development and change are viewed in lineal and timeless sequence, not dynamically.

Following Samir Amin, Mafeje refers to these areas as the 'Africa of labour reserves'. Strictly speaking, Amin refers only to the eastern and southern parts of the continent as labour reserves, referring to Central Africa as 'Africa of the concession-owning companies'.[53] It needs to be said, however, that East Africa (with the exception of Kenya) never had 'any serious white settler problem', as Mafeje asserts. Furthermore, although it has no big mining industries, it suffered from the 'dialectical effect' of labour migration and the 'underdevelopment of the African reserves', as did the other regions. This issue has colonial roots, although it intensified after the Second World War. The flow of international capital accentuated the problem. International companies, having controlled exports and imports, made 'common cause with domestic settler capital'.[54] So in spite of the dualistic theory of traditional and modern sectors, African people, 'whether peasant cultivators, wage earners, petty-traders, feckless layabouts, or intermittently all of these things, are subject to a pervading dialectic whose historical origins can scarcely be traced to anything called their past'. The problem lay squarely with colonialism and imperialism. Amin observes:

> Under these circumstances, the traditional society was distorted to the point of being unrecognisable, it lost its autonomy, and its main function was to produce for the world market under conditions which, because they impoverished it, deprived the members of any

prospects of radical modernisation. This traditional society was not, therefore, in transition to modernity, as a dependant society it was complete, peripheral, and hence at the dead end. It consequently retained certain 'traditional' appearances which constituted its only means of survival. The Africa of colonial trade economy includes all the subordination/domination relationships between this pseudo-traditional society, integrated into the world system, and the central capitalist economy which shaped and dominated it.[55]

The capitalist mode of production that emerged in Africa as a result of colonialism and imperialism shaped 'the specific socio-economic formations with which it is now supposed to be in competition or con-flict'; the supposedly traditional sector 'was a social emergence produced by *external forces*'.[56] The issue goes beyond economic imposition in that colonialism altered the social fabric of the African people and ushered in 'special formations which are not attributable to tradition'. As such, the idea emerging from dual theories about the so-called traditional and modern sectors amounts to a rationalisation, rather than an explanation. In short, a dialectical reading of African social formations reveals that one cannot conceive of the traditional outside the modern sector. They are a dialectical dynamic, rather than a binary or a dichotomy. Mafeje asserts that in underdeveloped countries 'the question of the exclusiveness of the capitalist mode of production over time is not a foregone conclusion nor its blockage a problem of traditionalism … capitalism in its external expansion … has not been able to sweep aside certain traditional institutions and modes of production … a serious historical contradiction and not a transient natural phenomenon'.

Dual theories misconceive the phenomenon they seek to explain and are therefore liable to the charge of studying appearance, rather than sub-stance. Apart from the Eurocentric assumption that the modern capitalist sector will absorb the traditional subsistence sector, this point of view is ahistorical in that none of its premises has been validated in any former colonial African country since the end of colonialism. Africa is still a largely agrarian continent.

Although dual theories and modernisation theories purported to deal with societies in transition, presumably from tradition to modernity, it is not clear why the traditional sector is seen as an impediment to progress. It is important to note, however, that this is where the Lewisian notion of 'traditional' should be demarcated from that contained in the modernisation theory. Arthur Lewis made no assumption or claim that the traditional sector was an impediment to development in the modern sector.[57] For Lewis, the two-sector economy model is more of a thought experiment than a description of actual economies. One of the basic assumptions is that you are dealing with a closed economy, one that clearly did not exist, and Lewis was well aware of this. Specifically, how exactly is the progressiveness of capitalism to be proved if it fails in Africa as a result of the 'backward' traditional sector? By its own logic, capitalism is meant to improve the supposedly backward sector.

The point of this discussion is that European analogies should not be used as a substitute for strict historical analysis. Mafeje concedes that, at one remove, the traditional sector can be a hindrance to capitalist transition. Yet the question still stands as to why colonial capitalism (as against classical capitalism) did not dissolve traditional structures overall. This is not a real question because colonialism was not meant to develop the colonised – according to Mafeje, it is a mere 'diversion' to look for answers in the traditional sector – one should rather study the structure and the mechanisms of modern capitalism itself. Mafeje observes that 'this is a logical starting-point since, historically, the so-called phenomenon of "dualism" did not occur until the *external expansion* of Western European capitalism'.[58] When it had reached its imperialist stage, Western European capitalism was not meant to transform traditional societies but, rather, to incorporate them as secure markets and suppliers of raw material. The point was not for capitalism to reproduce itself for the needs of those at the receiving end of colonialism, but to undermine their humanity and to produce a caricature of them. Capitalism 'contrived to maintain some semblance of traditional society on non-traditional terms'.[59] Notwithstanding the persistence of some traditional systems, 'the effect of the external expansion of capitalism in underdeveloped countries has been the *reconstruction* of the traditional societies to produce something other than the capitalist mode of production'. Following Laclau, Mafeje argues that because the world capitalist system exists, there is no reason to infer that the capitalist mode of production has been vindicated. From the point of view of underdevelopment, the primary contradiction, suitably understood, is the capitalist mode of production itself and not whether there exists a traditional sector and a modern sector. To emphasise the pervasiveness of colonial capitalism, Mafeje contends that in South Africa the development of the proletariat was forestalled in a variety of ways, chief among them the labour reserves system, which not only resulted in land alienation, but also created 'a permanent system of migrant labour and anti-black urban and industrial policies, creating a sense of insecurity and dependence on kin in the countryside'. The same could be said of Rhodesia.

A similar kind of issue was manifest in Kenya and Zambia. It resulted in the emergence of producers who assumed characteristics usually associated with two distinct social classes, the peasantry and the proletariat. Equally, what would have been a local bourgeoisie, became a class subordinate and heavily dependent on international finance capital. Although this is a disadvantage and even a handicap to underdeveloped countries, it is an advantage to developed countries. This framework ensured that there exists a readily available source of cheap unskilled labour for the benefit of foreign capital. This has been the case since the advent of colonialism. It is a known datum that underdeveloped countries are a source of cheap labour for international capital. What this means is that 'within the capitalist system itself there is an uneven rate of exploitation of labour by capital'.[60]

7 | Liberation Struggles in South Africa

E ven though Archie Mafeje published a paper in 1978 on the Soweto uprising, much of his work on South African politics appeared from the mid-1980s up to the late 1990s.[1] In making the distinction between Mafeje's earlier and later contribution to revolutionary theory and politics, I am not suggesting that the two are theoretically or politically distinct; I separate them purely on the basis of scope and focus, for there is in fact a strong connection and consistency between the earlier and later work.

In contributing to revolutionary theory and politics, Mafeje wanted fellow African intellectuals to avoid being dictated to by Euro-American scholars. He resisted derivative ideas and dogmas – succumbing to these weaknesses would alienate African intellectuals not only from the very same societies they are trying to understand, but also from each other as a community of intellectuals. In short, those African scholars who over-emphasise 'universal texts' cease to be 'authentic interlocutors'. Mafeje was interested in understanding the nature of the relationship between universal texts (referring to theory) and the 'vernacular' (referring to the historically concrete). Sometimes he spoke of nomothetic versus idiographic inquiry. He was interested, too, in the theory of society and theory of revolution.[2]

For Mafeje, 'authentic subjects' are neither automatically assumed to exist nor fully formed in the process of historical development of social formations. Instead, they exist in contradiction because 'in any given situation there is more than one truth'.[3] Mafeje also maintains that 'interacting subjects mutually create one another, whether in the positive or in the negative sense'. In the struggle for liberation, ideological standpoints imply diversity of opinion only insofar as they may be 'collective as well as exclusive or inward-looking'. It is important to remember, too, that in the struggle for self-discovery and self-assertion, there is the question of symbols, which are as important as the substantive issues they represent. In this instance, the matter of language immediately comes to mind. Mafeje argues that former colonial countries had to grapple with the distinction between universal languages and vernacular languages and, furthermore: 'In the context of domination, universal languages are a supreme instrument for indoctrination and in the context of liberation "vernacular" languages are a powerful instrument for self-assertion and self-rediscovery.'

It is partly for these reasons that African intellectuals called for indigenisation of the social sciences, but there was no agreement as to what indigenisation really means. For Mafeje, such disagreements are not a matter merely of theory, but also related to political choices – a terrain 'among classes and within classes', as he puts it. Mafeje believes that class contestation is of some value in understanding the petit bourgeoisie in Africa. Objectively, African intellectuals (revolutionary or otherwise) are members of the petit bourgeoisie, but what they seek to do with their objective class location is a different matter. Although deploying such Marxist terms as 'petit bourgeoisie', Mafeje is well aware that while Marxism has 'universalistic pretentions', it is in fact a product of 'European history at a particular juncture'. He asks two related questions: 'If Marxism is a universal scientific theory, how does it overcome its own syntactical as well as semantic limitations? How does it relate, methodologically, to vernacular languages, understood in the analytical, political sense?'[4] Mafeje argues that a number of Marxists were aware of the challenges arising from these questions, but chose to ignore them out of 'political expediency'.

Internal colonialism as colonialism of a special type
According to Mafeje, Marxism and socialist politics arrived in South Africa after the Twenty-One Points of the Third International or the

Comintern of 1920. Irina Filatova claims that in 1928 the Comintern sent an 'instruction' to the Communist Party of South Africa (CPSA) to work for an 'independent native republic'.[5] However, as Mafeje points out, many of the Comintern principles were designed by Lenin and his party, 'specifically for the leadership of the socialist movement in capitalist Europe, where schooled Marxists and an experienced working class existed'.[6] Allison Drew's *Discordant Comrades: Identities and Loyalties on the South African Left* suggests, however, that there were already socialist groups in South Africa at the very beginning of the twentieth century.[7] My sense is that while Mafeje was critical of the manner in which historians write about South African history and politics with a central focus on the CPSA and African National Congress (ANC), he inadvertently falls into the same trap insofar as he equates the history of socialism in South Africa with the formation of the CPSA.

According to Mafeje, the European immigrant workers in South Africa 'were more than presumptuous' in thinking that they could be authentic interlocutors in the local political situation. They were not adept at Marxist theory and the debates taking place in Europe nor were they familiar with the 'African political vernacular'. There was, too, an over-reliance on imported theoretical categories and European analogies, and concepts such as communal land, feudal landlords and tribal economy.[8] Mafeje says the upshot of the over-reliance on European analogies was two-fold. First, the CPSA, unlike other South African Marxist or left-leaning formations such as the Unity Movement, relied heavily on the Third International. Second, they were unable to appeal to black workers, whom they deemed 'semi-tribal'; hence they reached out to the black petit bourgeoisie, which characterised the ANC leadership. (I believe that Mafeje's second point is controversial and inaccurate. There are indications that by 1928, the CPSA had a sizeable black membership and some of its leaders in the late 1920s and 1930s [Moses Kotane, Albert Nzula and Edwin Thabo Mafutsanyana] were black.)[9] The CPSA adopted the 'native republic' thesis at the end of 1928. The black petit bourgeoisie, according to Mafeje, were authentic interlocutors insofar as they understood both the universal and the vernacular. Mafeje raises this issue primarily because he wishes to highlight the 'ambiguity of the relationship between black and white South Africa'.[10] He refers to one of the theoretical postulates of the South African Communist Party (SACP) that holds that South Africa was a case of 'colonialism of a special type', or 'internal colonialism'. Although the CPSA was disbanded in 1950, it re-emerged in 1953 as an underground organisation, the SACP, which adopted formally the concept of colonialism of a special type in 1962, although the concept of internal colonialism had a longer genealogy and continued to be used by South African intellectuals like Bernard Magubane and Harold Wolpe. The concept of internal colonialism was, to varying degrees, endorsed by liberals and Marxists alike, but if it was valid, its logical conclusion must apply *mutatis mutandis* to white immigrant workers at the turn of the twentieth century and the CPSA of the 1920s as well because liberals, Marxists and white immigrant workers set out not only to impose their ideas on black workers, but also to act as their mentors. Mafeje argues that although the Afrikaners, unlike their English counterparts, had no universal language to impose on black people, they were equally guilty of oppression. The Afrikaners fought in the vernacular to exclude black people from the white bourgeois civilisation that they themselves were not part of for a very long time. Mafeje even says that 'the class content of the struggle for the Afrikaners might not be different from that of the black nationalists'.[11]

The theory of internal colonialism or colonialism of a special type, in Mafeje's opinion, diverts our attention from a class analysis of the twentieth century. If one must use the theory, one ought to be consistent and make no exceptions. If the CPSA/SACP and the ANC accepted the premise that South Africa was a case of internal colonialism, or colonialism of a special type, they were bound to accept the conclusion that follows: white people overall are settler colonists and therefore to be driven out, as was the case elsewhere in former colonies and, logically, the internal colonialism thesis means that its white Marxist advocates must surrender the land and the means of production to the indigenous population. The colonialism of a special type or internal colonialism thesis 'makes nonsense of any claims about "our country" by groups other than Africans'.[12] The thesis comes close to saying that the white communists were themselves colonisers, which I believe comes close to being a self-defeating argument. Mafeje mentions that the white communists of the CPSA treated black workers as their underlings and sometimes as enemies, as they joined white vigilantes to attack black workers during the 1922 mine strike.[13] Elsewhere, Mafeje says: 'The white liberals (including the white communists in South Africa) reserved the right to exercise hegemonic power after independence. It is when this self-assigned prerogative is questioned or threatened that the white liberals take umbrage.'[14] The South African white leftist Heinrich Bohmke argues that, structurally, white people (wittingly or unwittingly) of all political persuasions continued to usurp black liberation.[15] Bohmke sets out to analyse what he takes to be the self-serving nature of the white left's political discourses. Instead of seeing the white left as revolutionaries in their own right, Bohmke insists that their continued prerogative to speak for the black majority only amounted to new forms of the 'civilising mission'. In short, for Bohmke, the white revolutionary is a missionary. Mafeje raises similar issues in his monograph *The National Question in Southern African Settler Societies*, referring to the patronising nature of the white left within the SACP. Mafeje, though, does not take the question of race to be central to his argument; in fact he takes it to be nothing more than a socially constructed epiphenomenon. In the Unity Movement, as he says, he was trained to believe that nationalism or the Africanist perspective was reactionary; the Movement was in favour not only of class analysis, but also of internationalism.

Mafeje contends that the internal colonialism thesis collapses different forms and stages/phases of oppression into 'one fixed category', colonialism – albeit 'of a special type'. At the level of epistemology, I believe that the internal colonialism thesis is liable to the charge of using taxonomic categorisations (rather than typologies) to understand social problems – however, as is known in the social sciences, the problem with taxonomic categorisations is that they are static and 'incapable of dealing with dynamic processes', as Mafeje argues.[16] Colonialism was not only a historically determined mode of political and economic domination, but also one whose method of extraction of economic value was extra-economic. Consistent with global political and economic trends, South Africa of the

1920s, paradoxically the period in which the CPSA adopted the internal colonialism thesis, had reached or entered what Lenin called the 'highest stage of capitalism': imperialism, or the monopoly stage.[17] The notion of internal colonialism was a case of superimposing theory on data, instead of using data to interrogate theory. In this regard (as has been noted), Mafeje insists that the CPSA were not authentic interlocutors. By the 1920s, South Africa did not 'thrive by exchange value but rather by *surplus-value*'.[18]

Given that Mafeje argued that South Africa of the 1920s had reached the stage of imperialism, I believe that it is important to define imperialism before the discussion goes any further. It is important to note that Mafeje was working with the Leninist definition of imperialism. Although imperialism is said to be an expression of colonialism, Lenin did not take it to be a mere question of annexation. Within Marxism, Karl Kautsky sees imperialism as 'a product of highly developed industrial capitalism. It consists in the striving of every industrial capitalist nation to bring under its control or to annex all large areas of *agrarian* territory, irrespective of what nations inhabit it.'[19] For Lenin, Kautsky's definition was not satisfactory because it was one-sided since it isolated the national question. Although the national question was important in its own right, Kautsky connected it only with the industrialised countries that annex agrarian countries. While annexation is an integral part of imperialism, annexation only highlights the *political* aspect of imperialism and ignores the equally violent aspect of *finance capital*. It is important to highlight the connection between the political part of imperialism and finance capital because, for Lenin, imperialism 'strives to annex *not only* agrarian territories, but even most highly industrialised regions'[20] and 'if it were necessary to give the briefest possible definition of imperialism we should have to say that imperialism is the monopoly stage of capitalism'. Yet even for Lenin this definition is incomplete. He argues that in talking about imperialism, we must give it a definition that includes five essential features. First, production and capital must be developed to the extent that they create monopolies that shape all aspects of economic life. Second, there must exist finance capital (bank capital and industrial capital), which in turn produces a 'financial oligarchy'. Third, there is an export of capital itself, rather than an export of commodities. Fourth, the world is characterised by a formation of international monopolist capitalist associations, which share the surplus value between themselves. The fifth stage relates to the division of the whole world among the major capitalist powers. In summary, for Lenin, imperialism refers to the complete dominance of the world by monopolies and finance capital.

Mafeje's critique of colonialism of a special type and his characterisation of post-1920 South Africa as having reached an imperialist stage must be understood against this background. It is not enough merely to point out that imperialism is consistent with colonialism, because, for Lenin, imperialism was to be distinguished from colonialism precisely because of monopoly capitalism and the five elements outlined above. Thus, for Mafeje, on the basis of the Leninist definition of imperialism, by the time the CPSA was formed, South Africa had, consistent with global capitalism, entered its highest stage: imperialism. Writing about Jack Simons and his popularisation of the internal colonialism thesis in the CPSA, his biographer Hugh Macmillan says: 'Jack used to say he borrowed the idea from Leo Marquard ... Jack intended this as no more than an analogy and was surprised that it became so well established ... It was restated in a much more elaborate form as "colonialism of a special type" (CST) in the South African Communist Party's manifesto, *The Road to South African Freedom*, in 1962.'[21]

Mafeje's contemporary Bernard Magubane took the opportunity to respond to Mafeje and other critics of internal colonialism and offered some defence of it, asserting: 'Contrary to the shallow misrepresentation and disingenuous attempts by Callinicos and Mafeje to discredit the theory of internal colonialism at the time it was formulated, the SACP and the ANC had no coherent theory on the character of black oppression, and no comprehensive strategy for intervention and leadership in the struggle for national liberation and social emancipation.'[22]

Magubane goes on to argue that the internal colonialism thesis, as borrowed by the CPSA from Comintern, grappled with the national question and highlighted the specificity of the South African state as it pointed out that black people in South Africa were oppressed and exploited in ways that the white working class was not. For Magubane, the internal colonialism thesis took seriously the fact that the oppression and exploitation of black people was so particular that it 'required a comprehensive and historical analysis in its own right, and a special political strategy and programme to overthrow it'.[23] The South African struggle was, Magubane argues, two-pronged: a struggle against both white minority rule and imperialism.

Instead of responding to the nuts and bolts of Mafeje's otherwise sophisticated critique of internal colonialism, Magubane mobilises well-known historical facts and proceeds to state the obvious. Not only does he avoid a direct confrontation with Mafeje's central argument, he simply presupposes the very point at issue, which is whether South Africa was still a colony after 1920. In my view, Magubane makes two separately important, but mutually contradictory claims. He affirms the idea that South Africa was a colony, while simultaneously acknowledging that South Africa had reached the imperialist stage, albeit burdened with white minority rule. The first claim is debatable, whereas the second is not only valid, but also accords with Mafeje's, as will be shown later on. Mafeje found fault with the internal colonialism thesis not only for lacking originality, but also for being Eurocentric since it was imported from the Comintern. Although the Comintern proposed for South African communists the notion of a 'native republic', the CPSA remained a largely white-dominated organisation, which was otherwise paternalistic and treated black people as underlings. Magubane's argument proceeds in circularity. Politically, it may have been effective because the notion of internal colonialism still holds sway among some South African intellectuals; intellectually, however, Magubane's defence lacks the theoretical subtlety and sophistication required to dispel Mafeje's argument. Magubane's assertion that 'the theses highlighted the fact that the struggle against white minority rule was also a struggle against imperialism' is in fact the weak point of his argument for Mafeje and other critics of internal colonialism. As Mafeje points out, to speak of internal colonialism after 1920 was not only to confuse different stages/phases of history and oppression, but also to ignore the fact that, consistent with global capitalism, South Africa had reached the stage of imperialism.

In my view, Magubane telescopes different stages of history into a single unit by arguing that colonialism was taking place concurrently with imperialism in South Africa after 1920. I believe that in cases where the two forms of oppression take place concurrently, the struggle needs to be waged in tandem, but the point is that South Africa had by the 1920s entered the phase of finance capital. Indeed, in his book *The Making of a Racist State*, Magubane himself points out that by 1875 the world had entered the imperialist stage.[24] Ultimately, Magubane advances a trans-historical claim that overlooks Mafeje's argument that oppression and exploitation are products of history and therefore change in accordance with economic and political development. Although colonialism is an expression of imperialism, the two represent different stages in history. This is even truer if one takes into account the fact that Mafeje was working with a Leninist definition of imperialism – the highest stage of imperialism – and not mere annexation. It is true that black workers in South Africa suffered acute oppression in ways their white counterparts did not. But, as I have pointed out above, Mafeje accepted this fact of history.

The nature of colonialism on the African continent was such that the indigenous population suffered more than the white working-class coloniser. The question I would like to ask is this: what kind of colonialists would colonialists be if they did not oppress and exploit the indigenous people more than poor whites? In his seminal 1972 paper, 'Underdevelopment and Dependence in Black Africa', Samir Amin points out that southern and eastern Africa exhibited similar characteristics of oppression and exploitation and calls these regions 'Africa of the labour reserves'. Furthermore, he says: 'This was because there was great mineral wealth to be exploited (gold and diamonds in South Africa, and copper in Northern Rhodesia), and an untypical settler agriculture in the tropical Africa of Southern Rhodesia, Kenya, and German Tanganyika. In order to obtain this proletariat quickly, the colonisers dispossessed the African rural communities – sometimes by violence – and drove them deliberately back into small, poor regions, with no means of modernising and intensifying their farming.'[25]

In the final analysis, as Mahmood Mamdani points out, the South African case may have been extreme, but it was not exceptional.[26]

Mafeje contends that if one were to follow the internal colonialism thesis to its logical conclusion, one would have to commit to 'racial classification and pedigree', the ideological commitment of the apartheid government. If the internal colonialism thesis were pushed to its logical conclusion, no racial group other than blacks and coloureds could lay claim to South Africa. On the basis of the internal colonialism thesis, Indians would have to be excluded, in spite of being as oppressed as blacks and coloureds. Yet this would have problems of its own since Indians have no history of colonising blacks (although some are known to discriminate against black people). Much more importantly, the term 'black' changed radically in South Africa of the 1970s, thanks to the Black Consciousness Movement. Coloureds and Indians were self-referentially black. What is important to note here is that Mafeje employs a *reductio ad absurdum* and attempts to show that if one were to follow the internal colonialism thesis, one would reach absurd conclusions such as excluding Indians and Cape Malays (coloureds) because they arrived with the colonisers. Mafeje is simply deriding the adherents of the internal colonialism or colonialism of a special type thesis. He seems to have had a great deal of foresight in that after having made the point that coloureds and Indians were self-referentially black in the 1970s and 1980s, he asks: 'Does this signify anything important or is it merely a passing phase?'[27] It is an important question because in the post-1994 dispensation, there has been a reversal of the gains of the Black Consciousness Movement, which sought to unite all the oppressed groups under 'Black'.

The national question

Having criticised the notion of internal colonialism, Mafeje discusses the national question. Although he does not define what a nation is, Mafeje seems to be working with the classical definition of what constitutes a nation – 'a historically evolved stable community of people, formed on the basis of a common language, territory, economic life and psychological make-up manifested in a common culture'.[28] Mafeje concedes, however, that because classical definitions of the national question derive from 'universal languages' (are imported from Europe), they are 'quickly getting antiquated'. Thandika Mkandawire agrees with Mafeje that the national question has been linked to the history of colonised or oppressed people of the world. Mkandawire argues that, for the best part of the twentieth century, the national question entailed asserting the humanity of African people, attaining independence and 'maintaining the unity and territorial integrity of the new state'.[29] During the struggle for independence and in the post-independence period, the question of national identity was always associated with land or territory. For Mkandawire, regardless of how the borders of a particular territory were drawn by the colonisers, the postcolonial or post-independence period was about 'how to hold the country together'.

Mafeje says that it is difficult to settle the national question in South Africa. He asserts that 'different waves of South Africans' have lived in this piece of land for over 500 years, the latest arrivals being the British and Indians who came more than 150 years ago – thus, the national question is not as self-evident as is assumed. According to Mafeje, precisely who constitutes a nation in South Africa is an object of inquiry and he finds that the SACP position on 'nationalities', although meant to be a radical position, is compatible with the bantustan policy of the apartheid government: 'From its inception the Communist Party has been guided by Stalin's thesis on the right of nations to self-determination and the recommendations of the Third International/Comintern to fraternal organisations.'[30]

For Mafeje, the universal texts or theories of the Comintern/Third International had to be translated into the vernacular. Before anything can be said about theory, one has to study conditions on the ground in order to ultimately reach an epistemological break. It is not enough to know what theory says – the point is that, where possible, one must transcend it in order to produce alternative knowledge systems. Mafeje is not committing himself to empiricism. On the contrary, he understands that the search for an epistemological break can only be made meaningful if social formations are studied on their own terms. In my view, the most glaring problem with Mafeje's argument, however, is that although he talks about learning from the local in order to arrive at the universal, he is actually relying on a universal text: Leninism. This is a much more devastating counter to Mafeje's argument than Magubane's claim about South Africa's being a case of white minority rule and imperialism – because with this claim Magubane is actually agreeing with Mafeje. The conceptual problem arising in Mafeje's argument is that he falls into the same trap that he accuses the CPSA/SACP of having fallen into. If the problem with the CPSA/SACP was relying on the Comintern to understand South African conditions, the problem with Mafeje's argument is that it relies on Leninism to understand South African conditions.

Mafeje highlights another instance in which the notion of internal colonialism comes up against limits it cannot overcome. In their struggle for liberation, South Africans, unlike Africans elsewhere on the continent, spoke not of independence but of 'non-racial democracy' and 'national democracy'. This may have been a tacit acknowledgement that South Africa was already an independent country – particularly after it pulled out of the Commonwealth in March 1961. Yet, according to Mafeje, to accept that South Africa was an existing state and still agitate for national democracy (which includes white people) was a contradiction in terms.[31] If South Africa was a case of internal colonialism, as the SACP/ANC suggested, how does one account for the inclusion of colonialists (that is, whites) in the notion of national democracy? The question arises precisely because, as everywhere else in the former colonies, 'imperialists and colonialists are worth driving out, as the Comintern had recommended in the 1930s'.[32] In general, the precise focus of the internal colonialism argument is on racial oppression; therefore, when all races are equal, it ceases to be a case of internal colonialism. Deracialisation becomes a solution to settler colonialism. Mafeje suggests that the ANC/SACP need to reconcile this contradictory position of diagnosing South Africa as a case of internal colonialism and accepting the coloniser as part of the non-racial national democracy.

The ultimate state of the internal colonialism thesis is the two-stage theory of the revolution – the liberation of black people, first as the oppressed racial category and then as an exploited class. Mafeje's problem with the two-stage theory is that it was untenable for both theoretical and historical reasons. As he puts it, what constitutes a colony are political and economic relations, chief among them the domination or oppression of pre-capitalist formations by a capitalist formation, and the 'extraction of value by largely extra-economic means'.[33] Importantly, however, extraction of value by extra-economic means was not unique to South Africa. Similar patterns of oppression and exploitation obtained in Southern and Northern Rhodesia, Kenya and Tanganyika. Although in *South Africa: From Soweto to Uitenhage* Magubane tries to defend the notion of internal colonialism, in *The Making of a Racist State* he argues at some length that blackness is not a necessary condition for racism.[34] Indeed, he uses the case of Ireland, 'the Irish Question', to clinch his argument and argues that Ireland could legitimately be called the first colony of England. Moreover, as Mafeje argues: 'Both the United States and Australia (and the Cape as is shown by the Great Trek) were *white* colonies of Britain and suffered the same ravages as everybody else.'[35] Although Mafeje neglects to mention the extermination of the native peoples of both countries, the point is clear – South Africa is not exceptional. Elsewhere, he argues that 'it is apparent that "colonialism of a special type" *is a non-concept and not even a descriptive term*. It is unwieldy and has no analytic value. Judged by its own terms, there would be no difference between Rhodesia, a great many of the Latin-American states and even the United States, where blacks or "reds" are dominated, oppressed and exploited by whites.'[36] Magubane makes the same point in his book *The Ties That Bind* when he says that 'experiences of Afro-Americans and of the black people of South Africa share a great deal in common'.[37] In his paper 'Race and Class Revisited: The Case of North America and South Africa', Magubane argues that 'it is in these societies that race and class and class and race are primary issues of sociological, philosophical and political discourse'.[38] It is not altogether clear to me, therefore, why he strains to defend the notion of internal colonialism when he readily acknowledges that South Africa and the United States have much in common. Mafeje's verdict on the South African situation is that perhaps South Africa should be characterised as a case of *'racial oppression* in an age of capitalism or imperialism',[39] rather than the transhistorical characterisations that telescope different stages of oppression and mutually contradictory claims about internal colonialism. To object to Mafeje by pointing out that this is not different from Magubane's position is to overlook the fact that Mafeje had already argued that apartheid South Africa had entered the Leninist imperialist stage and had therefore gone beyond colonialism – when he said South Africa was a case of racial oppression in the age of imperialism, he did not need to address 'the colonial dimension'. In his view, this question did not arise. He denied that apartheid was colonialism of a special type from the beginning.

Towards a socialist democracy

Mafeje contends that the struggle for liberation and the ANC/SACP theoretical positions said little about what black people would do once in power. He argues that non-racial democracy was the common denominator: 'This is a demand for inclusion in the body polity of the country and guarantees the national integration that has been frustrated by apartheid hitherto.'[40] Indeed, the inclusion in the body polity is precisely what took place after 1994 since there was no major overhaul of the structural determinants of apartheid. Black people are still largely poor while whites still own the land and have control over the means of production. For Mafeje, notions of majority rule and non-racial democracy are perfectly consistent with liberal democracy and therefore the kind of non-racialism adopted by the ANC says very little about socialism. To respond by saying the ANC is not a socialist organisation – because it is primarily a nationalist movement with a primary focus on racial oppression – is to overlook the fact that the ANC/SACP are in pursuit of the two-stage theory of a revolution (national liberation) followed by class liberation of the workers. I believe that it would be fair to evaluate whether the ANC has a socialist programme, and my sense is that to evaluate the ANC's socialist programme would be to take the ANC on its own terms, otherwise to object to such an evaluation would be to make nonsense of the ANC's own stance of a 'national democratic revolution' in pursuit of the 'second transition' to 'economic liberation in our lifetime'. If the current posturing about the nationalisation of mines, expropriation of land and radical economic transformation is not a gesture towards a socialist path (even if rhetorically), then what is it about?

What seems to have mattered for Mafeje is that those waging the struggle for liberation must win the support of oppressed classes. Whether or not the struggle is socialist-orientated, history shows that the former colonies pursued their national democratic revolution through the unification of the oppressed classes. The communist parties of China and Vietnam relied on the support of the peasants as well as the progressive elements of the petit bourgeoisie. According to Mafeje, this bears testimony 'to the leading role of the petit-bourgeoisie in underdeveloped countries'.[41] Based on this, he concludes that all nationalist or national movements in underdeveloped countries are likely to be shaped by the interests of the petit bourgeoisie. I agree with Mafeje that there exists a progressive section of the petit bourgeoisie in underdeveloped countries, but it does not follow that they are or will be sympathetic to a socialist struggle. The African continent has not had a progressive petit bourgeoisie since the 1980s. The 1980s and the adoption of structural adjustment programmes signalled the end of progressive policies and an adoption of neoliberal policies. The situation has not changed two decades into the twenty-first century. If there is a progressive petit bourgeoisie on the African continent at the moment, it operates outside of state power.

Mafeje argues that, unlike the bourgeoisie and the proletariat, the state petit bourgeoisie cannot reproduce itself. He says its only available option is to win over the working class and the peasants and other disgruntled sectors of the population. This is precisely what the Afrikaners did through policy protectionism and economic nationalism and they were therefore able to appease the working class, business and farmers. Consequently, there developed an Afrikaner bourgeoisie in the true sense of the word. The Afrikaner bourgeoisie was, in Mafeje's words, the 'foster-child' of the Afrikaner petit bourgeoisie. But this is cold comfort to the black majority. The black petit bourgeoisie was always much more conciliatory in its political and theoretical orientation, as evidenced by the notion of non-racial democracy. In spite of its rhetorical flair, the non-racial democracy slogan does not 'represent a nation in itself and by itself, as happened elsewhere in Africa (barring Zimbabwe)'.[42] According to Mafeje, the South African state is 'a state without a nation'. Although the nature of oppression was always known, there was no real agreement on the nature of the national democratic revolution. For example, the ANC/SACP has always been keen on the notion of the two-stage theory of the revolution. Yet 'the grounds for supposing that a socialist revolution is implicit in the South African national liberation struggle are as tenuous as the postulated link between the national democratic revolution and the social revolution in the two-stage theory'.

Consistent with Mafeje's search for an epistemological break, this was not a matter merely of political struggles, but also a contribution to revolutionary theory and, therefore, to knowledge production. Thus the question of the two-stage theory as favoured by the ANC/SACP was a case of using universal texts without sufficient attention to local history. Politically, the danger of such a practice is that it 'underestimated the capacity of the petit bourgeoisie in the new states to mount their own political enterprise and frustrate any attempts towards a socialist transformation'.[43] Post-1994 South Africa provides a good example of this. Significantly, 'under conditions of monopoly capitalism, imperialism will abort the national democratic revolution by imposing a petit-bourgeois comprador class whose interests will be opposed to those of the majority of the people'. The workers and the peasants both have no option but to prevail on the petit bourgeoisie to adopt radical programmes.

One of the problems of the two-stage theory is the un-Marxist assumption that socialism itself is a finite stage. For Mafeje, socialism was not a mode of production, but a transitional phase towards communism. This notwithstanding, in the South African context, as Mafeje says, '*Socialist democracy* is on the agenda precisely because of the unrealisability of bourgeois democracy under conditions of imperialism and monopoly capitalism.'[44] Socialist democracy, contrary to the ANC/SACP second transition, is on the agenda primarily because of the failures of the liberal democracy they have chosen, not because of the successes of their chosen path. Mafeje notes that in South Africa and Namibia a party-state model would not succeed because of a combination of internal and external forces, and the idea of a single party being the sole representative of the people had become obsolete. Mafeje observed, in the late 1980s, a conscious effort by the apartheid government to negotiate with 'pliant petit bourgeois organisations' in order to establish a reconciliation government that would be amenable to the interests of finance capital. He contends that the negotiated settlement meant the black petit bourgeois leadership would have to ensure the 'inviolability of the property of the South African white bourgeoisie'.[45] In Mafeje's schema, the black petit bourgeoisie and the white bourgeoisie became 'strange bedfellows'. The negotiated settlement meant that 'a foundation [was] being laid for an undemocratic alliance between the right fractions of the Black petit bourgeoisie and the White bourgeoisie in order to outflank those forces which might insist on majority rule'. What makes the African petit bourgeoisie attractive to imperialism is the fact that it is corruptible.

In trying to understand black struggles, Mafeje speaks about three kinds of nationalism. First, there is black nationalism in South Africa. Second, there is black nationalism on the African continent (both black and African nationalism are a response to white structural racism). Third, there is Third World nationalism against imperialism. All of these forms of nationalism overlap, just as the dialectical units they respond to overlap. In its various forms, nationalism can be part of socialist struggles 'without contradicting itself'. This is an important point because black/African nationalism and European nationalism proceed from different logics. Contrary to the conventional view – which not only sees black/African nationalism as reactionary, but also sees it as akin to European nationalism – black nationalism was more of a response to oppression and exploitation than it was an attempt to dominate others. The assumption that black/African nationalism is the flipside of European nationalism is not only ahistorical, but also comes very close to suggesting that Napoleon Bonaparte and Jean-Jacques Dessalines or Toussaint L'Ouverture are fellow travellers – although it seems extraordinary that this could be so. One cannot make such an assumption without drawing a moral equivalent between the black liberation struggle and the oppression and exploitation to which it was a response. It is for this reason, for example, that Jimi Adesina says that the concept of nationalism is a misnomer on the African continent. For Adesina, categories such as the nation, nation state, nationalism or nationalist are not very helpful in making sense of post-independence Africa. He argues that the so-called nationalist movements in Africa were not nationalist but, rather, anti-colonial and anti-imperialist, because they were not concerned with constructing nations along the lines of shared ethnolinguistic and cultural heritage. What the African liberation movements aspired to was the undoing of the ethnic and religious divisions created by colonialism. According to Adesina: 'The commitment they espoused had more to do with state-territory than the nation-state.'[46]

Similarly, Magubane says about black nationalism that it 'lacks a territorial base'.[47] Unlike European nationalism, which was not only a super-imposition on others, but also an attempt to construct nations along ethnolinguistic lines within specifically defined geographical boundaries, black nationalism transcended borders or geographical boundaries. Strictly speaking, the trans-border and transcontinental nature of black liberation struggles, not only call into question the veracity of the notion of 'black nationalism', but also render it a contradiction in terms. Perhaps the time is ripe to reconsider altogether the appropriateness of this term.

At any rate, Mafeje says: 'Socialism is part of universal history by virtue of having been put on the agenda by the negations of capitalism and imperialism which are a universal force.'[48] He concludes that universal and local histories are not in conflict. He was interested in building theory and therefore learning from the socio-historically concrete. The idea that universal and local history are mutually contradictory is founded on the assumption that historical materialism is a 'model rather than a method of analysis whose subject matter is determined by actual struggles'. Mwesiga Baregu shares this sentiment and argues that African scholars ought to 'depart from the received and largely hackneyed wisdom handed down either by sympathetic but idealistic Africanists or by the doctrinaire neoMarxists. While the former have tended to confuse advocacy with analysis and ended up with disillusionment, *the latter have suffered from a proclivity to mis-apply Marx to historically different situations*.[49]

Perhaps Mafeje is correct to point out that Marx's analytical categories were rooted in the European historical struggles of his time and that before those categories can be used in other parts of the world they should be subjected to critical scrutiny in line with new or different experiences. This is the level at which new knowledge occurs – and Mafeje is well aware of it. He makes an important distinction between what he understood as 'theory of revolution' and 'theory of society'. The latter is in fact what Marx's revolutionary theory was about – Marx wrote a theory of history itself while Lenin and Mao Tse-Tung were theorising history in Russia and in China. Mafeje concedes that both of these were revolutionary theory in spite of the qualitative and analytical distinction he makes. The suggestion seems to be that Marx's revolutionary theory may have been pitched at a meta-theoretical level. Mafeje concludes: 'If the point of departure of dialectical materialism is the rules of social reproduction and production within finite modes of production, then dialectical materialism cannot, within its terms of reference, have a theory of societies in transition. It is one thing to elucidate dialectical principles and another to predict their concrete expression.'[50]

Mafeje is suggesting here that socialism is transitory. He does not clarify the corollary of the claim that dialectical materialism cannot contain a theory of societies in transition. The idea that dialectical materialism cannot have a theory of socialism is likely to startle some Marxists; his explanation is that this is a problem of history, of a process of change, and the kind of change that comes with socialism is subject to the struggle between contending forces. A theory of change cannot occur in a vacuum: it is a matter of 'interpretation' and 'subjective representation', as Mafeje puts it. Short of committing himself to relativism, Mafeje remedies his formulation by saying the winner will win on the basis of his 'correct reading of historical conjuncture and the formulation of an appropriate strategy'.[51] He credits Lenin and Mao for having excelled in reading historical conjunctures, implying that both brought the concrete realities of their locales to bear on historical materialism. It is at this point that Mafeje cautions against over-reliance on classical concepts. For him, relying on local history was much more rewarding than superimposing theory on local history.

A socialist conception of the national democratic revolution

Mafeje briefly discusses the revolutionary strategy of South African political organisations that made up the liberation movement in his book *In Search of an Alternative*, focusing on the ANC/SACP, the Pan Africanist Congress (PAC) and the Unity Movement. He argues that the Unity Movement rejected the notion of the ANC's multiracialism as an acknowledgement or recognition of races. The Unity Movement, moreover, had reservations about the progressiveness of 'black nationalism', which they considered progressive to the extent that it was anti-colonialist. On the other hand, the Unity Movement denounced black nationalism as reactionary to the extent that it was not anti-imperialist. But Mafeje points out three levels of nationalism and concludes that it *can* be read as anti-imperialist. (The Unity Movement position referred to here was specifically a memorandum to the Organisation of African Unity in which the Unity Movement accused the Organisation of being party to an 'imperialist conspiracy' to keep Africa in bondage.)

In a 1975 theoretical and policy document, published as *The New Road of Revolution*, the PAC invokes the Maoist concept of the 'new democracy'.[52] The PAC speaks of anti-imperialism and the leading role of the workers and peasants as an essential condition for socialist and nationalist liberation, which the PAC saw as intrinsically linked. The ANC, on the other hand, although well aware of the existence of imperialism and the presence of a large and growing working class in South Africa, confined itself to the national question. The ANC 'Strategy and Tactics' document of 1969 says: 'We in South Africa are part of the zone in which national liberation is the chief content of the struggle.'[53] In this formulation, Mafeje saw the influence of the SACP's two-stage theory of revolution and that one could infer that for the ANC anti-imperialism and the leading role of the workers and peasants 'are not a necessary condition for national liberation but a sequel to it'.[54] He claims that the ANC strategy showed lack of awareness of what had happened in the rest of the continent and asks rhetorically: 'What are its grounds for supposing that things will be different in South Africa? Is the ANC on the basis of those grounds, prepared to settle for another Lancaster House Agreement?'

Mafeje makes a distinction between a nationalist and a socialist conception of the national democratic revolution: the former is bourgeois or capitalist and therefore consistent with imperialism; the latter is anti-capitalist and anti-imperialist. He finds it 'ironical' that the nationalist conception of the national democratic revolution is 'advocated by the ANC, the only Black organisation in South Africa that has been associated with the SACP'.[55] For me, this position is not ironic at all, since the ANC is a nationalist organisation with bourgeois and capitalist inclinations. In contrast, the Unity Movement and the PAC, both of which were very critical of the ANC and SACP at different stages, endorsed the socialist concept of the national democratic revolution. Then, the Black Consciousness Movement 'must be credited with some radicalism… Insofar as its stalwarts have stood firm against severe odds … and rendered the country ungovernable, they must be credited with a militancy which far exceeds that of the liberation movements'.[56] There was, too, the United Democratic Front (UDF), which 'calls for the destruction of a pernicious system, without putting forward a clear alternative … From what we know, none of the constituent factions of the UDF has a comprehensive programme for the South African revolution'.[57]

Mafeje points out that South Africans had a stark choice between 'two contending tendencies', the 'petit-bourgeois constituency' and the 'worker/peasant constituency'. He makes this distinction on the basis of the liberation movements' programmes of demands and potential supporters. As such, 'there is now growing realisation that within each liberation movement there are different constituencies, whose development or lack of it will determine the character of the new state'.[58] The realisation of different camps within the liberation movement led some radicals to call for 'national socialism'. Curiously, the SACP was opposed to this as incompatible with its two-stage theory of revolution. Mafeje concludes that the 'class character of its constituency is therefore clear and consistent with petit-bourgeois interests. In fact, the ANC had for its own convenience, officially accepted this theoretical position'.[59]

Although Mafeje makes all these distinctions between the South African political organisations, he points out that in spite of their differences – theoretically, politically and otherwise – their programmes had been conceived in the period of petit bourgeois nationalism of the independence movement on the rest of the continent. This is an important sociological insight as it relates the South African experience to the rest of the African continent, yet at the time when South Africans were nego-tiating democracy, the rest of the continent was in the process of negating the historical period that influenced the programmes of the South African liberation movements. The message was to learn from the history of the independent African states. Mafeje's proposal is that the South African revolutionaries should not get stuck on 'formal bourgeois rights', but should attempt 'participatory democracy i.e. the right of the people to act on their own behalf', even though he knew that 'this category of people will be shunted off, as has happened elsewhere in Africa'.[60] The notion of power-sharing was empty rhetoric since it did not include the redistribu-tion of wealth. In any case, 'logically, the ANC could not accept a dialogue with the white capitalists ("businessmen") and liberals and at the same time threaten to expropriate them'.[61]

Apart from the maturation of South Africa's internal contradictions, there was a constellation of regional and international events. The Cold War meant that the liberation movements were faced with difficult tac-tical and strategic questions. This was more acute in the case of liber-ation movements stationed outside of their countries, which had to rely on sympathetic countries in order to survive in exile. Inherent in this is a contradiction between 'progressive states' and revolutionary movements. For Mafeje, states set out to consolidate their power base and, as a con-sequence, 'they cannot be revolutionary but at best be progressive' and the Trotskyist or Maoist notion of permanent revolution cannot refer to the state, but to forces outside of state power.[62] Mafeje thus took the opportunity to ask, in the context of what appeared to be an incongruous alliance between the SACP and the ANC: 'After the "negotiated settlement" where will the communists and their celebrated programme be? In jail or in the new bourgeois government?'[63] The latter has not only proven to be the case, but also serves to highlight Mafeje's point that it would take forces outside of state power for a permanent revolution to occur. Mafeje suggests that for the Trotskyist or Maoist permanent revolution to be realised, one would have to take seriously Lenin's theory and emphasis on the revolutionary potential of the alliance between workers and peasants. In the Chinese revolution, the peasants (not the petit bourgeois or communist government as such) expropriated property. Equally, in the urban areas the workers took over foreign enterprises; what the communist government accomplished upon getting into power was to declare this expropriation a fait accompli and to legalise it.

Open-ended remarks

Mafeje argues that liberation struggles in Africa and the global South turned on the national question. Although he recognises that the national question meant different things to different people, the tie that binds all discussions of it is nationalism, and a thread running through the forms of nationalism mentioned by Mafeje is the attempt to combat colonialism and imperialism, which call for 'qualitatively different types of nationalism'.[64] The two types of nationalism are proto-nationalism and meta-nationalism, the former concerned primarily with political domination by aliens ('without relating it to its modal foundations since the end of the nineteenth century'), the latter coming about as a result of disillusionment with proto-nationalism and of an 'understanding of imperialist domination'. In Africa, the two types of nationalism represent pre- and post-independence political struggles. In some countries – particularly in countries that attained independence after 1975 – there was an overlap of the two.

Mafeje makes a much stronger claim: that the economic collapse of the 1980s meant that the national question was not resolved anywhere in Africa. The kind of disillusionment with neocolonialism meant that there was a second phase of national struggles with a twin project – to fight imperialism and the comprador class. In contrast, the earlier nationalists were fighting colonialism. According to Mafeje, the anti-imperialist and anti-comprador struggles in Africa are best understood as nationalist, rather than socialist in character. This distinction was important for Mafeje, for at least two reasons:

> First, to justify their self-motivated interventions in under-developed countries, the imperialist countries have always found it ideologically convenient to brand any anti-imperialist movement in Africa and elsewhere in the Third World as 'communist' or 'Marxist-Leninist'. In the context of the Cold War this was credible. It also suited the comprador proto-nationalists in Africa whose position has become more and more precarious. Second, as a response to the historically-determined meta-nationalism, anti-imperialist movements in Africa confirmed the illusion of 'socialism' through their own rhetoric and Marxist-Leninist pretensions. As would be expected, this manifested itself more blatantly in those countries which were approaching their independence at this point in time.[65]

African states such as Angola, Mozambique and Zimbabwe are working examples of what Mafeje has in mind here. It is notable that in raising these issues at all Mafeje is not quibbling about chronological matters such as which country achieved independence before the others. He is interested in historically determined contradictions on the African continent. Specifically, he is concerned to understand whether the national question had been resolved in the historical period of anti-imperialism and anti-comprador. Although South Africans generally tend to think that what applies to other African countries does not apply to them, Mafeje argues that the distinction he makes between proto- and meta-nationalists applied to them as well. The exclusion of blacks by the whites in their own country was an invitation to nationalism. The formation of the ANC in 1912 made proto-nationalists of them and this remained so until 1955. What strengthened their commitment to proto-nationalism came from an unlikely source in the form of the SACP and its advance of the 'colonialism of a special type' or 'internal colonialism' thesis. Furthermore, it meant that prior to 1955 and the adoption of the Freedom Charter, the ANC never raised the question of imperialism and 'its local agents'. Following the recognition of imperialism, the national question was therefore understood in meta-nationalist terms.

Mafeje concludes that nationalist struggles against colonialism and imperialism 'are decidedly progressive and might even be a necessary condition for would-be socialism'.[66] He argues that history reveals that even in countries with an advanced proletariat, there is always nationalism of some kind. (Perhaps it is for this reason that Adesina says the Chinese Communist Party is best understood as a nationalist party.) For Mafeje, the problem with socialist internationalists had always been to universalise the European historical experience. In the southern African settler societies, 'black nationalism is not only an important last line of defence but also a liberating and transcendent force'. Mafeje is quick to point out that the kind of nationalism he is talking about should not be associated with classical definitions that derive from European history. He does not, however, offer an alternative definition, save to say that nationalism 'will mean different things in different historical epochs and in different social contexts'.[67] It is for this reason that such Eurocentric concepts as nation state or nations are becoming antiquated through cross-border migration and regional integration. This is possibly the best thing to happen in post-independence Africa as it undermines and threatens colonial borders and the idea of the state formalised at the 1884 Berlin Conference. While the national question initially referred to liberation from colonial domination and oppression, the post-independence African state had to contend with ethnic conflicts and the notion of the nation state remained elusive.

In South Africa, the wealth of the country is still in the hands of the white minority. This is 'the juxtaposition of a settler splendour of swimming pools, picnics, fishing and hunting trips and a squalid black world of drudgery and grinding poverty in southern Africa'.[68] This is what ANC/SACP theorists refer to as 'colonialism of a special type' or 'internal colonialism'. As has already been noted, Mafeje rejects this characterisation of South Africa for several reasons. On logical grounds, he refers to it as nonsensical; colonialism cannot be internal because the term connotes historically determined external imposition. The phrase 'of a special type' does not render the ANC/SACP argument valid. The white liberal and communist proponents of the 'internal colonialism' would not think of themselves as colonialists, in spite of the implications of the concept, yet liberals and communists 'cannot prove that they are not liable because in practice they are as much of white supremacists as the openly racist whites'. The only difference is that the liberals and communists absolve themselves by pointing out that they are on the side of the black people. This is part of the reason that led Steve Biko, when talking about liberals and leftists, to declare: 'A number of whites in this country adopt the class analysis, primarily because they want to detach us from anything relating to race.'[69] In contending with the dispossession of black people, it is not uncommon in intellectual discourse to come across the notion of two economies or nations, 'an oppressing and exploiting white nation and an oppressed and exploited black nation'.[70] In defending and protecting ill-gotten wealth, Mafeje says, whites cannot be said to be a nation so long as they live in the same land that is contested by blacks – and in fighting oppression and exploitation black people cannot constitute a nation 'while the "white problem" pervades all society'.

For Mafeje, those would count, rightly or wrongly, as ethnic groups. It is for this reason that the national question in the region turns on anti-racial domination and redistribution of wealth. There can be no social democracy in South Africa while there is racial domination and without the redistribution of wealth because social democracy would involve 'a conscious and continuing improvement of the conditions of livelihood of the oppressed and exploited mass of the population'.[71] He concludes that 'the policy of reconciliation in three white settler societies in Southern Africa is a social and economic fraud'. The national question, as Mafeje conceived of it, remains unresolved. He argues that, theoretically, the national question cannot be subsumed under socialism, which is about a struggle between two irreconcilable forces such as capital and labour, whereas the national question is about a coalition of classes against a common oppressor.[72] This is why the ANC/SACP speak of a two-stage theory: the two stages can be carried out at the same time. However, to subsume the national question under a socialist perspective is to presuppose that socialism was on the cards to begin with, whereas in South Africa that was not the case. Notwithstanding the existence of a proletariat and a trade union movement, Mafeje reasons that this is not a socialist constituency, but a 'militant nationalist constituency' – not revolutionary, but progressive insofar as it espouses social democracy. Material conditions in South Africa may be ripe for a socialist transformation, but what is lacking are committed agents to advance it.

Strategically and tactically, Mafeje argues, there is no value in socialists marching ahead of the popular classes, insisting on socialism on their behalf. Mafeje seems to have wanted the revolutionary situation to arise of its own accord, rather than socialists having actively created conditions for it. But he goes on to argue that, in the meantime, the available avenue for African socialists was not only social democracy, but also regional integration, which would 'obviate the negative implications of "socialism" in one country, as Cuba got to know in its torturous path to socialism'.[73] Mafeje is saying that socialism in a country is meaningless without regional integration – socialism in its neighbouring countries. In spite of putting forward social democracy as a placeholder for socialism, Mafeje is well aware that social democracy 'is not a panacea for all social ills in society'.

It is extremely important to contextualise this apparent deviation by Mafeje, from socialism to social democracy. He advanced these ideas in the mid-1990s in the wake of liberal democracy, at a time when radical intellectuals like him felt defeated. His words are instructive: 'My plea is that under the determinate conditions in Southern Africa in particular, and in Africa in general, social democracy should be seen, if not as a necessary condition for a socialist transformation, as a necessary condition for testing the limits of the capitalist model of accumulation and distribution of value. This is more of a strategic consideration than a theoretical postulate.'[74]

It makes sense to call it a tactical rather than a strategic consideration because a strategy is long-standing or permanent, whereas tactics change over time, based on the best possible way to achieve the strategy. Therefore, for Mafeje: 'If in the face of apparent defeat we cannot maximise our gains, then it is imperative that we minimise our losses.'[75]

In his foreword to Mafeje's *In Search of an Alternative*, Ibbo Mandaza says: 'For Archie Mafeje, therefore, *the search for an alternative* is but this search for that *lost identity, the inner self*.'[76] Insofar as this is true, Mafeje's writings are grounded not only in the search for political and economic freedom, but also in the search for intellectual and cultural liberation. Mafeje understood very well that in the post-independence period Africans had to deal with a society that suffered not only from economic poverty, but also from intellectual and cultural poverty. Intellectual and cultural liberation is worth fighting for, a struggle as legitimate as any other.

The genius of Mafeje is that he was never content merely to regurgitate received theory. It is partly because of this that some readers could doubt that he was a Marxist. Although he *was* a Marxist, Mafeje wanted to think *with* Marx, rather than to apply Marx's ideas. In this regard, he saw Marx as an intellectual peer, rather than an intellectual leader. Although he learned a great deal from the European canon, Mafeje also wanted African intellectuals and revolutionaries to liberate themselves from it. Mafeje's intellectual vigilance told him that liberation was not only about marching through the streets, but also about contributing to knowledge through a critique of orthodox or dominant narratives.

Notes

Introduction

1   I give credit to the Rhodes Must Fall and Fees Must Fall movements for centring knowledge decolonisation, but I take seriously the Fanonian view that knowledge can never be completely decolonised in a society that is not itself decolonised – see Frantz Fanon, *The Wretched of the Earth* (London: Penguin Books, 1963), especially the chapters 'Concerning Violence' and 'On National Culture'.

2   Jimi Adesina, 'Realising the Vision: The Discursive and Institutional Challenges of Becoming an African University', *African Sociological Review* 9.1 (2005), 32.

3   Functionalism in anthropological and sociological literature is the theoretical perspective that holds that society is a 'complex system' whose parts operate to promote stability and solidarity. Theoretically, the works of social anthropologists of the 1950s and 1960s (such as Monica Wilson) were of this intellectual persuasion. Politically, they were of a liberal bent. Mafeje argued that this work was not only complicit in colonialism and imperialism, but also termed it 'liberal functionalism'. Note, however, that Mafeje adopted Marxism and rejected functionalism as inherently liberal, even though some kinds of Marxist frameworks are functionalist. This is not to say he adopted functionalist Marxism.

4   Archie Mafeje, *The Theory and Ethnography of African Social Formations: The Case of the Interlacustrine Kingdoms* (Dakar: Codesria Book Series, 1991), 11.

5   For use of this terminology, see South African Communist Party, *The Road to South African Freedom* (London: Inkululeko Publications, 1962).

Chapter 1

1   Archie Mafeje, 'The Ideology of "Tribalism"', *Journal of Modern African Studies* 9 (1971), 252–261.

2   Archie Mafeje, *The Theory and Ethnography of African Social Formations: The Case of the Interlacustrine Kingdoms* (Dakar: Codesria Book Series, 1991).

3   An article of 1998 agreed that 'it is important to recall that Mafeje has never said that tribes were simply a figment of the European imagination, but rather that European observers generalised the notion of tribe to be an inherent feature of all African social formations'. John Sharp, 'Who Speaks for Whom? A Response to Archie Mafeje's *Anthropology and Independent Africans: Suicide or End of an Era?*' *African Sociological Review* 2.1 (1998), 69.

4   Jimi Adesina, 'Archie Mafeje and the Pursuit of Endogeneity: Against Alterity and Extroversion', *Africa Development* 33.4 (2008), 133–152.

5   Monica Wilson and Archie Mafeje, *Langa: A Study of Social Groups in an African Township* (Cape Town: Oxford University Press, 1963), 11.

6   Jimi Adesina, 'Realising the Vision: The Discursive and Institutional Challenges of Becoming an African University', *African Sociological Review* 9.1 (2005), 23–39.

7   Bernard Magubane, 'Whose Memory – Whose History? The Illusion of Liberal and Radical Historical Debates', in *History Making and Present-Day Politics: The Meaning of Collective Memory in South Africa*, ed. Hans Erik Stolten (Uppsala: The Nordic Africa Institute, 2007), 254.

8   Bernard Magubane, 'Crisis in African Sociology', *East African Journal* 5.12 (1968), 23.

9   Magubane, 'Crisis', 33.

10 Archie Mafeje, 'A Chief Visits Town', *Journal of Local Administration Overseas* 2 (1963), 88.

11 Mafeje, 'Chief Visits', 93.

12 Mafeje, 'Chief Visits', 97.

13 Archie Mafeje, 'The Role of the Bard in a Contemporary African Community', *Journal of African Languages* 6.3 (1967), 193–223.

14 In the isiXhosa word *imbongi*, the '*i*' means 'the', so it would be tautological to include the English article before the word.

15 Mafeje, 'Role of the Bard', 193.

16 Mafeje, 'Role of the Bard', 195.

17 Mafeje, 'Role of the Bard', 196–197.

18 Isaac Schapera, *Praise Poems of Tswana Chiefs* (Oxford: Clarendon Press, 1965).

19 Mafeje, 'Ideology', 253.

20 Philip Hugh Gulliver, 'Introduction', in *Tradition and Transition in East Africa: Studies of the Tribal Element in the Modern Era*, ed. Philip Hugh Gulliver (London: Routledge & Kegan Paul, 1969), 5–40.

21 Quoted in Mafeje, 'Ideology', 254; emphasis in original.

22 Magubane, 'Crisis'; Bernard Magubane, 'Pluralism and Conflict Situations in Africa: A New Look', *African Social Research* 7 (1969), 529–554; Bernard

Magubane, 'A Critical Look at Indices Used in the Study of Social Change in Colonial Africa', *Current Anthropology* 12.4–5 (1971), 419–445.

23 Arnold L. Epstein, *Politics in an Urban African Community* (Manchester: Manchester University Press, 1958).

24 Mafeje, 'Ideology', 256.

25 Mafeje, 'Ideology', 257.

26 Meyer Fortes and Edward E. Evans-Pritchard, eds, *African Political Systems* (London: Oxford University Press, 1940).

27 Quoted in Mafeje, 'Ideology', 257.

28 Gulliver, 'Introduction', 24.

29 Mafeje, 'Ideology', 258; emphasis added.

30 Archie Mafeje, 'Tribalism', in *The Oxford Companion to Politics of the World*, ed. Joel Krieger (New York: Oxford University Press, 1993), 919; emphasis in original.

31 Adesina, 'Archie Mafeje', 137.

32 Mafeje, 'Ideology', 258–259.

33 Mafeje, 'Ideology', 259.

34 Mafeje, *Theory and Ethnography*, 107.

35 Mafeje, *Theory and Ethnography*, 108.

36 Mafeje, *Theory and Ethnography*, 39.

37 Mafeje, 'Tribalism'.

38 Mafeje, 'Tribalism', 919; emphasis in original.

39 Archie Mafeje, 'The Bathos of Tendentious Historiography: A Review of Joe Slovo's *Has Socialism Failed?' Southern Africa Political & Economic Monthly* (*SAPEM*) 3.10 (1990), 43; emphasis in original.

40 Epstein, *Politics*; Max Gluckman, *Order and Rebellion in Tribal Africa* (London: Oxford University Press, 1963); Leo Kuper and Garfield Smith, *Pluralism in Africa* (Los Angeles: University of California Press, 1965); Philip Mayer, *Townsmen or Tribesmen (Xhosa in Town)* (Cape Town: Oxford University Press, 1961); Pierre van den Berghe, ed., *Africa: Social Problems of Conflict and Change* (San Francisco: Chandler Publishing, 1965).

41 Magubane, 'Pluralism', 529.

42 Epstein, *Politics*; Gluckman, *Order*; Kuper and Smith, *Pluralism*; Mayer, *Townsmen*; Van den Berghe, *Africa*.

43 Magubane, 'Pluralism', 534; emphasis in original.

44 John S. Furnivall, *Colonial Policy and Practice* (Cambridge: Cambridge University Press, 1948).

45 Magubane, 'Pluralism', 546.

46 Archie Mafeje, 'Multi-Party Democracy and Ethnic Divisions in Africa: Are They Compatible?' in *Breaking Barriers, Creating New Hopes: Democracy, Civil*

Society and Good Governance in Africa, ed. Abdalla S. Bujra and Said Adejumobi (Trenton, NJ: Africa World Press, 2002), 55.

47   Peter Ekeh, 'Social Anthropology and Two Contrasting Uses of Tribalism in Africa', *Comparative Studies in Society and History* 32.4 (1990), 661.

48   Mafeje, 'Multi-Party Democracy', 56.

49   Mafeje, 'Multi-Party Democracy', 57.

50   Mafeje, 'Multi-Party Democracy', 57.

51   Mafeje, 'Multi-Party Democracy', 57.

52   Mafeje, 'Multi-Party Democracy', 58; emphasis in original.

53   Mafeje, 'Multi-Party Democracy', 60.

54   Mafeje, 'Multi-Party Democracy', 63.

55   In Kenya, *majimboism* is a kiSwahili word that refers to political devolution or decentralisation of power from national level to the country's provinces or regions. The controversy around the term is that devolution of power is ethno-regional and therefore it cemented ethnicity, rather than doing away with it.

56   Claude Ake, 'What Is the Problem of Ethnicity in Africa?' *Transformation* 22.1 (1993), 1–14; Okwudiba Nnoli, *Ethnic Politics in Nigeria* (Enugu: Fourth Dimension, 1978); Okwudiba Nnoli, *Ethnic Politics in Africa* (Ibadan: Vintage Press, 1989); Okwudiba Nnoli, *Ethnic Conflict in Africa* (Dakar: Codesria Book Series, 1998).

57   Mafeje, 'Multi-Party Democracy', 73.

58   Mafeje, 'Multi-Party Democracy', 74.

59   Mafeje, 'Multi-Party Democracy', 80.

60   Mafeje, 'Multi-Party Democracy', 81.

61   Mafeje, 'Multi-Party Democracy', 83.

Chapter 2

1   See Archie Mafeje, 'Large-Scale Farming in Buganda', in *The Anthropology of Development in Sub-Saharan Africa*, ed. David Brokensha and Marion Pearsall (Lexington: University Press of Kentucky, 1969), 22–30; Archie Mafeje, 'The Ideology of "Tribalism"', *Journal of Modern African Studies* 9.1 (1971), 252–261; Archie Mafeje, 'The Fallacy of Dual Economies Revisited: A Case of East, Central and Southern Africa', *East Africa Journal* 9.2 (1972), 30–34; Archie Mafeje, 'Agrarian Revolution and the Land Question in Buganda', in *A Century of Change in Eastern Africa*, ed. William Arens (The Hague: Mouton Publishers, 1976), 23–46.

2   Archie Mafeje, 'Religion, Class and Ideology in South Africa', in *Religion and Social Change in Southern Africa: Anthropological Essays in Honour of Monica Wilson*, ed. Michael Whisson and Martin West (Cape Town: David Philip, 1975), 164–184; Archie Mafeje, 'The Problem of Anthropology in Historical

Perspective: An Inquiry into the Growth of the Social Sciences', *Canadian Journal of African Studies* 10.2 (1976), 307–333.

3   Mafeje, 'Problem of Anthropology'; Archie Mafeje, *Anthropology and Independent Africans: Suicide or End of an Era?* (Dakar: Codesria Monograph Series No. 4/96, 1996).

4   Mafeje, 'Religion, Class and Ideology', 164.

5   Mafeje, 'Religion, Class and Ideology', 164–165.

6   Mafeje, 'Religion, Class and Ideology', 165.

7   Philip Mayer, 'A Comment on Magubane's "Indices of Social Change in Africa"', *Current Anthropology* 12.4–5 (1971), 433.

8   Lewis R. Gordon, 'The Problem of Biography in the Study of the Thought of Black Intellectuals', *Small Axe* 4 (1998), 47–63; Lewis R. Gordon, *Existentia Africana: Understanding Africana Existential Thought* (New York: Routledge, 2000).

9   Archie Mafeje, 'Development Literature and Writers from Underdeveloped Countries: A Comment on Ayse Trak', *Current Anthropology* 26.1 (1985), 97.

10   Bernard Magubane, 'A Critical Look at Indices Used in the Study of Social Change in Colonial Africa', *Current Anthropology* 12.4–5 (1971), 419.

11   Magubane, 'Critical Look', 419–420.

12   Archie Mafeje, *Science, Ideology and Development: Three Essays on Development Theory* (Uppsala: Scandinavian Institute of African Studies, 1978), 43, footnote 1.

13   Mafeje, 'Religion, Class and Ideology', 175.

14   Mafeje, 'Religion, Class and Ideology', 182; emphasis in original.

15   Mafeje, 'Religion, Class and Ideology', 184.

16   Mafeje, 'Problem of Anthropology', 308.

17   Mafeje, 'Problem of Anthropology', 309; emphasis in original.

18   Mafeje, 'Problem of Anthropology', 310.

19   Frantz Fanon, *The Wretched of the Earth* (London: Penguin Books, 1963), 76.

20   Mafeje, 'Problem of Anthropology', 311.

21   Mafeje, 'Problem of Anthropology', 312.

22   Mafeje, 'Problem of Anthropology', 314.

23   Mafeje, 'Problem of Anthropology', 312.

24   Archie Mafeje, *The National Question in Southern African Settler Societies* (Harare: SAPES Monograph Series No. 6, 1997).

25   Mafeje, *National Question*, 7.

26   Mafeje, 'Problem of Anthropology', 332–333.

27   Mafeje, *Anthropology and Independent Africans*, 26.

28   The idiographic approach emphasises an individual's unique subjective experience, whereas the nomothetic approach focuses on the numerical and statistical to draw universal conclusions.

29 Archie Mafeje, 'On the Articulation of Modes of Production', *Journal of Southern African Studies* 8.1 (1981), 123–138.

30 Michael Morris, 'The Development of Capitalism in South African Agriculture: Class Struggle in the Countryside', in *The Articulation of Modes of Production*, ed. Harold Wolpe (London: Routledge & Kegan Paul, 1980), 425–456; Harold Wolpe, 'Capitalism and Cheap Labour-Power in South Africa: From Segregation to Apartheid', in *The Articulation of Modes of Production*, ed. Harold Wolpe (London: Routledge & Kegan Paul, 1980), 289–320.

31 Mafeje, 'On the Articulation', 132.

32 Mafeje, 'On the Articulation', 133.

33 Harold Wolpe, 'Introduction', in *The Articulation of Modes of Production*, ed. Harold Wolpe (London: Routledge & Kegan Paul, 1980), 35.

34 Quoted in Mafeje, 'On the Articulation', 133.

35 Mafeje, 'On the Articulation', 127; emphasis in original.

36 Mafeje, 'On the Articulation', 127.

37 See, for example, Claude Meillassoux, 'From Reproduction to Production', *Economy & Society* 1.1 (1972), 93–105; Claude Meillassoux, 'The Social Organisation of the Peasantry: The Economic Basis of Kinship', *Journal of Peasant Studies* 1.1 (1973), 81–90; Pierre-Philippe Rey, 'The Lineage Mode of Production', *Critique of Anthropology* 1 (1975), 27–79.

38 Even during the peasant rebellions of the late 1950s and the early 1960s, the peasants were *not* protesting for halving of their quit-rent land, which they knew was associated with individual family units, but with limitation of stock and fencing of grazing grounds.

39 Mafeje, 'On the Articulation', 130.

40 Archie Mafeje, *Studies in Imperialism: A Discourse in Methodology, Research Methods and Techniques* (Harare: University of Zimbabwe Department of Economics, Law and Political & Administrative Studies Discussion Paper Series, 1986), 10.

41 Mafeje, *Studies in Imperialism*, 11.

42 Mafeje, *Studies in Imperialism*, 11–12.

43 Mafeje, *Studies in Imperialism*, 12.

44 Mafeje, *Studies in Imperialism*, 16.

45 Jimi Adesina, 'Archie Mafeje and the Pursuit of Endogeneity: Against Alterity and Extroversion', *Africa Development* 33.4 (2008), 133–152.

46 Mafeje, *Studies in Imperialism*, 16–17.

47 Mafeje, *Studies in Imperialism*, 17–18; emphasis in original.

48 Mafeje, *Studies in Imperialism*, 18.

49 Mafeje, *Studies in Imperialism*, 19; emphasis in original.

50   Oyeronke Oyewumi, *The Invention of Women: Making an African Sense of Western Gender Discourse* (Minneapolis, MN: University of Minnesota Press, 1997).

51   Mafeje, *Anthropology and Independent Africans*, 1.

52   Mafeje, *Anthropology and Independent Africans*, 2; emphasis in original.

53   Godwin Murunga, 'Review: Archie Mafeje's *Anthropology and Independent Africans: Suicide or End of an Era?' Africa Development* 23.1 (1998), 177.

54   Helen MacDonald, 'A Conversation: Subaltern Studies in South Asia and Post-Colonial Anthropology in Africa', *Anthropology Southern Africa* 23.1–2 (2009), 59–68.

55   Adesina, 'Archie Mafeje', 144.

56   Dani Nabudere, 'Archie Mafeje and the Social Sciences in Africa', *Coedesria Bulletin* 3/4 (2008), 8–10; Dani Nabudere, *Archie Mafeje: The Scholar and Political Activist* (Pretoria: AISA Archie Mafeje Memorial Lecture Series No. 1, 2010); Dani Nabudere, *Archie Mafeje: Scholar, Activist and Thinker* (Pretoria: AISA, 2011); Helmi Sharawy, 'The End of Anthropology: The African Debate on the Universality of Social Research and its "Indigenisation" – A Study Dedicated to Archie Mafeje', *Codesria Bulletin* 3/4 (2008), 15–20; Helmi Sharawy, *Political and Social Thought in Africa* (Dakar: Codesria Book Series, 2014).

57   Sharawy, 'End of Anthropology', 19.

58   Mafeje, *Anthropology and Independent Africans*, 28; emphasis in original.

59   Archie Mafeje, 'Conversations and Confrontations with My Reviewers', *African Sociological Review* 2.2 (1998), 102.

60   Mafeje, *Anthropology and Independent Africans*, 19; emphasis added.

61   Akinsola Akiwowo, 'Trend Report: Sociology in Africa Today', *Current Sociology* 28.2 (1980), 3–73; Akinsola Akiwowo, 'Indigenous Sociologies: Extending the Scope of the Argument', *International Sociology* 14.2 (1999), 115–138.

62   Ifi Amadiume, *Male Daughters, Female Husbands: Gender and Sex in an African Society* (London: Zed Books, 1987).

63   Mafeje, *Anthropology and Independent Africans*; Archie Mafeje, *Anthropology in Post-Independence Africa: End of an Era or the Problem of Self-Redefinition* (Nairobi: Heinrich Boll Foundation, 2001).

64   Archie Mafeje, 'African Socio-Cultural Formations in the 21st Century', *African Development Review* 7.2 (1995), 168.

Chapter 3

1   Samir Amin, 'Homage to Archie Mafeje', *Codesria Bulletin* 3–4 (2008), 12.

2   'Interlacustrine' refers to an area that is situated between lakes. In this particular instance, it refers to the eastern African region bounded by lakes Victoria, Kyoga, Albert, Edward and Tanganyika.

3   Archie Mafeje, *The Theory and Ethnography of African Social Formations: The Case of the Interlacustrine Kingdoms* (Dakar: Codesria Book Series, 1991), 18–19.

4   Audrey Isabel Richards, ed., *East African Chiefs: A Study of Political Development in Some Uganda and Tanganyika Tribes* (London: Faber & Faber, 1960).

5   The same holds true in the Eastern Cape, South Africa, where amaXhosa speak the same language but in practice are divided into independent chiefdoms, such as amaMpondo and amaBhaca.

6   Mafeje, *Theory and Ethnography*, 14. Bahima and Bahuma refer to pastoralists and the two terms are of the same linguistic group but different dialects. In this chapter I use them interchangeably.

7   Samir Amin, 'Underdevelopment and Dependence in Black Africa: Origins and Contemporary Forms', *Journal of Modern African Studies* 10.4 (1972), 503–524; Étienne Balibar, 'The Basic Concepts of Historical Materialism', in *Reading Capital*, ed. Louis Althusser and Étienne Balibar (London: New Left Books, 1970), 199–209.

8   Balibar, 'Basic Concepts', 207; emphasis in original.

9   Amin, 'Underdevelopment and Dependence', 507; emphasis in original.

10 Mafeje, *Theory and Ethnography*, 33.

11 Amin, 'Homage to Archie Mafeje', 14.

12 Mafeje, *Theory and Ethnography*, 17.

13 Mafeje, *Theory and Ethnography*, 18.

14 Bernard Magubane, 'Crisis in African Sociology', *East African Journal* 5.12 (1968), 21–40.

15 Mafeje, *Theory and Ethnography*, 5; emphasis in original.

16 Mafeje, *Theory and Ethnography*, 21.

17 Mahmood Mamdani, *When Victims Become Killers: Colonialism, Nativism, and the Genocide in Rwanda* (Princeton: Princeton University Press, 2001), 46.

18 Mafeje, *Theory and Ethnography*, 19.

19 Mafeje, *Theory and Ethnography*, 22.

20 Mafeje, *Theory and Ethnography*, 22.

21 John Hanning Speke, *Journal of the Discovery of the Source of the Nile* (Edinburgh: William Blackwood and Sons, 1863).

22 Mafeje, *Theory and Ethnography*, 32.

23 Mafeje, *Theory and Ethnography*, 11.

24 Mafeje, *Theory and Ethnography*, 37.

25 Richards, *East African Chiefs*.

26 Mafeje, *Theory and Ethnography*, 38.

27 Claude Meillassoux, 'From Reproduction to Production', *Economy & Society* 1.1 (1972), 93–105; Claude Meillassoux, 'The Social Organisation of the Peasantry: The Economic Basis of Kinship', *Journal of Peasant Studies* 1.1 (1973), 81–90.

28 Mafeje, *Theory and Ethnography*, 47.

29 Mafeje, *Theory and Ethnography*, 49.

30 Mafeje, *Theory and Ethnography*, 52.

31 Mafeje, *Theory and Ethnography*, 52–53.

32 Mafeje, *Theory and Ethnography*, 56.

33 Mafeje, *Theory and Ethnography*, 58.

34 Mafeje, *Theory and Ethnography*, 60.

35 Mafeje, *Theory and Ethnography*, 61.

36 Mafeje, *Theory and Ethnography*, 65.

37 Mafeje, *Theory and Ethnography*, 66.

38 Jack Goody, *Technology, Tradition and the State in Africa* (London: Oxford University Press, 1971).

39 Mafeje, *Theory and Ethnography*, 68.

40 Mafeje, *Theory and Ethnography*, 70.

41 Mafeje, *Theory and Ethnography*, 73.

42 Mafeje, *Theory and Ethnography*, 76.

43 Mafeje, *Theory and Ethnography*, 82.

44 Mafeje, *Theory and Ethnography*, 84.

45 Mafeje, *Theory and Ethnography*, 85.

46 Mafeje, *Theory and Ethnography*, 85.

47 Catherine Coquery-Vidrovitch, 'Research on an African Mode of Production', in *African Social Studies: A Radical Reader*, ed. Peter C.W. Gutkind and Peter Waterman (London: Heinemann, 1977), 77–92.

48 Meillassoux, 'Social Organisation'.

49 Samir Amin, *Class and Nation: Historically and in the Current Crisis* (London: Heinemann, 1980).

50 Mafeje, *Theory and Ethnography*, 86.

51 Mafeje, *Theory and Ethnography*, 87.

52 Amin, *Class and Nation*, 50.

53 Mafeje, *Theory and Ethnography*, 92.

54 Amin, *Class and Nation*, 49–50.

55 Mafeje, *Theory and Ethnography*, 94.

56 Mafeje, *Theory and Ethnography*, 98.

57 Mafeje, *Theory and Ethnography*, 99.

58 Mafeje, *Theory and Ethnography*, 105.

59 Mafeje, *Theory and Ethnography*, 107.

60 Mafeje, *Theory and Ethnography*, 116.

61 Archie Mafeje, 'On the Articulation of Modes of Production', *Journal of Southern African Studies* 8.1 (1981), 130.

62 Mafeje, *Theory and Ethnography*, 116.

63 Mafeje, *Theory and Ethnography*, 122.

64 Mafeje, *Theory and Ethnography*, 122–123.

65 Mafeje, *Theory and Ethnography*, 123.

66 Mafeje, *Theory and Ethnography*, 124.

67 Archie Mafeje, *Anthropology and Independent Africans: Suicide or End of an Era?* (Dakar: Codesria Monograph Series No. 4/96, 1996), 23.

68 Mafeje, *Anthropology and Independent Africans*, 26.

69 Mafeje, *Anthropology and Independent Africans*, 28.

70 Mafeje, *Anthropology and Independent Africans*, 28.

71 Mafeje, *Anthropology and Independent Africans*, 33.

Chapter 4

1 Archie Mafeje, 'Large-Scale Farming in Buganda', in *The Anthropology of Development in Sub-Saharan Africa*, ed. David Brokensha and Marion Pearsall (Lexington: University Press of Kentucky, 1969), 22–30; Archie Mafeje, 'Agrarian Revolution and the Land Question in Buganda' (The Hague: Institute of Social Studies Occasional Paper No. 32, 1973), hereafter 'OP'; Archie Mafeje, 'Agrarian Revolution and the Land Question in Buganda', in *A Century of Change in Eastern Africa*, ed. William Arens (The Hague: Mouton Publishers, 1976), 23–46, hereafter 'Arens'; Archie Mafeje, *'African Agriculture: The Next 25 Years*: Old Problems, Old Solutions and Scientific Foibles', *Africa Development* 12.2 (1987), 5–34; Archie Mafeje, 'African Households and Prospects for Agricultural Revival in Sub-Saharan Africa' (Dakar: Codesria Working Paper No. 22/91, 1991); Archie Mafeje, *The Agrarian Question, Access to Land, and Peasant Responses in Sub-Saharan Africa* (Geneva: UNRISD, 2003).

2 Samir Amin, 'Contemporary Imperialism and the Agrarian Question', *Agrarian South: Journal of Political Economy* 1.1 (2012), 11–26; Sam Moyo, Praveen Jha and Paris Yeros, 'The Classical Agrarian Question: Myth, Reality and Relevance Today', *Agrarian South: Journal of Political Economy* 2.1 (2013), 93–119.

3 Sam Moyo, 'Debating the African Land Question with Archie Mafeje', *Agrarian South: Journal of Political Economy* 7.2 (2018), 214.

4 Moyo, 'Debating the African Land Question', 211.

5 Amin, 'Contemporary Imperialism', 19–20.

6 Mafeje, *'African Agriculture'*, 56.

7 Moyo, Jha and Yeros, 'Classical Agrarian Question', 93.

8 Amin, 'Contemporary Imperialism', 20.

9 Syed Farid Alatas, 'Academic Dependency and Global Division of Labour', *Current Sociology* 51.6 (2003), 599–613.

10   Paulin Hountondji, 'Scientific Dependence: Its Nature and Ways to Overcome It', in *Cultural Development, Science and Technology in Sub-Saharan Africa*, ed. Klaus Gottstein and Gotz Link (Baden-Baden: Nomos, 1986), 109–113; Paulin Hountondji, 'Scientific Dependence in Africa Today', *Research in African Literatures* 21.3 (1990), 5–15.

11   Syed Hussein Alatas, 'Intellectual Imperialism: Definition, Traits, and Problems', *Southeast Asian Journal of Social Science* 28.1 (2000), 23–45.

12   Mafeje, *Agrarian Question*, 94.

13   Moyo, Jha and Yeros, 'Classical Agrarian Question', 94.

14   Mafeje, *Agrarian Question*.

15   Mafeje, 'Agrarian Revolution', OP.

16   Mafeje, 'Agrarian Revolution', Arens, 23.

17   Mafeje, 'Agrarian Revolution', OP, 5.

18   Mafeje, 'Agrarian Revolution', OP, 6.

19   The basic unit of the mailo system is a square mile, hence the derivation of mailo, which is also equivalent to 640 acres.

20   Mafeje, 'Agrarian Revolution', Arens, 28.

21   Mafeje, 'Agrarian Revolution', OP, 8; emphasis in original.

22   Mafeje, 'Agrarian Revolution', Arens, 30.

23   Mafeje, 'Agrarian Revolution', OP, 10.

24   Mafeje, 'Agrarian Revolution', Arens, 33.

25   Mafeje, 'Agrarian Revolution', OP, 12.

26   Mafeje, 'Agrarian Revolution', Arens, 34; emphasis in original.

27   Mafeje, 'Large-Scale Farming', 22.

28   Mafeje, 'Agrarian Revolution', Arens, 36; emphasis in original.

29   Mafeje, 'Agrarian Revolution', OP, 15; emphasis in original.

30   Christopher C. Wrigley, 'The Changing Economic Structure in Buganda', in *The King's Men: Leadership and Status in Buganda on the Eve of Independence*, ed. Lloyd A. Fallers (London: Oxford University Press, 1964), 16–63.

31   Mafeje, 'Agrarian Revolution', OP, 16; emphasis in original. 'Jim Crow' refers to the racial segregation or anti-black laws that operated mainly in the southern states of the United States between 1877 and 1965. These laws meant that better-paying jobs were reserved for whites while small and low-paid jobs were reserved for black people.

32   Mafeje, 'Agrarian Revolution', OP, 17.

33   Mafeje, 'Agrarian Revolution', OP, 19.

34   Mafeje, 'Agrarian Revolution', Arens, 44; emphasis in original.

35   FAO (Food and Agriculture Organization), *African Agriculture: The Next 25 Years* (Rome: FAO, 1986).

36 Mafeje, 'African Agriculture', 9.

37 Mafeje, 'African Agriculture', 12.

38 Mafeje, 'African Agriculture', 13.

39 Moyo, Jha and Yeros, 'Classical Agrarian Question', 95.

40 Mafeje, 'African Agriculture', 14.

41 Mafeje, 'African Agriculture', 14.

42 Mafeje, 'African Agriculture', 14–15.

43 Mafeje, 'African Agriculture', 16.

44 Amin, 'Contemporary Imperialism'; Moyo, 'Debating the African Land Question'; Moyo, Jha and Yeros, 'Classical Agrarian Question'.

45 Amin, 'Contemporary Imperialism', 14.

46 Mafeje, 'African Households'.

47 Mafeje, 'African Agriculture', 18.

48 Amin, 'Contemporary Imperialism', 16.

49 Mafeje, 'African Agriculture', 18.

50 Mafeje, 'African Agriculture', 19.

51 Mafeje, Agrarian Question.

52 Sam Moyo, 'African Land Questions, Agrarian Transitions and the State' (Dakar: Codesria Working Paper Series, 2008), 1.

53 Sam Moyo, interview with the author, 25 May 2015, Pretoria, South Africa. According to Moyo, the term 'peasant' is used very casually in liberal bourgeois social sciences; he says people are referred to as peasants merely because they live in the countryside. For him and Mafeje, the concept is not just an abstract category; it has a concrete referent and the two of them use it in the classical Leninist sense to mean petty landholders.

54 Mafeje, Agrarian Question, 4.

55 FAO (Food and Agriculture Organization), The Dynamics of Land Tenure and Agrarian Systems in Africa: Case Studies from Ghana, Kenya, Madagascar and Togo (Rome: FAO, 1989).

56 Mafeje, Agrarian Question, 4.

57 Mafeje, Agrarian Question, 5.

58 Mafeje, Agrarian Question, 5.

59 Mafeje, Agrarian Question, 6.

60 Mafeje, Agrarian Question, 6.

61 Mafeje, Agrarian Question, 7.

62 Samir Amin, Class and Nation: Historically and in the Current Crisis (London: Heinemann, 1980).

63 Mafeje, Agrarian Question, 8.

64 Thandika Mkandawire, 'Economic Crisis in Malawi', in *Recession in Africa*, ed. Jerker Carlsson (Uppsala: Scandinavian Institute of African Studies, 1983), 28–47.

65 Mafeje, *Agrarian Question*, 8.

66 Mafeje, *Agrarian Question*, 9.

67 Mafeje, *Agrarian Question*, 10.

68 Cited in Mafeje, *Agrarian Question*, 11.

69 Mafeje, *Agrarian Question*, 11.

70 Mafeje, *Agrarian Question*, 11.

71 Mafeje, *Agrarian Question*, 11.

72 Mafeje, *Agrarian Question*, 13.

73 Elliot Berg, *Accelerated Development in Sub-Saharan Africa: An Agenda for Africa* (Washington: World Bank, 1981).

74 Economic Commission for Africa (United Nations), *African Alternative Framework to Structural Adjustment Programmes for Socio-Economic Recovery and Transformation* (Addis Ababa: United Nations Economic Commission for Africa, 1990); Thandika Mkandawire and Charles Soludo, *Our Continent, Our Future: African Perspectives on Structural Adjustment* (Dakar: Codesria Book Series, 1999).

Chapter 5

1 Archie Mafeje, 'Peasant Organisations in Africa: A Potential Dialogue between Economists and Sociologists – Some Theoretical/Methodological Observations', *Codesria Bulletin* 1 (1993), 14–17.

2 Mafeje, 'Peasant Organisations', 14.

3 Dessalegn Rahmato, 'On Peasant Studies: A Reply to Archie Mafeje', *Codesria Bulletin* 2 (1993), 23.

4 Sam Moyo, 'Peasant Organisations and Rural Civil Society in Africa: An Introduction', in *Peasant Organisations and Democratisation in Africa*, ed. Sam Moyo and Mahmoud Romdhane (Dakar: Codesria Book Series, 2002), 1–26.

5 Archie Mafeje, 'Peasants in Sub-Saharan Africa', *Africa Development* 10.3 (1985), 28–39.

6 Monica Wilson, 'The Growth of Peasant Communities', in *The Oxford History of South Africa*, ed. Monica Wilson and Leonard M. Thompson (Oxford: Oxford University Press, 1971), 49–103.

7 Wilson, 'Growth of Peasant Communities', 49.

8 Wilson, 'Growth of Peasant Communities', 50.

9 Mafeje, 'Peasants in Sub-Saharan Africa', 29.

10 John Saul and Roger Woods, 'African Peasantries', in *Peasants and Peasant Societies*, ed. Teodor Shanin (Harmondsworth: Penguin, 1971), 106.

11 Ken Post, 'Peasantisation in Western Africa', in *African Social Studies: A Radical Reader*, ed. Peter C.W. Gutkind and Peter Waterman (London: Heinemann, 1977), 242; emphasis in original.

12 Mafeje, 'Peasants in Sub-Saharan Africa', 30.

13 Colin Bundy, *The Rise and Fall of the South African Peasantry* (London: Heinemann, 1979); Stanley Trapido, 'Landlord and Tenant in a Colonial Economy: The Transvaal 1880–1910', *Journal of Southern African Studies* 5.1 (1978), 26–58; Wilson, 'Growth of Peasant Communities'.

14 Mafeje, 'Peasants in Sub-Saharan Africa', 31.

15 Archie Mafeje, 'On the Articulation of Modes of Production', *Journal of Southern African Studies* 8.1 (1981), 123–138.

16 Mafeje, 'Peasants in Sub-Saharan Africa', 32.

17 *Ujamaa* was a Tanzanian quasi-socialist economic system from the 1960s to the mid-1980s based on village self-help collectives and co-operatives. Then president of Tanzania, Julius Nyerere referred to it as 'African socialism'. However, there is no agreement among Marxists that this was socialism in the Marxist sense.

18 Mafeje, 'Peasants in Sub-Saharan Africa', 32–33.

19 Samir Amin, 'Underdevelopment and Dependence in Black Africa: Origins and Contemporary Forms', *Journal of Modern African Studies* 10.4 (1972), 503–524; Samir Amin, 'The Dynamic and Limitations of Agrarian Capitalism in Black Africa', in *African Social Studies: A Radical Reader*, ed. Peter C.W. Gutkind and Peter Waterman (London: Heinemann, 1977), 154–159; Catherine Coquery-Vidrovitch, 'Research on an African Mode of Production', in *African Social Studies: A Radical Reader*, ed. Peter C.W. Gutkind and Peter Waterman (London: Heinemann, 1977), 77–92; Polly Hill, *Studies in Rural Capitalism in West Africa* (Cambridge: Cambridge University Press, 1970); Post, 'Peasantisation in Western Africa'.

20 Mafeje, 'Peasants in Sub-Saharan Africa', 36.

21 Sam Moyo, Praveen Jha and Paris Yeros, 'The Classical Agrarian Question: Myth, Reality and Relevance Today', *Agrarian South: Journal of Political Economy* 2.1 (2013), 94.

22 Archie Mafeje, 'Food for Security and Peace in the SADCC Region', in *Africa: Perspectives on Peace and Development*, ed. Emmanuel Hansen (London: Zed Books, 1987), 183–211.

23 Mafeje, 'Food for Security', 205.

24 Archie Mafeje, 'The Agrarian Question and Food Production in Southern Africa', in *Food Security Issues in Southern Africa*, ed. Kwesi K. Prah (Maseru: Institute of Southern African Studies Series, 1988), 92–124.

25   Mafeje, 'Agrarian Question', 92.

26   Amin, 'Underdevelopment and Dependence'; Amin, 'Dynamic and Limitations'; Coquery-Vidrovitch, 'Research on an African Mode of Production'; Claude Meillassoux, 'The Social Organisation of the Peasantry: The Economic Basis of Kinship', *Journal of Peasant Studies* 1.1 (1973), 81–90; Pierre-Philippe Rey, 'The Lineage Mode of Production', *Critique of Anthropology* 1.3 (1975), 27–79.

27   Amin, 'Underdevelopment and Dependence'; Amin, 'Dynamic and Limitations'.

28   Mafeje, 'Agrarian Question', 94.

29   Mafeje, 'Agrarian Question', 95.

30   Mafeje, 'Agrarian Question', 96.

31   Mafeje, 'Agrarian Question', 97.

32   Mafeje, 'Agrarian Question', 99.

33   Mafeje, 'Agrarian Question', 100.

34   Bundy, *Rise and Fall*; Trapido, 'Landlord and Tenant'.

35   Mafeje, 'Agrarian Question', 101.

36   Mafeje, 'Agrarian Question', 101.

37   Mafeje, 'Agrarian Question', 105.

38   Mafeje, 'Agrarian Question', 106.

39   Mafeje, 'Agrarian Question', 117.

40   Mafeje, 'Agrarian Question', 118–119.

41   Mafeje, 'Agrarian Question', 122.

42   Arthur Lewis, 'Economic Development with Unlimited Supplies of Labour', *The Manchester School* 22.2 (1954), 139–191.

43   Arthur Lewis, 'The Dual Economy Revisited', *The Manchester School* 47.3 (1979), 213.

44   Archie Mafeje, *The Agrarian Question, Access to Land, and Peasant Responses in Sub-Saharan Africa* (Geneva: UNRISD, 2003), 15.

45   Mafeje, *Agrarian Question*, 15.

46   Bundy, *Rise and Fall*.

47   Michael Neocosmos, *The Agrarian Question in Southern Africa and 'Accumulation from Below'* (Uppsala: Scandinavian Institute of African Studies, 1993).

48   Mafeje, *Agrarian Question*, 17.

49   Mahmood Mamdani, 'Extreme but Not Exceptional: Towards an Analysis of the Agrarian Question in Uganda', *The Journal of Peasant Studies* 14.2 (1987), 191–225.

50   Mafeje, *Agrarian Question*, 18.

51   Mafeje, *Agrarian Question*, 19.

52   Coquery-Vidrovitch, 'Research on an African Mode of Production'; Rey, 'Lineage Mode of Production'.

53   Mafeje, *Agrarian Question*, 20.

54 Mafeje, *Agrarian Question*, 20.
55 Mafeje, *Agrarian Question*, 20.
56 Mafeje, *Agrarian Question*, 23.
57 Mafeje, *Agrarian Question*, 24.
58 Mafeje, *Agrarian Question*, 30.
59 Archie Mafeje, 'Conceptual and Philosophical Predispositions', in *Poverty Reduction: What Role for the State in Today's Globalized Economy?* ed. Francis Wilson, Nazneen Kanji and Einar Braathen (London: Zed Books, 2001), 15–32.
60 Mafeje, 'Conceptual and Philosophical Predispositions', 15.
61 Mafeje, 'Conceptual and Philosophical Predispositions', 16.
62 Economic Commission for Africa (United Nations), *African Alternative Framework to Structural Adjustment Programmes for Socio-Economic Recovery and Transformation* (Addis Ababa: United Nations Economic Commission for Africa, 1990).
63 Ismail Seragaldin, *Poverty, Adjustment, and Growth in Africa* (Washington, DC: World Bank, 1989), http://documents.worldbank.org/curated/en/18161146819 4652323/Poverty-adjustment-and-growth-in-Africa.
64 Mafeje, 'Conceptual and Philosophical Predispositions', 18.
65 Mafeje, 'Conceptual and Philosophical Predispositions', 19; emphasis in original.
66 Mafeje, 'Conceptual and Philosophical Predispositions', 21.
67 I. Jazairy, M. Alamgir and T. Panuccio, *The State of World Rural Poverty: An Inquiry into Its Causes and Consequences* (Rome: International Fund for Agricultural Development, 1992).
68 Ravi Kanbur, *Poverty and Development: The Human Development Report and the World Development Report, 1990 (English)*. Policy, Research, and External Affairs Working Papers No. WPS 618 (Washington, DC: World Bank, 1991). http://documents.worldbank.org/curated/en/241631468766795984/Poverty-and-development-the-Human-Development-Report-and-the-World-Development-Report-1990.
69 Mafeje, 'Conceptual and Philosophical Predispositions', 27.
70 Mafeje, 'Conceptual and Philosophical Predispositions', 28.
71 Mafeje, 'Conceptual and Philosophical Predispositions', 29–30.

Chapter 6

1 His early work includes: Archie Mafeje, 'The Fallacy of Dual Economies Revisited: A Case of East, Central and Southern Africa', *East Africa Journal* 9.2 (1972), 30–34; Archie Mafeje, 'Neo-Colonialism, State Capitalism, or Revolution?' in *African Social Studies: A Radical Reader*, ed. Peter C.W. Gutkind

and Peter Waterman (London: Heinemann, 1977), 412–422; Archie Mafeje, *Science, Ideology and Development: Three Essays on Development Theory* (Uppsala: Scandinavian Institute of African Studies, 1978); Archie Mafeje, 'Soweto and Its Aftermath', *Review of African Political Economy* 5.11 (1978), 17–30.

2   Mafeje, 'Neo-Colonialism', 412.

3   Mafeje, 'Neo-Colonialism', 413.

4   Ernesto Laclau, 'Feudalism and Capitalism in Latin America', *New Left Review* 67 (1971), 19–38; Ernesto Laclau, *Politics and Ideology in Marxist Theory: Capitalism, Fascism and Populism* (London: New Left Books, 1977); Andre Gunder Frank, *Capitalism and Underdevelopment in Latin America* (New York: Monthly Review Press, 1967); Andre Gunder Frank, *Latin America: Underdevelopment or Revolution* (New York: Monthly Review Press, 1969).

5   Mafeje, 'Neo-Colonialism', 414.

6   Mafeje, 'Neo-Colonialism', 414.

7   Fernando H. Cardoso and Enzo Faletto, *Dependency and Development in Latin America* (Berkeley: University of California Press, 1979).

8   Mafeje, 'Neo-Colonialism', 415.

9   Mafeje, 'Neo-Colonialism', 417.

10 Mafeje, 'Neo-Colonialism', 417; emphasis in original.

11 Mafeje, 'Neo-Colonialism', 422.

12 Govan Mbeki, *South Africa: The Peasants' Revolt* (Harmondsworth: Penguin, 1964); Isaac B. Tabata, *The Awakening of a People* (Nottingham: Spokesman Books, 1974).

13 Mafeje, 'Neo-Colonialism', 419.

14 Mafeje, 'Neo-Colonialism', 420.

15 Mafeje, 'Neo-Colonialism', 420.

16 Mafeje, 'Neo-Colonialism', 421.

17 Mafeje, *Science, Ideology and Development*, 13.

18 Vijay Prashad, *The Darker Nations: A People's History of the Third World* (New York: The New Press, 2007), xv–xvi.

19 Mafeje, *Science, Ideology and Development*, 14.

20 Mafeje, *Science, Ideology and Development*, 14.

21 Mafeje, *Science, Ideology and Development*, 16.

22 Mafeje, *Science, Ideology and Development*, 16.

23 Mafeje, *Science, Ideology and Development*, 17.

24 Mafeje, *Science, Ideology and Development*, 17.

25 Mafeje, *Science, Ideology and Development*, 18.

26 Mafeje, *Science, Ideology and Development*, 18.

27 Mafeje, *Science, Ideology and Development*, 19.

28 Mafeje, *Science, Ideology and Development*, 19.

29 Mafeje, *Science, Ideology and Development*, 20.

30 Mao Tse-Tung, *Selected Works, Vol. II* (Peking: Foreign Languages Press, 1967), 353.

31 Mafeje, *Science, Ideology and Development*, 22.

32 Vladimir I. Lenin, *Materialism and Empirio-Criticism* (Moscow: Progress Publishers, 1967); Mao, *Selected Works, Vol. II*, 353.

33 Paul M. Sweezy and Charles Bettelheim, eds., *On the Transition to Socialism* (New York: Monthly Review Press, 1972).

34 Mafeje, *Science, Ideology and Development*, 23; emphasis in original.

35 Mafeje, *Science, Ideology and Development*, 23.

36 Mafeje, *Science, Ideology and Development*, 28.

37 Mafeje, *Science, Ideology and Development*, 29.

38 Paul M. Sweezy, 'Toward a Program of Studies of the Transition to Socialism', in *On the Transition to Socialism*, ed. Paul M. Sweezy and Charles Bettelheim (New York: Monthly Review Press, 1972), 130; emphasis in original.

39 Mafeje, *Science, Ideology and Development*, 34.

40 Mafeje, *Science, Ideology and Development*, 35.

41 Mafeje, *Science, Ideology and Development*, 35.

42 Mafeje, *Science, Ideology and Development*, 36.

43 Mafeje, *Science, Ideology and Development*, 36; emphasis in original.

44 Nikolai Bukharin, *The Politics and Economics of the Transition Period* (London: Routledge & Kegan Paul, 1979), 134.

45 Mafeje, *Science, Ideology and Development*, 39.

46 Mafeje, *Science, Ideology and Development*, 40.

47 Mafeje, *Science, Ideology and Development*, 41.

48 Mafeje, *Science, Ideology and Development*, 41–42.

49 Mafeje, *Science, Ideology and Development*, 42.

50 Mafeje, *Science, Ideology and Development*, 47.

51 Mafeje, *Science, Ideology and Development*, 47.

52 Luthando Funani, 'State, Democracy and Development: An Exploration of the Scholarship of Professor Archie Monwabisi Mafeje' (Master's thesis, University of the Western Cape, 2016).

53 Samir Amin, 'Underdevelopment and Dependence in Black Africa: Origins and Contemporary Forms', *Journal of Modern African Studies* 10.4 (1972), 504.

54 Mafeje, *Science, Ideology and Development*, 64.

55 Amin, 'Underdevelopment and Dependence', 520–521.

56 Mafeje, *Science, Ideology and Development*, 66; emphasis in original.

57 Arthur Lewis, 'Economic Development with Unlimited Supplies of Labour', *The Manchester School* 22.2 (1954), 139–191; Arthur Lewis, 'The Dual Economy Revisited', *The Manchester School* 47.3 (1979), 211–229.

58 Mafeje, *Science, Ideology and Development*, 67; emphasis in original.

59 Mafeje, *Science, Ideology and Development*, 68.

60 Mafeje, *Science, Ideology and Development*, 69.

Chapter 7

1 Archie Mafeje, 'South Africa: The Dynamics of a Beleaguered State', *African Journal of Political Economy* 1.1 (1986), 95–119; Archie Mafeje, *In Search of an Alternative: A Collection of Essays on Revolutionary Theory and Politics* (Harare: SAPES Books, 1992); Archie Mafeje, *The National Question in Southern African Settler Societies* (Harare: SAPES Monograph Series No. 6, 1997); Archie Mafeje, 'White Liberals and Black Nationalists: Strange Bedfellows', *Southern Africa Political & Economic Monthly (SAPEM)* 11.13 (1998), 45–48.

2 Mafeje, 'South Africa', 95.

3 Mafeje, 'South Africa', 95.

4 Mafeje, 'South Africa', 97.

5 Irina Filatova, 'Communism in South Africa', in *Oxford Research Encyclopaedia of African History*, ed. Thomas Spear (Oxford: Oxford University Press, 2017), 1.

6 Mafeje, 'South Africa', 97.

7 Allison Drew, *Discordant Comrades: Identities and Loyalties on the South African Left* (Pretoria: Unisa Press, 2002).

8 Harold Wolpe, ed., *The Articulation of Modes of Production* (London: Routledge & Kegan Paul, 1980).

9 Brian Bunting, ed., *South African Communists Speak, 1915–1980* (London: Inkululeko Publications, 1981).

10 Mafeje, 'South Africa', 98.

11 Mafeje, 'South Africa', 98.

12 Mafeje, 'South Africa', 98–99.

13 Historian Keith Breckenridge notes: 'Far from being a spontaneous white working-class uprising against capitalist power, a major strand of the 1922 strike was a deliberate, violent assault on the political organisation of their African working-class peers.' See Keith Breckenridge, 'Fighting for a White South Africa: White Working-Class Racism and the 1922 Rand Revolt', *South African Historical Journal* 57.1 (2007), 230.

14 Mafeje, 'White Liberals and Black Nationalists', 47.

15 Heinrich Bohmke, 'The White Revolutionary as a Missionary? Contemporary Travels and Researches in Caffraria', *New Frank Talk* 5 (2010), 9–28.

16 Archie Mafeje, 'The Agrarian Question and Food Production in Southern Africa', in *Food Security Issues in Southern Africa*, ed. Kwesi K. Prah (Maseru: Institute of Southern African Studies Series, 1988), 93.

17 Vladimir I. Lenin, *Imperialism: The Highest Stage of Capitalism* (Sydney: Resistance Books, 1999).

18 Mafeje, 'South Africa', 98; emphasis in original.

19 Kautsky quoted in Lenin, *Imperialism*, 92; emphasis in original.

20 Lenin, *Imperialism*, 93–94; emphasis in original.

21 Hugh Macmillan, *Jack Simons: Teacher, Scholar, Comrade* (Johannesburg: Jacana Media, 2016), 48.

22 Bernard Magubane, *South Africa: From Soweto to Uitenhage* (Trenton, NJ: Africa World Press, 1989), 203–204.

23 Magubane, *South Africa*, 204.

24 Bernard Magubane, *The Making of a Racist State: British Imperialism and the Union of South Africa, 1875–1910* (Trenton, NJ: Africa World Press, 1996).

25 Samir Amin, 'Underdevelopment and Dependence in Black Africa: Origins and Contemporary Forms', *Journal of Modern African Studies* 10.4 (1972), 519.

26 Mahmood Mamdani, *Citizen and Subject: Contemporary Africa and the Legacy of Late Colonialism* (Princeton: Princeton University Press, 1996).

27 Mafeje, 'South Africa', 99.

28 Joseph Stalin, 'Marxism and the National Question', in *Marxism and Nationalism*, ed. Vladimir I. Lenin (Sydney: Resistance Books, 2002), 197.

29 Thandika Mkandawire, 'From the National Question to the Social Question', *Transformation: Critical Perspectives on Southern Africa* 69.1 (2009), 132.

30 Mafeje, 'South Africa', 100–101.

31 Mafeje, 'South Africa', 101.

32 Mafeje, 'South Africa', 102.

33 Mafeje, 'South Africa', 102.

34 Magubane, *South Africa*; Magubane, *Making of a Racist State*.

35 Mafeje, 'South Africa', 102; emphasis in original.

36 Archie Mafeje, 'The National Question in South Africa', *Southern Africa Political & Economic Monthly (SAPEM)* 2.8 (1988), 21; emphasis in original.

37 Bernard Magubane, *The Ties That Bind: African-American Consciousness of Africa* (Trenton, NJ: Africa World Press, 1987), 207.

38 Bernard Magubane, 'Race and Class Revisited: The Case of North America and South Africa', *Africa Development* 12.1 (1987), 6.

39 Mafeje, 'South Africa', 103; emphasis in original.

40   Mafeje, 'South Africa', 103.

41   Mafeje, 'South Africa', 112.

42   Mafeje, 'South Africa', 116.

43   Mafeje, 'South Africa', 117.

44   Mafeje, 'South Africa', 119; emphasis in original.

45   Mafeje, *In Search of an Alternative*, 40.

46   Jimi Adesina, 'Social Policy in Sub-Saharan Africa: A Glance in the Rear-View Mirror', *International Journal of Social Welfare* 18 (2009), 37, footnote 1.

47   Magubane, *The Ties That Bind*, 1.

48   Mafeje, *In Search of an Alternative*, 43.

49   Mwesiga Baregu, 'Review of *Zimbabwe: The Political Economy of Transition, 1980–1986*, by Ibbo Mandaza', *African Journal of Political Economy* 1.2 (1987), 124; emphasis added.

50   Mafeje, *In Search of an Alternative*, 44.

51   Mafeje, *In Search of an Alternative*, 44.

52   PAC (Pan Africanist Congress), *The New Road of Revolution* (Dar es Salaam: Pan Africanist Congress of Azania, 1975).

53   African National Congress, 'Strategy and Tactics of the ANC', policy document adopted at the Morogoro Conference, Morogoro, Tanzania, 25 April–1 May 1969, 1.

54   Mafeje, *In Search of an Alternative*, 50.

55   Mafeje, *In Search of an Alternative*, 50–51.

56   Mafeje, *In Search of an Alternative*, 56.

57   Mafeje, *In Search of an Alternative*, 55.

58   Mafeje, *In Search of an Alternative*, 57.

59   Mafeje, *In Search of an Alternative*, 58.

60   Mafeje, *In Search of an Alternative*, 65.

61   Mafeje, *In Search of an Alternative*, 67.

62   Mafeje, *In Search of an Alternative*, 69.

63   Mafeje, *In Search of an Alternative*, 83.

64   Mafeje, *In Search of an Alternative*, 90; emphasis in original.

65   Mafeje, *In Search of an Alternative*, 91.

66   Mafeje, *National Question*, 7.

67   Mafeje, *National Question*, 8.

68   Mafeje, *National Question*, 9.

69   Steve Biko, 'Interview' by Gail Gerhart, in *Biko Lives! Contesting the Legacies of Steve Biko*, ed. Andile Mngxitama, Amanda Alexander and Nigel C. Gibson (Basingstoke: Palgrave Macmillan, 2008), 34.

70   Mafeje, *National Question*, 10.

71 Mafeje, *National Question*, 11.

72 Mafeje, *National Question*, 15.

73 Mafeje, *National Question*, 18.

74 Mafeje, *National Question*, 19.

75 Mafeje, *National Question*, 18.

76 Ibbo Mandaza, 'Foreword', in Archie Mafeje, *In Search of an Alternative: A Collection of Essays on Revolutionary Theory and Politics* (Harare: SAPES Books, 1992), viii; emphasis in original.

Bibliography

Adesina, Jimi. 'Archie Mafeje and the Pursuit of Endogeneity: Against Alterity and Extroversion'. *Africa Development* 33.4 (2008): 133–152.

Adesina, Jimi. 'Realising the Vision: The Discursive and Institutional Challenges of Becoming an African University'. *African Sociological Review* 9.1 (2005): 23–39.

Adesina, Jimi. 'Social Policy in Sub-Saharan Africa: A Glance in the Rear-View Mirror'. *International Journal of Social Welfare* 18 (2009): 37–51.

African National Congress. 'Strategy and Tactics of the ANC'. Policy document adopted at the Morogoro Conference, Morogoro, Tanzania, 25 April–1 May 1969.

Ake, Claude. 'What is the Problem of Ethnicity in Africa?' *Transformation* 22.1 (1993): 1–14.

Akiwowo, Akinsola. 'Indigenous Sociologies: Extending the Scope of the Argument'. *International Sociology* 14.2 (1999): 115–138.

Akiwowo, Akinsola. 'Trend Report: Sociology in Africa Today'. *Current Sociology* 28.2 (1980): 3–73.

Alatas, Syed Farid. 'Academic Dependency and Global Division of Labour'. *Current Sociology* 51.6 (2003): 599–613.

Alatas, Syed Hussein. 'Intellectual Imperialism: Definition, Traits, and Problems'. *Southeast Asian Journal of Social Science* 28.1 (2000): 23–45.

Amadiume, Ifi. *Male Daughters, Female Husbands: Gender and Sex in an African Society.* London: Zed Books, 1987.

Amin, Samir. *Class and Nation: Historically and in the Current Crisis.* London: Heinemann, 1980.

Amin, Samir. 'Contemporary Imperialism and the Agrarian Question'. *Agrarian South: Journal of Political Economy* 1.1 (2012): 11–26.

Amin, Samir. 'The Dynamic and Limitations of Agrarian Capitalism in Black Africa'. In *African Social Studies: A Radical Reader,* edited by Peter C.W. Gutkind and Peter Waterman, 154–159. London: Heinemann, 1977.

Amin, Samir. 'Homage to Archie Mafeje'. *Codesria Bulletin* 3–4 (2008): 12–14.

Amin, Samir. 'Underdevelopment and Dependence in Black Africa: Origins and Contemporary Forms'. *Journal of Modern African Studies* 10.4 (1972): 503–524.

Balibar, Étienne. 'The Basic Concepts of Historical Materialism'. In *Reading Capital*, edited by Louis Althusser and Étienne Balibar, 199–209. London: New Left Books, 1970.

Baregu, Mwesiga. 'Review of *Zimbabwe: The Political Economy of Transition, 1980–1986*, by Ibbo Mandaza'. *African Journal of Political Economy* 1.2 (1987): 124–128.

Berg, Elliot. *Accelerated Development in Sub-Saharan Africa: An Agenda for Africa*. Washington, DC: World Bank, 1981.

Biko, Steve. 'Interview' by Gail Gerhart. In *Biko Lives! Contesting the Legacies of Steve Biko*, edited by Andile Mngxitama, Amanda Alexander and Nigel C. Gibson, 21–42. Basingstoke: Palgrave Macmillan, 2008.

Bohmke, Heinrich. 'The White Revolutionary as a Missionary? Contemporary Travels and Researches in Caffraria'. *New Frank Talk* 5 (2010): 9–28.

Breckenridge, Keith. 'Fighting for a White South Africa: White Working-Class Racism and the 1922 Rand Revolt'. *South African Historical Journal* 57.1 (2007): 228–243.

Bukharin, Nikolai. *The Politics and Economics of the Transition Period*. London: Routledge & Kegan Paul, 1979.

Bundy, Colin. *The Rise and Fall of the South African Peasantry*. London: Heinemann, 1979.

Bunting, Brian, ed. *South African Communists Speak, 1915–1980*. London: Inkululeko Publications, 1981.

Cardoso, Fernando H. and Enzo Faletto. *Dependency and Development in Latin America*. Berkeley: University of California Press, 1979.

Coquery-Vidrovitch, Catherine. 'Research on an African Mode of Production'. In *African Social Studies: A Radical Reader*, edited by Peter C.W. Gutkind and Peter Waterman, 77–92. London: Heinemann, 1977.

Drew, Allison. *Discordant Comrades: Identities and Loyalties on the South African Left*. Pretoria: Unisa Press, 2002.

Economic Commission for Africa (United Nations). *African Alternative Framework to Structural Adjustment Programmes for Socio-Economic Recovery and Transformation*. Addis Ababa: United Nations Economic Commission for Africa, 1990.

Ekeh, Peter. 'Social Anthropology and Two Contrasting Uses of Tribalism in Africa'. *Comparative Studies in Society and History* 32.4 (1990): 660–700.

Epstein, Arnold L. *Politics in an Urban African Community*. Manchester: Manchester University Press, 1958.

Fanon, Frantz. *The Wretched of the Earth*. London: Penguin Books, 1963.

FAO (Food and Agriculture Organization). *African Agriculture: The Next 25 Years*. Rome: FAO, 1986.

FAO (Food and Agriculture Organization). *The Dynamics of Land Tenure and Agrarian Systems in Africa: Case Studies from Ghana, Kenya, Madagascar and Togo*. Rome: FAO, 1989.

Filatova, Irina. 'Communism in South Africa'. In *Oxford Research Encyclopaedia of African History*, edited by Thomas Spear, 1–37. Oxford: Oxford University Press, 2017.

Fortes, Meyer and Edward E. Evans-Pritchard, eds. *African Political Systems*. London: Oxford University Press, 1940.

Funani, Luthando. 'State, Democracy and Development: An Exploration of the Scholarship of Professor Archie Monwabisi Mafeje'. Master's thesis, University of the Western Cape, 2016.

Furnivall, John S. *Colonial Policy and Practice*. Cambridge: Cambridge University Press, 1948.

Gluckman, Max. *Order and Rebellion in Tribal Africa*. London: Oxford University Press, 1963.

Goody, Jack. *Technology, Tradition and the State in Africa*. London: Oxford University Press, 1971.

Gordon, Lewis R. *Existentia Africana: Understanding Africana Existential Thought*. New York: Routledge, 2000.

Gordon, Lewis R. 'The Problem of Biography in the Study of the Thought of Black Intellectuals'. *Small Axe* 4 (1998): 47–63.

Gulliver, Philip Hugh. 'Introduction'. In *Tradition and Transition in East Africa: Studies of the Tribal Element in the Modern Era*, edited by Philip Hugh Gulliver, 5–40. London: Routledge & Kegan Paul, 1969.

Gunder Frank, Andre. *Capitalism and Underdevelopment in Latin America*. New York: Monthly Review Press, 1967.

Gunder Frank, Andre. *Latin America: Underdevelopment or Revolution*. New York: Monthly Review Press, 1969.

Hill, Polly. *Studies in Rural Capitalism in West Africa*. Cambridge: Cambridge University Press, 1970.

Hountondji, Paulin. 'Scientific Dependence in Africa Today'. *Research in African Literatures* 21.3 (1990): 5–15.

Hountondji, Paulin. 'Scientific Dependence: Its Nature and Ways to Overcome It'. In *Cultural Development, Science and Technology in Sub-Saharan Africa*, edited by Klaus Gottstein and Gotz Link, 109–113. Baden-Baden: Nomos, 1986.

Jazairy, I., M. Alamgir and T. Panuccio. *The State of World Rural Poverty: An Inquiry into Its Causes and Consequences*. Rome: International Fund for Agricultural Development, 1992.

Kanbur, Ravi. *Poverty and Development: The Human Development Report and the World Development Report, 1990 (English)*. Policy, Research, and External Affairs Working Paper No. WPS 618. Washington, DC: World Bank, 1991. http://documents.worldbank.org/curated/en/241631468766795984/Poverty-and-development-the-Human-Development-Report-and-the-World-Development-Report-1990.

Kuper, Leo and Garfield Smith. *Pluralism in Africa*. Los Angeles: University of California Press, 1965.

Laclau, Ernesto. 'Feudalism and Capitalism in Latin America'. *New Left Review* 67 (1971): 19–38.

Laclau, Ernesto. *Politics and Ideology in Marxist Theory: Capitalism, Fascism and Populism*. London: New Left Books, 1977.

Lenin, Vladimir I. *Imperialism: The Highest Stage of Capitalism*. Sydney: Resistance Books, 1999.

Lenin, Vladimir I. *Materialism and Empirio-Criticism*. Moscow: Progress Publishers, 1967.

Lewis, Arthur. 'The Dual Economy Revisited'. *The Manchester School* 47.3 (1979): 211–229.

Lewis, Arthur. 'Economic Development with Unlimited Supplies of Labour'. *The Manchester School* 22.2 (1954): 139–191.

Macdonald, Helen. 'A Conversation: Subaltern Studies in South Asia and Post-Colonial Anthropology in Africa'. *Anthropology Southern Africa* 23.1–2 (2009): 59–68.

Macmillan, Hugh. *Jack Simons: Teacher, Scholar, Comrade*. Johannesburg: Jacana Media, 2016.

Mafeje, Archie. 'African Agriculture: The Next 25 Years: Old Problems, Old Solutions and Scientific Foibles'. *Africa Development* 12.2 (1987): 5–34.

Mafeje, Archie. 'African Households and Prospects for Agricultural Revival in Sub-Saharan Africa'. Dakar: Codesria Working Paper No. 22/91, 1991.

Mafeje, Archie. 'African Socio-Cultural Formations in the 21st Century'. *African Development Review* 7.2 (1995): 154–172.

Mafeje, Archie. *The Agrarian Question, Access to Land, and Peasant Responses in Sub-Saharan Africa*. Geneva: UNRISD, 2003.

Mafeje, Archie. 'The Agrarian Question and Food Production in Southern Africa'. In *Food Security Issues in Southern Africa*, edited by Kwesi K. Prah, 92–124. Maseru: Institute of Southern African Studies Series, 1988.

Mafeje, Archie. 'Agrarian Revolution and the Land Question in Buganda'. The Hague: Institute of Social Studies Occasional Paper No. 32, 1973.

Mafeje, Archie. 'Agrarian Revolution and the Land Question in Buganda'. In *A Century of Change in Eastern Africa*, edited by William Arens, 23–46. The Hague: Mouton Publishers, 1976.

Mafeje, Archie. *Anthropology and Independent Africans: Suicide or End of an Era?* Dakar: Codesria Monograph Series No. 4/96, 1996.

Mafeje, Archie. *Anthropology in Post-Independence Africa: End of an Era or the Problem of Self-Redefinition.* Nairobi: Heinrich Boll Foundation, 2001.

Mafeje, Archie. 'The Bathos of Tendentious Historiography: A Review of Joe Slovo's *Has Socialism Failed?' Southern Africa Political & Economic Monthly (SAPEM)* 3 (1990): 40–44.

Mafeje, Archie. 'A Chief Visits Town'. *Journal of Local Administration Overseas* 2 (1963): 88–99.

Mafeje, Archie. 'Conceptual and Philosophical Predispositions'. In *Poverty Reduction: What Role for the State in Today's Globalized Economy?* edited by Francis Wilson, Nazneen Kanji and Einar Braathen, 15–32. London: Zed Books, 2001.

Mafeje, Archie. 'Conversations and Confrontations with My Reviewers'. *African Sociological Review* 2.2 (1998): 95–107.

Mafeje, Archie. 'Development Literature and Writers from Underdeveloped Countries: A Comment on Ayse Trak'. *Current Anthropology* 26.1 (1985): 97–98.

Mafeje, Archie. 'The Fallacy of Dual Economies Revisited: A Case of East, Central and Southern Africa'. *East Africa Journal* 9.2 (1972): 30–34.

Mafeje, Archie. 'Food for Security and Peace in the SADCC Region'. In *Africa: Perspectives on Peace and Development,* edited by Emmanuel Hansen, 183–211. London: Zed Books, 1987.

Mafeje, Archie. 'The Ideology of "Tribalism"'. *Journal of Modern African Studies* 9.1 (1971): 252–261.

Mafeje, Archie. *In Search of an Alternative: A Collection of Essays on Revolutionary Theory and Politics.* Harare: SAPES Books, 1992.

Mafeje, Archie. 'Large-Scale Farming in Buganda'. In *The Anthropology of Development in Sub-Saharan Africa,* edited by David Brokensha and Marion Pearsall, 22–30. Lexington: University Press of Kentucky, 1969.

Mafeje, Archie. 'Leadership and Change: A Study of Two South African Peasant Communities'. Master's thesis, University of Cape Town, 1963.

Mafeje, Archie. 'Multi-Party Democracy and Ethnic Divisions in Africa: Are They Compatible?' In *Breaking Barriers, Creating New Hopes: Democracy, Civil Society and Good Governance in Africa,* edited by Abdalla S. Bujra and Said Adejumobi, 53–87. Trenton, NJ: Africa World Press, 2002.

Mafeje, Archie. 'The National Question in South Africa'. *Southern Africa Political & Economic Monthly (SAPEM)* 2.8 (1988): 20–22.

Mafeje, Archie. *The National Question in Southern African Settler Societies.* Harare: SAPES Monograph Series No. 6, 1997.

Mafeje, Archie. 'Neo-Colonialism, State Capitalism, or Revolution?' In *African Social Studies: A Radical Reader,* edited by Peter C.W. Gutkind and Peter Waterman, 412–422. London: Heinemann, 1977.

Mafeje, Archie. 'On the Articulation of Modes of Production'. *Journal of Southern African Studies* 8.1 (1981): 123–138.

Mafeje, Archie. 'Peasants in Sub-Saharan Africa'. *Africa Development* 10.3 (1985): 28–39.

Mafeje, Archie. 'Peasant Organisations in Africa: A Potential Dialogue between Economists and Sociologists – Some Theoretical/Methodological Observations'. *Codesria Bulletin* 1 (1993): 14–17.

Mafeje, Archie. 'The Problem of Anthropology in Historical Perspective: An Inquiry into the Growth of the Social Sciences'. *Canadian Journal of African Studies* 10.2 (1976): 307–333.

Mafeje, Archie. 'Religion, Class and Ideology in South Africa'. In *Religion and Social Change in Southern Africa: Anthropological Essays in Honour of Monica Wilson,* edited by Michael Whisson and Martin West, 164–184. Cape Town: David Philip, 1975.

Mafeje, Archie. 'The Role of the Bard in a Contemporary African Community'. *Journal of African Languages* 6.3 (1967): 193–223.

Mafeje, Archie. *Science, Ideology and Development: Three Essays on Development Theory.* Uppsala: Scandinavian Institute of African Studies, 1978.

Mafeje, Archie. 'South Africa: The Dynamics of a Beleaguered State'. *African Journal of Political Economy* 1.1 (1986): 95–119.

Mafeje, Archie. 'Soweto and Its Aftermath'. *Review of African Political Economy* 5.11 (1978): 17–30.

Mafeje, Archie. *Studies in Imperialism: A Discourse in Methodology, Research Methods and Techniques.* Harare: University of Zimbabwe Department of Economics, Law and Political & Administrative Studies Discussion Paper Series, 1986.

Mafeje, Archie. *The Theory and Ethnography of African Social Formations: The Case of the Interlacustrine Kingdoms.* Dakar: Codesria Book Series, 1991.

Mafeje, Archie. 'Tribalism'. In *The Oxford Companion to Politics of the World,* edited by Joel Krieger, 918–920. New York: Oxford University Press, 1993.

Mafeje, Archie. 'White Liberals and Black Nationalists: Strange Bedfellows'. *Southern Africa Political & Economic Monthly (SAPEM)* 11.13 (1998): 45–48.

Magubane, Bernard. 'Crisis in African Sociology'. *East African Journal* 5.12 (1968): 21–40.

Magubane, Bernard. 'A Critical Look at Indices Used in the Study of Social Change in Colonial Africa'. *Current Anthropology* 12.4–5 (1971): 419–445.

Magubane, Bernard. *The Making of a Racist State: British Imperialism and the Union of South Africa, 1875–1910.* Trenton, NJ: Africa World Press, 1996.

Magubane, Bernard. 'Pluralism and Conflict Situations in Africa: A New Look'. *African Social Research* 7 (1969): 529–554.

Magubane, Bernard. 'Race and Class Revisited: The Case of North America and South Africa'. *Africa Development* 12.1 (1987): 5–40.

Magubane, Bernard. *South Africa: From Soweto to Uitenhage*. Trenton, NJ: Africa World Press, 1989.

Magubane, Bernard. *The Ties That Bind: African-American Consciousness of Africa*. Trenton, NJ: Africa World Press, 1987.

Magubane, Bernard. 'Whose Memory – Whose History? The Illusion of Liberal and Radical Historical Debates'. In *History Making and Present-Day Politics: The Meaning of Collective Memory in South Africa*, edited by Hans Erik Stolten, 253–279. Uppsala: The Nordic Africa Institute, 2007.

Mamdani, Mahmood. *Citizen and Subject: Contemporary Africa and the Legacy of Late Colonialism*. Princeton: Princeton University Press, 1996.

Mamdani, Mahmood. 'Extreme but Not Exceptional: Towards an Analysis of the Agrarian Question in Uganda'. *The Journal of Peasant Studies* 14.2 (1987): 191–225.

Mamdani, Mahmood. *When Victims Become Killers: Colonialism, Nativism, and the Genocide in Rwanda*. Princeton: Princeton University Press, 2001.

Mandaza, Ibbo. 'Foreword'. In *In Search of an Alternative: A Collection of Essays on Revolutionary Theory and Politics*, by Archie Mafeje, v–viii. Harare: SAPES Books, 1992.

Mayer, Philip. 'A Comment on Magubane's "Indices of Social Change in Africa"'. *Current Anthropology* 12.4–5 (1971): 419–445.

Mayer, Philip. *Townsmen or Tribesmen (Xhosa in Town)*. Cape Town: Oxford University Press, 1961.

Mbeki, Govan. *South Africa: The Peasants' Revolt*. Harmondsworth: Penguin, 1964.

Meillassoux, Claude. 'From Reproduction to Production'. *Economy & Society* 1.1 (1972): 93–105.

Meillassoux, Claude. 'The Social Organisation of the Peasantry: The Economic Basis of Kinship'. *Journal of Peasant Studies* 1.1 (1973): 81–90.

Mkandawire, Thandika. 'Economic Crisis in Malawi'. In *Recession in Africa*, edited by Jerker Carlsson, 28–47. Uppsala: Scandinavian Institute of African Studies, 1983.

Mkandawire, Thandika. 'From the National Question to the Social Question'. *Transformation* 69.1 (2009): 130–160.

Mkandawire, Thandika and Charles Soludo. *Our Continent, Our Future: African Perspectives on Structural Adjustment*. Dakar: Codesria Book Series, 1999.

Morris, Michael. 'The Development of Capitalism in South African Agriculture: Class Struggle in the Countryside'. In *The Articulation of Modes of Production*, edited by Harold Wolpe, 425–456. London: Routledge & Kegan Paul, 1980.

Moyo, Sam. 'African Land Questions, Agrarian Transitions and the State'. Dakar: Codesria Working Paper Series, 2008.

Moyo, Sam. 'Debating the African Land Question with Archie Mafeje' *Agrarian South: Journal of Political Economy* 7.2 (2018): 211–233.

Moyo, Sam. 'Peasant Organisations and Rural Civil Society in Africa: An Introduction'. In *Peasant Organisations and Democratisation in Africa*, edited by Sam Moyo and Mahmoud Romdhane, 1–26. Dakar: Codesria Book Series, 2002.

Moyo, Sam, Praveen Jha and Paris Yeros. 'The Classical Agrarian Question: Myth, Reality and Relevance Today'. *Agrarian South: Journal of Political Economy* 2.1 (2013): 93–119.

Murunga, Godwin. 'Review: Archie Mafeje's *Anthropology and Independent Africans: Suicide or End of an Era?*' *Africa Development* 23.1 (1998): 173–177.

Nabudere, Dani. 'Archie Mafeje and the Social Sciences in Africa'. *Codesria Bulletin* 3/4 (2008): 8–10.

Nabudere, Dani. *Archie Mafeje: Scholar, Activist and Thinker*. Pretoria: AISA, 2011.

Nabudere, Dani. *Archie Mafeje: The Scholar and Political Activist*. Archie Mafeje Memorial Lecture Series No. 1. Pretoria: AISA, 2010.

Neocosmos, Michael. *The Agrarian Question in Southern Africa and 'Accumulation from Below'*. Uppsala: Scandinavian Institute of African Studies, 1993.

Nnoli, Okwudiba. *Ethnic Conflict in Africa*. Dakar: Codesria Book Series, 1998.

Nnoli, Okwudiba. *Ethnic Politics in Africa*. Ibadan: Vintage Press, 1989.

Nnoli, Okwudiba. *Ethnic Politics in Nigeria*. Enugu: Fourth Dimension, 1978.

Oyewumi, Oyeronke. *The Invention of Women: Making an African Sense of Western Gender Discourse*. Minneapolis, MN: University of Minnesota Press, 1997.

PAC (Pan Africanist Congress). *The New Road of Revolution*. Dar es Salaam: Pan Africanist Congress of Azania, 1975.

Post, Ken. 'Peasantisation in Western Africa'. In *African Social Studies: A Radical Reader*, edited by Peter C.W. Gutkind and Peter Waterman, 241–250. London: Heinemann, 1977.

Prashad, Vijay. *The Darker Nations: A People's History of the Third World*. New York: The New Press, 2007.

Rahmato, Dessalegn. 'On Peasant Studies: A Reply to Archie Mafeje'. *Codesria Bulletin* 2 (1993): 23.

Rey, Pierre-Philippe. 'The Lineage Mode of Production'. *Critique of Anthropology* 1.3 (1975): 27–79.

Richards, Audrey Isabel, ed. *East African Chiefs: A Study of Political Development in Some Uganda and Tanganyika Tribes*. London: Faber & Faber, 1960.

Saul, John and Roger Woods. 'African Peasantries'. In *Peasants and Peasant Societies*, edited by Teodor Shanin, 103–114. Harmondsworth: Penguin, 1971.

Schapera, Isaac. *Praise Poems of Tswana Chiefs*. Oxford: Clarendon Press, 1965.

Seragaldin, Ismail. *Poverty, Adjustment, and Growth in Africa*. Washington, DC: World Bank, 1989. http://documents.worldbank.org/curated/en/181611468194652323/Poverty-adjustment-and-growth-in-Africa.

Sharawy, Helmi. 'The End of Anthropology: The African Debate on the Universality of Social Research and Its "Indigenisation" – A Study Dedicated to Archie Mafeje'. *Codesria Bulletin* 3/4 (2008): 15–20.

Sharawy, Helmi. *Political and Social Thought in Africa*. Dakar: Codesria Book Series, 2014.

Sharp, John. 'Who Speaks for Whom? A Response to Archie Mafeje's *Anthropology and Independent Africans: Suicide or End of an Era?*' *African Sociological Review* 2.1 (1998): 66–73.

South African Communist Party. *The Road to South African Freedom*. London: Inkululeko Publications, 1962.

Speke, John Hanning. *Journal of the Discovery of the Source of the Nile*. Edinburgh: William Blackwood and Sons, 1863.

Stalin, Joseph. 'Marxism and the National Question'. In *Marxism and Nationalism*, edited by Vladimir I. Lenin, 192–242. Sydney: Resistance Books, 2002.

Sweezy, Paul M. 'Toward a Program of Studies of the Transition to Socialism'. In *On the Transition to Socialism*, edited by Paul M. Sweezy and Charles Bettelheim, 123–135. New York: Monthly Review Press, 1972.

Sweezy, Paul M. and Charles Bettelheim, eds. *On the Transition to Socialism*. New York: Monthly Review Press, 1972.

Tabata, Isaac B. *The Awakening of a People*. Nottingham: Spokesman Books, 1974.

Trapido, Stanley. 'Landlord and Tenant in a Colonial Economy: The Transvaal 1880–1910'. *Journal of Southern African Studies* 5.1 (1978): 26–58.

Tse-Tung, Mao. *Selected Works, Vol. II*. Peking: Foreign Languages Press, 1967.

Van den Berghe, Pierre, ed. *Africa: Social Problems of Conflict and Change*. San Francisco: Chandler Publishing, 1965.

Wilson, Monica. 'The Growth of Peasant Communities'. In *The Oxford History of South Africa*, edited by Monica Wilson and Leonard M. Thompson, 49–103. Oxford: Oxford University Press, 1971.

Wilson, Monica and Archie Mafeje. *Langa: A Study of Social Groups in an African Township*. Cape Town: Oxford University Press, 1963.

Wolpe, Harold, ed. *The Articulation of Modes of Production*. London: Routledge & Kegan Paul, 1980.

Wolpe, Harold. 'Capitalism and Cheap Labour-Power in South Africa: From Segregation to Apartheid'. In *The Articulation of Modes of Production*, edited by Harold Wolpe, 289–320. London: Routledge & Kegan Paul, 1980.

Wolpe, Harold. 'Introduction'. In *The Articulation of Modes of Production*, edited by Harold Wolpe, 1–41. London: Routledge & Kegan Paul, 1980.

Wrigley, Christopher C. 'The Changing Economic Structure in Buganda'. In *The King's Men: Leadership and Status in Buganda on the Eve of Independence*, edited by Lloyd A. Fallers, 16–63. London: Oxford University Press, 1964.

Index

A

abaThembu 7, 9, 16
'acculturation' 27, 33
accumulation 38, 80, 142
    capital 84, 188
    capitalist model 227
    expanded 165
    from below 158–162, 165
    in pastoral kingdoms 84
    internal 176, 183
    of cattle 78
    primary 165
    primitive 106–107
    rapid 190, 192
achikumbe 128
acts
    Bantu Authorities Act of 1951 48
    Land Act of 1913 48, 149
    Master and Servants Act of 1845 148
Adesina, Jimi xii–xiii, 3, 5, 15, 51,
    54, 218, 225, 229 (n 2)
African Agriculture: The Next 25 Years 113
*African Alternative Framework to
    Structural Adjustment Programmes
    for Socio-Economic Recovery and
    Transformation* 133, 166
African Council of Ministers 133
African National Congress (ANC) 5,
    203–204, 207, 212, 214, 216, 220–226
'African Peasantries' 138
African Union (AU) 144
Africanus: Journal of Development Studies 195
agrarian
    African systems 105

economies/economy 103, 116, 132, 143
issues in sub-Saharan Africa 101–170
policies/policy 121, 126, 167
question 127–133, 143–165
reform 126, 155–165
revolution 105–113, 143, 153–155
settings 136
social formations 146
social settings 135
societies in Europe 79
structures 151
studies 103–105, 145
territories/territory 206
transformation 103, 154
*The Agrarian Question, Access to
    Land and Peasant Responses
    in Sub Saharan Africa* 59
*The Agrarian Question in Southern Africa
    and 'Accumulation from Below'* 158
agricultural
    capitalists 110, 128
    economies 47, 117–118, 141, 146
    economists 144–145
    production 87, 90, 108, 122, 124,
        127–128, 130, 143, 149, 152, 158, 167
agriculture
    capitalist *see* capitalist, agriculture
    colonialism *see* colonialism, agriculture
    division of labour 156
    settler *see* settler, agriculture
    subsistence *see* subsistence, agriculture
Ake, Claude 26
Akiwowo, Akinsola 56
Alatas, Syed Farid 104

Alatas, Syed Hussein 105
Alexandratos, Nikos 130
Algeria 178, 193
All Saints 34
alterity 37, 49, 52–53, 56
Amadiume, Ifi 56
amadlelo (grazing grounds) 125
amaqaba 34
amaqheya 47
amarhanuga 47
amasimi (plots of arable land) 125
amaSwati 74
amaXhosa 74, 82, 236 (n 5)
amaZulu 16, 74
Amin, Samir 59, 62–63, 85–92, 95, 104,
    119–120, 125, 141, 145, 161, 196, 209
ANC *see* African National Congress
Anderson, Perry 18
Angola 179, 189, 193, 224
Ankole 61, 63–69, 72, 75–76, 81–83
annexation 206, 209
anthropological
    atomisation of societies 61
    notion of feudal aristocracy 83
anthropologists 7, 10–15, 17, 24, 32–34,
    44, 60–73, 86–88, 98, 145
    African 53, 55
    British 39
    colonial 10, 32–33, 40, 60, 67
    French 36, 87
    French Marxist 88
    pluralist 18–19
    social 10, 14, 32–33, 137, 144, 229 (n 3)
anthropology 5–6, 29–31, 44, 49–57, 98
    African 53, 57
    colonial 31–32, 37, 40, 51, 53, 68
    colonial writings 15
    discipline/science 29, 38
    functionalism 5, 7, 36–43
    liberal 5
    liberal functionalist *see* liberal,
      functionalist anthropology
    liberal writings 5
    Marxism/Marxist *see* Marxist,
      anthropology
    non-Marxist 36
    pluralist 18
    politics *see* politics, in anthropology
    positivism and functionalism 36–43

    radical 37
    role in colonialism and
      imperialism 30, 37, 98
    social/socialist 37, 92
    writings 17, 72
Anthropology and Independent Africans 53, 55
anti-colonialism 184
anti-comprador struggles 224
anti-imperialism 183, 185, 220, 224
anti-imperialist
    ideology 190
    struggles 30, 65, 182–183, 188
apartheid 6, 158, 214
    government 7, 151, 210–211, 217
aristocracies/aristocracy
    feudal *see* feudal, aristocracy
    pastoral *see* pastoral, aristocracies
Arrighi, Giovanni 65
Asia 136
AU *see* African Union

B
Babito 66–67, 69, 74–75
Bachwezi 66–68, 74
Bahima/Bahuma 61, 66–76, 80–84, 236 (n 6)
bahuma (pastoralists) 74
Bahutu 61, 76–77, 83, 90
Bahutu-Batutsi clash 25
Bairu 61, 68–70, 72, 75, 80–84
bairu (agriculturalists) 74
Baker, Samuel 68
bakungu (territorial chiefs) 75, 82
Balibar, Étienne 46, 62
Bank, Andrew xiii
Bank, Leslie xiii
Bantu
    authorities 6
    communities/kingdoms 63
    councils 6
    languages 64
    origin 71
Bantu Authorities Act of 1951 48
bantustan 48, 211
Banyankole 82
banyaruguru (privileged stratum
    in society) 76
Bataga 76
bataka (village chiefs) 75
Batare 76

batongole (district chiefs) 75
'The Bathos of Tendentious
    Historiography' 17
Batutsi 25, 61, 76–78, 83–84
Berg Report 133, 166
Berlin Conference 225
Bettelheim, Charles 188
Bezi 76
Black Consciousness Movement
    210, 221
black nationalism 217–218, 220, 225–226
black nationalists 204
blue-collar workers 178–179
Bohmke, Heinrich 205
Bond, Patrick 195
Botswana 116, 150–151, 169
Bretton Woods institutions 131
Brittany 8
Buganda 63–64, 66, 70–72, 75,
    78–83, 87, 105–114
    see also Uganda
Buha 64, 66, 70, 72, 81, 84
Buhaya 63–64, 66, 69–70, 72, 81, 84, 87
Bukharin, Nikolai 192
Bundy, Colin 139, 158
Bunyoro 61–72, 74–75, 80–83, 87
Burkina Faso 169
Burundi 61, 66, 69, 72, 76, 81, 83–84, 189
Busoga 63–64, 66, 70–72, 80
busulu (dues) 109
Busulu and Envujjo Law 109
Buzinza 64, 66, 69–70, 72, 81, 84

C
Callinicos, Luli 207
Cameroon 115, 154
Cape 139, 148–149, 213
Cape Malays 210
Cape Town 4, 6–7
capital
    accumulation 84, 188
    allocation and utilisation 177
    colonial 118, 150, 190
    flight 184
    foreign 176, 186–187, 190, 199
    international 143, 174, 190, 196, 199
    monopoly 182
    settler 196
    white 147

capitalism 85, 90, 104, 112,
    156, 174–199, 206
    Africa 143, 157
    as mode of accumulation 38
    classical 169, 177, 198
    colonial 118, 150, 152, 198–199
    European 38, 198
    global 156, 192, 207–208
    growth 114
    imperialist 119
    industrial 206
    international 138, 173
    Kenya 140
    monopoly 206–207, 216
    Russia 159
    state *see* state capitalism
    Western *see* Western, capitalism
capitalist
    agriculture 90, 117, 141, 156
    class 141, 152–153
    domination 175
    economy 138, 197
    expansion/expansionism 111, 188
    farmers/farming 115, 127–131,
        140, 151–153, 159–160
    labour market 114
    market 120, 129–131, 162–163
    model of accumulation 227
    modes of production 45, 47,
        118–119, 137, 176, 197, 199
    production 46, 111, 117, 187, 191
    relations 44, 46
    revolutions 109, 112–113, 143
    utilitarianism 40
    West 16, 175
capitalists
    agricultural 110, 128
    labour-employing 149
    local 160
    rural 110
    village 160
cash crop production 108, 116, 127, 139
cash crops 107, 122, 131, 146, 158, 162–163
Celtic people 8
'A Chief Visits Town' 6
Chile 186
China 178, 185, 193, 215, 219
Christianity/Christians 34, 36, 92, 139
Chwezi 66

'civilisation' 12, 35
civilisation 25, 35, 204
civilising mission(s) 13, 35, 37–38, 137, 205
class
    agricultural capitalist 141
    and ideology 31
    black agricultural 152
    bourgeois 40, 184
    capitalist *see* capitalist, class
    comprador *see* comprador, class
    consciousness 13
    differentiation 13, 23, 77, 161
    discrimination 151
    distinctions 69
    division 65, 75
    employing 110
    exploited/exploiting 73, 89–92, 213
    formation 13, 65, 81, 94, 161
    hegemonic 21, 24
    labouring 81
    land-owning/property-owning 48, 80
    middle 178
    non-producing 83
    peasant 138
    privileges 5
    ruling 11–12, 75, 89
    self-producing 128
    societies/society 76, 93
    structure 65
    struggle(s) 45, 62, 89, 183, 187–188
    system 80
Cold War 104, 174, 176, 183, 222, 224
colonial
    capital 118, 150, 190
    capitalism 118, 150, 152, 198–199
    economy 145, 154
    historiography 68
    mode of production 147
    underdevelopment 190
colonialism 4, 6, 10, 17, 32–33, 35, 38,
        40–41, 51–52, 56, 73, 85, 103,
        117–118, 137, 146–148, 150, 156–157,
        164, 174, 185, 189–190, 196–199,
        210, 214, 223–226, 229 (n 3)
    agriculture 115, 146
    battles against 182
    British 107
    European 10, 38
    impact in Great Lakes region 60

    internal xv, 202–213, 225–226
    land reform 126
    'of a special type' (CST) xv, 202,
        204–205, 207, 210, 213–214, 225
    religious divisions 218
    rise of the peasantry 137
    role of anthropology 30, 37, 98
    settler 204, 212
    Uganda 106
'Colonialism and the Two Publics in
        Africa: A Theoretical Statement' 195
coloureds 210
Comintern (Third International)
        202–203, 207–208, 211–212
commodity production 128, 132
communal land 47–48, 78, 89–90, 93,
        124–125, 138–139, 141, 145, 153, 203
communal social formations 90, 93
communalism 189
Communist Party of South Africa
        (CPSA) 203–208, 212
communists 184, 208, 223, 226
    white 204–205
comprador 187
    class 175, 216, 224
    proto-nationalists 224
Comte, August 38–39
'Conceptual and Philosophical
        Predispositions' 167
concessionaries/concession-owning
        companies 145, 195
Congo 63, 189
conservatism 51, 85
Constitution of South Africa 155
'Conversations and Confrontations
        with My Reviewers' 55
Coquery-Vidrovitch, Catherine 141, 145
Côte d'Ivoire 115–116, 126, 154, 175
CPSA *see* Communist Party of South Africa
crop-sharing *see* sharecropping
Crosse-Upcott, A.R.W. 5
CST *see* colonialism, 'of a special type'
Cuba 174, 178, 186, 193, 227
cultural
    continuities and reproduction 61
    creativity 61
    heritage 218
    institutions 39
    liberation 228

pluralism 17
poverty 228
practices 34, 63
relativity 44
values toward land and its use 123

D
Dalindyebo, Chief Sabata 9
Das Kapital 43
decentralisation of power 27, 232 (n 55)
decentralised agricultural communities 63
decolonisation 173
   and neocolonialism 146
   curriculum 51
   epistemological xii, 51, 56
   of knowledge xi–xii, xvi, 42, 229 (n 1)
deconstruction 53, 56, 97–100
democracy 28, 159–160, 191
   liberal *see* liberal, democracy
   national 212
   new 183, 185, 220
   non-racial 212, 214–215
   participatory 222
   social *see* social democracy
   socialist 214–220
determinism 185–186, 194–195
The Development of Capitalism in Russia 159
Dhlomo, Herbert Isaac Ernest xi
Dike, Kenneth Onwuka xi
Diop, Cheikh Anta xi, 56
Discordant Comrades: Identities and Loyalties
   on the South African Left 203
division of labour 69, 111, 119, 176–177
   in agriculture 156
   intellectual 104
   kinship-based 120
   social 22
Drew, Allison 203
dual theories
   of economic growth 173, 194–199
   of the neoclassical theorists 157
Durkheim, Émile 39
The Dynamics of Land Tenure and
   Agrarian Systems in Africa 122

E
Eastern Cape 47
Eastern religion 92
ECA *see* Economic Commission for Africa

economic
   counter-revolution 188
   domination 182, 186, 205
   freedom 228
   growth 86, 167
      theories 173, 194–199
   instance 62, 69, 71, 96
   laws 195
   liberation 214
   models 167
   nationalism 215
   organisation 71, 103
   plunder 38
   poverty 228
   power 60
   production 72, 74, 190
   protectionism 177
   reform 164
   relations 95
   self-sufficiency 151
   surplus 84, 94, 96
   transformation 215
   trickle-down theory 156, 166
Economic Commission for
   Africa (ECA) 133, 166
economics 71
   neoliberal 156
   trickle-down 156, 166
   welfare 168
economies/economy
   African 120–121, 133, 137, 143, 146
   African redistributive 45, 47
   agrarian *see* agrarian, economies 103
   agricultural *see* agricultural, economies
   Asian village economy 93
   Bugandan 106, 108–109, 111
   capitalist *see* capitalist, economy
   colonial *see* colonial, economy
   dual 195
   export-orientated 191
   global 165
   household 92–93, 106, 119, 138
   imperialist 136
   left-leaning 177
   market 139, 143
   modern 116
   monetised 146
   of predation 106
   political *see* political, economy

economies/economy (*continued*)
  semi-pastoral 81
  settler 147
  socialist-orientated 177
  subsistence 14
  tribal 84, 203
  two-sector 198
  underdeveloped 177
economists
  agricultural *see* agricultural, economists
  liberal *see* liberal, economists
  political 79
Egypt 64, 126
Ekeh, Peter 19, 195
El-Baz, Shahida xii
Engels, Friedrich 11
Enlightenment 37–38, 40
epistemological
  break 49–57, 59, 103, 211, 216
  decolonisation xii, 51, 56
  rupture(s) 49–50, 52, 55–56
epistemology xiv, 54, 97–99, 194, 205
  Euro-American 54
  materialism as 93
  of alterity 56
  of subject(s)-object(s) 42–43, 49, 104
  of the sociology of religion 30
Epstein, Arnold 12
Ethiopia 64, 66–67, 70, 121,
    126, 135–136, 189
ethnic
  antagonisms 22
  categorisation 82
  classification 72
  competition 22
  conflict(s) 18, 21–22, 25–26, 28, 225
  diversity 22
  divisions 19–28, 77, 218
  group(s) 18–28, 61, 74, 78, 226
  identities/identity 7, 25–27, 61
  integration 28
  jingoism 23
  multi-ethnic kingdoms 74
  nomenclature 72
  origin 75–76
  social formations 26
ethnicity xiv, 19–28, 61, 69, 78, 232 (n 55)
ethnography xiv, 9, 56–57, 60–62
  African 56

in the social sciences 30
of the interlacustrine region 60–71, 145
Eurocentric
  concepts such as nation
    state or nations 225
  models of government 155
  modes of production 105
  paradigms 103
  theories and definitions 60
  view on property 123
Eurocentrism xi–xii, xiv, 14, 28, 30, 42
  alternative modes of social
    organisation 125
  in social sciences 30, 49, 55–56
  in the study of the agrarian question 105
'Europeanisation' 12, 33, 35
Evans-Pritchard, E.E. 14
expansion/expansionism 38, 111, 188
exploitation 5–6, 15, 25, 40, 77, 88–95,
    110, 112, 127, 129, 161, 192, 217–218
  by capital 142–143, 179, 199
  by the state 78
  by white farmers 152
  by white landlords 149
  by white people 213, 226
  of Africans 35
  of black people 34, 207–208, 226
  of labour 75, 81, 83–85, 107, 119,
    190, 199
  of land 127
  of mineral wealth 209
  of peasantry/peasants 160,
    165, 178–180, 193–194
  of primary producers 147
  of small producers/migrant
    workers 179
  of subjects 84
  of women 163–164
expropriation 91, 180, 190, 223
  of cultivators 126
  of farmers 132
  of land *see* land expropriation
extra-economic
  coercion 165
  extraction of value 94, 205
  means 213
  policies 157
  relations 12
extraction of value 77, 90, 94, 205, 213

'Extreme but Not Exceptional: Towards
an Analysis of the Agrarian
Question in Uganda' 160

F
FAO *see* Food and Agriculture Organization
farmers/farming
    capitalist *see* capitalist, farmers
    expropriation 132
    subsistence *see* subsistence, farmers
feudal
    aristocracy 83, 159
    bondage 159
    landlordism 170
    landlords 203
    lords 87, 106, 148
    societies 87
    system 81
feudalism 47, 60, 79, 84, 86–89,
    95, 107, 145, 159, 189
feudalist and capitalist relations 46
Filatova, Irina 203
finance capital 179, 194, 199,
    206–207, 209, 217
First World 183
First World War 183
Food and Agriculture Organization
    (FAO) xiii, 113–115, 117, 122,
    128, 166
food production 166
    and food security issues 143–155
    crisis 113
    neglect of 128
    role of commercial farmers 115
food security 121, 135–170
    deteriorating 144
    for black people 153
    in post-independence Africa 113
Fortes, Meyer 14
fragmentation
    among citizens 27
    of African estates 126
France 36, 38
Freedom Charter 225
Funani, Luthando 195
functionalism 3–32, 36, 52, 99,
    229 (n 3)
    early writings 4
    in anthropolgy 36–43

liberal *see* liberal, functionalism
functionalist
    anthropology 5, 7
    sociologists 39
Furnivall, John 19

G
Gabon 175
Galla 70
gender discrimination 151
The German Ideology 11
Gezira Scheme 116
Ghana 116, 129
global North 50, 168
global South 40, 44, 50–51, 56,
    85, 168, 170, 173, 181, 185,
    188, 223
Goody, Jack 79
Gordon, Lewis R. 32
Gqoba, William Wellington xi
Great Lakes region 59–60, 67
    see also interlacustrine region
Grundrisse 43, 99
Guam 174
Guinea Bissau 178–179, 193
Gulliver, Philip Hugh 14
Gunder Frank, Andre 65–66, 174

H
Hamitic
    genetic stock 70
    invaders 66
    pastoralists 64, 68
    people 66
Hendricks, Fred xiii
Hill, Polly 141
historical
    approach 32
    conjuncture 219
    determinism 194
    experience 188, 195, 225
    Marxism 119
    materialism 43, 93, 99, 218–219
    sociology 56, 103, 194
    struggles (European) 219
    time 65–66
    transformation 31
historiography xi, 5–6, 68
Homans, George 39

I

'The Ideology of "Tribalism'" 3, 30, 145
idiographic inquiry 44–48,
   87, 201, 233 (n 28)
IFAD *see* International Fund for
   Agricultural Development
iinkuni (firewood trees) 125
imbongi (bard/praise-singer)
   xiv, 7–10, 230 (n 14)
imbongi yakomkhulu (the poet of
   the main residence) 8
imbongi yesizwe (the poet of the nation) 8
imbongi yomthonyama (the poet who
   recites his poems from memory) 9
imbongi yosiba (the poet who writes
   down his poems) 9
IMF *see* International Monetary Fund
imperial rule 18
imperialism 30, 37–38, 41, 44, 51,
   56, 85, 175, 184, 192, 196–197,
   206–209, 212–225, 229 (n 3)
   British 85, 107–109
   intellectual 105
   Western 169
imperialist
   capitalism 119
   economies 136
   social sciences 32, 53
   Western powers 28
In Search of an Alternative 220, 228
India 126
Indians 38, 210–211
indigenisation 202
   of knowledge xi
   of the social sciences 202
individualisation
   of agricultural production 130, 167
   of land rights/rights in land
      108, 122–123, 167
   of production 123
   resistance to 123
individualism
   bourgeois 161, 164
   sociological 40
   Western 156
industrial
   capitalism 206
   policies 199
   production 190

proletariat 179
   workers 179–181, 193
Industrial Revolution 38, 105
industrialisation 104–105, 117, 152,
   156, 177
industrialised
   countries 206
   peasantry 143
industrialising countries 168
intellectual
   activity 49
   division of labour 104
   force 12
   freedom 5
   imperialism 105
   liberation 228
   poverty 228
   prejudice 51
   systems 49
intellectuality 49
intellectuals
   African 16–17, 201–202, 228
   black 32
   community of 201
   in the West 168
   South African 204, 208
inter-cropping 114
interdisciplinarity 54–55, 98
interlacustrine region 56, 58
   (map), 59–99, 235 (n 2)
   ethnography and social
      formations 60–71, 145
   modes of political organisation
      71–78
   social and economic character
      78–85
   social formations 60–71, 87, 95
   see also Great Lakes region
interlocutors
   authentic 99, 201, 203, 206
   intellectual 67
International Fund for Agricultural
   Development (IFAD) 166, 168
International Labour Organisation 166
International Monetary Fund
   (IMF) 133, 156
internationalism 205
Ireland 8, 38, 213
isiXhosa 7, 9

J

Japan 175–176
Jha, Praveen 104–105, 117, 143
Johnston, Sir Harry 106–107
Jordan, Pallo 42
Joyi, Chief 7

K

Kautsky, Karl 206
Kenya 25, 114–115, 123–129, 135, 140–141,
      150, 154, 157, 162, 175–176, 189,
      196, 199, 209, 213, 232 (n 55)
kinship mode of social
      organisation 160–161
knowledge
      decolonisation *see* decolonisation,
            of knowledge
      indigenisation xi
      making 32, 49–50, 68, 98
      production xvi, 54, 104, 216
Korea 193
kulaks 110, 128, 140–141, 160

L

labour
      allocation 120, 161
      aristocrats 179
      as a commodity 191
      black 114, 148–150
      bonded 148
      cheap 110, 141, 143, 148–149, 199
      corvee 87
      discharged 157
      division of 22, 69, 78, 90, 104,
            111, 119–120, 156, 176–177
      dues 83
      efficiency 111
      efficient utilisation 196
      employment 149, 158
      exchange 160
      exploitation *see* exploitation, of labour
      family 110, 121, 140–141, 143
      farm 149
      foreign 110
      full-time 128
      hired 107, 110, 119, 129, 140, 163
      household 119, 162–163
      internal 81
      land as instrument of 90

market 114
migrancy 119
migrant *see* migrant, labour
migration 46, 120, 142, 150, 196
      of relatives and clients 127, 129
      of wives and domestic slaves 87
      of women 110
      power 26, 46, 83, 110, 179–180, 193
      relations 76–77, 90–92, 94–95, 103
      rent 47
      reproduction 44, 46, 48, 120, 143, 150
      reserves 145, 152, 196, 199, 209
      service(s) 77, 81
      tenancies/tenancy 45–47, 75, 126, 149
      unskilled 184, 199
      wage 47–48
Laclau, Ernesto 45, 174, 199
Lagos Plan of Action 132–133, 166–167
Land Act of 1913 48, 149
land alienation 103, 147, 199
land allocation 122, 162
land dispossession 5
land distribution 103, 106, 114, 126, 147
land expropriation 114, 124, 155, 215
land grabs 124
land question 103, 121–122, 163
      Buganda 105–113
      in sub-Saharan Africa 103, 140, 155
land reform 124, 126–128, 151, 154
land redistribution *see* redistribution of land
land rights/rights in land 122–126,
            138–140, 142, 164, 167
      bourgeois 140
      family 120
      hereditary 106
      individual/individualisation
            see individualisation, of land rights
      juridical 142
      property 82, 90, 139, 142
      usufruct 138
land tenure 79–80, 87, 93, 151, 155, 163
      African systems 78, 103, 115, 119, 121–127
      communal 125, 138, 141, 145, 153
      customary 127, 130, 140, 142, 147
      dynamics of 138
      individual 124–128, 141, 145,
            147, 153–154, 156
      lineage(s) 76, 138
      studies 79

land tenure (*continued*)
  sub-Saharan systems 105, 140
  systems 138
  types (Buganda) 107
Langa: A Study of Social Groups in an
    African Township 4–5, 30
Langa township 4, 6–7, 29–30, 33–34
languages 202–204, 211
Latin America 65, 105, 136, 154,
    175, 182–183, 186, 213
'Leadership and Change: A Study of Two
    South African Peasant Communities' 4
Lenin, Vladimir I. 159, 188,
    206–207, 219, 223
Leninism 212
Leninist definition of imperialism
    206–207, 209
Leninist imperialist stage in South Africa 214
Leninist notion of a 'revolutionary
    situation' 50
Lesotho 124
Lévi-Straussian structuralism 36
Lewis, Arthur 156, 198
liberal
  academics 4–5
  democracy 214, 216, 227
  determinism 194–195
  development theory 195
  economists 86, 93
  empiricism/empiricists 144
  functionalism xiv, 3, 5, 229 (n 3)
  functionalist 32
  functionalist anthropology 5, 7
  idealists 10, 32
  ideology 34–35
  positivist sociologists 32
  relativism 36
  scholars 153–154, 156
  social scientists 25, 79
  theorists/theory 35, 142
liberalisation policies (World Bank) 132
liberalism 5
liberals xiii, 35, 78, 86, 138,
    142, 204, 222, 226
  Western European 184
  white 205, 226
liberation
  black 205, 212, 217–218
  cultural 228

  economic 214
  intellectual 228
  movements 22, 187, 218, 220–222
  nationalist 220
  socialist 220
  struggles 22, 173–174, 183, 201–228
  women 164
Liberia 175
lineage(s) 11, 16, 20, 63, 73, 75–77,
    81, 123, 160, 190
  affiliations 147
  African 161
  assets 162
  boundaries 122
  form of political organisation 63
  land tenure systems 138
  minimal 125, 161
  mode of production 48, 86, 96, 161
  mode of social organisation 124, 161, 164
  organisation 145
  principle 84, 154
  royal 73
  ruling 73
  security of 122
  social reproduction 48, 163
  structure of segmentary societies 71
  supervision 80
lobola (bride wealth) 48
Luganda 71
Lukiiko (the Bugandan Legislative
    Assembly) 108
Luo speakers 68
Luoland 129
Lusoga 71

M

Macdonald, Helen 53
Macmillan, Hugh 207
Mafeje Affair xii
Mafeje, Archie
  biography xii–xvi
Magubane, Bernard 5–6, 17–19, 29–41,
    50, 65, 204, 207–209, 212–214, 218
majimbo (regions) movement 123
majimboism 25, 232 (n 55)
The Making of a Racist State 209, 213
Malawi 114, 116, 126, 128, 150–152,
    154, 157
  Tangatha system 148

Malinowski, Bronisław 39
Mambutsa 76
Mamdani, Mahmood 66–68, 160, 162, 210
Mandaza, Ibbo 228
Mao Tse-Tung 26, 187–188, 219
Maoist permanent revolution 222–223
market economy 139, 143
Marquard, Leo 207
Marshall Islands 174
Marx, Karl 11, 42, 46, 99, 219, 228
Marxism 3, 41–45, 48–49, 55, 119,
     157, 188, 202, 206, 229 (n 3)
Marxist
    anthropologists 88
    anthropology 36, 43, 55
    determinism 195
    materialism/materialists 10, 41, 99
    rhetoric 190
    social scientists 79
    sociology 43
    theorists/theory 43, 119,
        173, 194–195, 203
    universalism 161
Marxist(s) 31, 62, 71, 73, 78–79, 86,
     93–94, 99, 125, 138, 142, 145,
     153, 156, 161, 168, 174, 179, 204,
     219, 228
Master and Servants Act of 1845 148
materialism
    historical see historical, materialism
    Marxist see Marxist, materialism
matrilineages 163
matrilineal societies 162–163
Mauritius 163
Mayer, Philip 31–32
Mbeki, Thabo 195
Mbutuma, Melikhaya 9–10
Meillassoux, Claude 48, 73, 86, 145
mercantilism 189
Merton, Robert K. 39
Mesopotamia 126
Messianism 142
meta-nationalism 223–224
Mexico 178, 193
migrant
    cocoa growers in Ghana 116
    farmers in West Africa 122
    labour 7, 12, 46, 120–121,
        131–132, 158, 193, 199

workers 6, 34, 120, 129, 143, 147,
     157–159, 177, 179, 194
Mills, C. Wright 6
Mkandawire, Thandika 133, 211
Mlangeni, Patrick 58
modernisation 13, 51, 197
    theories 136, 198
modernity xi, 13, 105, 191, 197–198
modes of political organisation 71–79
modes of production 44–47, 60,
     62–63, 78–96, 105, 157, 161,
     175, 188–189, 197, 219
    Africa(n) 86–97, 161, 189
    articulation of 45, 62, 157
    articulation theory of 60
    Asiatic 86–88, 161
    capitalist see capitalist,
        modes of production
    colonial 147
    combination of 46
    communal 89
    domestic 88
    dominant 62
    expanded 165
    expanded petty 123, 157, 162–163
    finite 219
    lineage see lineage, mode of production
    pastoral 80
    peasant see peasant, mode of production
    pre-capitalist 46
    social 78
    subsistence 87
    theory 44
    tributary 86, 88–89, 91, 95–96, 161
modes of social organisation 125, 155
    kinship 160–161
    lineage 124, 161, 164
monocropping/monoculture 114, 154
Morris, Michael 44–47
Moyo, Sam 103–105, 117, 119, 121,
     136, 143
Mozambique 179, 193, 224
Mpondoland 179
Mtikrakra, Chief Zwelihle 7
multi-ethnic kingdoms 74
multi-ethnicity 21, 25
multi-kingdom tribes 69, 72
'Multi-Party Democracy and Ethnic
     Divisions in Africa' 20

multi-partyism 17, 28
Murunga, Godwin 53
mwami (king) 76

N
Nabudere, Dani 54–55
Namibia 64, 216
Natal 139, 148–149
national question 25, 206–207,
      210–214, 220, 223–227
*The National Question in Southern
      African Settler Societies* 205
nationalisation 182–184, 190
   of mines 215
   policies 182
nationalism 42, 205, 217–225
   black/African 217–218, 220, 225
   economic 215
   European 217–218
   meta-nationalism 223–224
   petit bourgeois 222
   proto-nationalism 223–224
   Third World 217
nationalist liberation 220
neocolonialism 19, 55, 146, 173–199, 223
neocolonialist
   production structure 191
   regimes 186, 189
   states 186
   strategy for development 186
Neocosmos, Michael 158–160
neoliberal
   economics 156
   paradigm 133
   period 104
   policies 215
   theories 132
neoliberalism 168
neoMarxists 218
neopositivism 36
NEUM *see* Unity Movement of South Africa
The New Road of Revolution 220
nganzi (chief minister) 75
Nguni 74, 99
Nigeria 124, 136
Nnoli, Okwudiba 26
nomothetic inquiry 44–48,
      87, 201, 233 (n 28)
non-disciplinarity 30, 42, 54–59, 97–98

Non-European Unity Movement
      see Unity Movement of South Africa
non-Marxist anthropology 36
Ntsebeza, Lungisile xiii
nvujjo (tithe) 109
Nyamnjoh, Francis 29

O
Omugabe 76
'On the Articulation of Modes
      of Production' 44
one-kingdom tribes 72
oomantshingilane (police spies) 7
Orange Free State 139, 149
Organisation of African Unity 220
Our Continent, Our Future 133
Oyewumi, Oyeronke 52, 56

P
PAC *see* Pan Africanist Congress
'pagans' 12, 34
Pan Africanist Congress (PAC) 5, 220–221
Panama Canal Zone 174
parasitism 108–109, 112, 127
Parsons, Talcott 39
particularism 144, 161
pastoral
   aristocracies 76, 78, 83–84, 189
   kingdoms 77–78, 83–84
   mode of production 80
   societies 78
pastoralism 22, 60, 63–71, 78,
      81, 84, 96, 114, 189
pastoralist invaders 64
pastoralists 66, 68–77, 81–85,
      90, 114, 122, 138
   Bahima/Bahuma 66, 82, 236 (n 6)
   Batutsi 84
   dominant 70, 81
   empire-building 63
   Hamitic 64, 68
   immigrant 71
   nomadic 70
patrilineage(s) 76, 82
patron-client relationship
      75–76, 83–84, 90, 93
P'Bitek, Okot 53
'Peasant Organisations in Africa:
      A Potential Dialogue between

Economists and Sociologists – Some Theoretical/Methodological Observations' 135
'Peasantisation in Western Africa' 138
peasant(s)/peasantry 104, 141, 136, 153, 190, 199
   African 132, 135, 138, 142
   black 139, 152
   classical 132
   differentiation of 158
   European 193
   exploitation *see* exploitation, of peasantry
   industrialised 143
   Kenyan 141
   mode of production 139–140
   proletarianisation of 158
   South Africa 137
   Ugandan 160
'Peasants in Sub-Saharan Africa' 136
Peru 186
petit bourgeoisie 179, 190–192, 202–203, 215–217
   Africa 147, 202, 217
   Afrikaner 215
   black 153, 215, 217
   urban-based 162
Philippines 174–176
'plantocracy' 116
pluralism 17–19
political
   action 65, 178
   centralisation 65, 69, 72, 79
   economists 79
   economy 64, 78, 113, 138–139
   mobilisation 178
   organisation 16, 61, 63, 71–79, 94, 103
   power 69
   relations 95
politics
   and revolutionary theory 171–228
   in anthropology 32, 36–43
   modern African 22
   of ethnicity 69
   revolutionary *see* revolutionary, politics
   separation from economics 71
   socialist 202
positivism 36–43, 49, 55, 99
positivist
   conception of science 30–31

sociologists/sociology 31–32, 39
Post, Ken 138–139, 141
post-independence 174
   Africa 22, 113–114, 218, 225
   African governments 153
   African states 185, 225
   dispensation 183
   era/period 15, 50, 53, 103, 112, 114, 116, 123, 126, 131, 177, 186, 211, 228
   land distribution 114
   Malawi 150
   political struggles 223
   states 159, 173, 185, 187
   underdeveloped countries 185
post-structuralism 99
postmodernism 99
poverty 115, 117, 133
   alleviation 165–170
   allowances 169
   cultural 228
   economic 228
   eradication 135–170
   in southern Africa 225
   in subsistence sector 154
   increase in global South 168
   intellectual 228
   rural 121, 135
Poverty, Adjustment, and Growth in Africa 167
Prashad, Vijay 182
pre-capitalist
   formations 213
   mode of production 46
   modes of economic and political organisation 103
   technology 113
privatisation 127
'The Problem of Anthropology in Historical Perspective' 36, 54
production
   agricultural *see* agricultural, production
   Buganda 111
   capitalist *see* capitalist, production
   capitalist mode *see* capitalist, modes of production
   cash crop 108, 116, 127, 139
   collective 110, 125
   colonial mode 147
   commercialisation 162
   commodity 128, 132

production (*continued*)
  communal mode of 89
  domestic mode of 88
  economic *see* economic, production
  expanded mode of 163, 165
  expanded petty mode of 122, 162
  export 132
  financing from remittances 162
  food *see* food production
  individualisation 123
  individualised 110
  individualism of 162
  industrial 190
  instruments 47–48, 85, 140
  intensification 163
  knowledge *see* knowledge, production
  mode(s) *see* modes of production
  neocolonialist 191
  peasant 108, 110, 119–120
  peasant mode *see* peasant,
    mode of production
  primary 79, 190
  relations/relationship 44, 46, 65,
    79, 81–82, 110, 113, 128, 141,
    143, 153, 160, 176–177, 180
  small-scale 108, 120
  subsistence *see* subsistence, production
  surplus 113, 121
proletarian insurrection 191
proletarianisation 141, 158–159, 179
proletariat 13, 141–143, 159, 178–179, 187,
  192, 194, 199, 209, 215, 225, 227
property rights 82, 87, 138–140, 142
  absence of 93
  individual 90, 95
  lack of 142
  private 75
protectionism 177, 215
proto-nationalism 223–224
PSC study 130
pseudo-feudal systems 145
Puerto Rico 174

R
'Race and Class Revisited: The Case of
  North America and South Africa' 213
racial discrimination 153
Radcliffe-Brown, Alfred 39

reconstruction 10, 53, 56, 97–100, 198
'red people' 12
redistribution of land 48, 124, 151, 177
redistribution of wealth 222, 226
reform
  agrarian *see* agrarian, reform
  economic 164
  land *see* land reform
reformism 30, 41, 155, 164, 168
relativism 36, 97, 219
'Religion, Class and Ideology in
  South Africa' 29, 30
reserves 48, 150–152, 154, 157, 196
  black 139
  labour *see* labour, reserves
  native 150
revolutionaries
  African 41, 228
  of the global South 188
  South African 222
revolutionary
  agrarian transformation 154
  changes in social scientific theories 52
  crisis in the social sciences 50,
  politics 43, 201
  romanticism 153
  struggle 159, 183
  theory 26, 100, 171–228
'revolutionary situation' 50, 227
Rey, Pierre-Philippe 48
Rhodesia 148–149, 152, 199, 209, 213
rights in land *see* land rights
*The Rise and Fall of the South
  African Peasantry* 139
The Road to South African Freedom 207
'The Role of the Bard in a Contemporary
  African Community' 7, 9
Roscoe, John 68
Russia 47, 159, 183, 185, 219
Rwanda 25, 61, 63–64, 66, 69, 72,
  76–78, 81–84, 87, 189

S
SACP *see* South African Communist Party
SADC *see* Southern African
  Development Community
Samoa 174
Sankara, Thomas 169
SAPs *see* structural adjustment programmes

Printed and bound by CPI Group (UK) Ltd, Croydon, CR0 4YY
09/06/2025
14685827-0002

Saul, John 138
Schapera, Isaac 10, 14
Second World 183
Second World War 111, 167, 196
Senegal 129
settler(s) 103
   agriculture 209
   agricultural economy 141
   colonial/colonists 126, 204
   colonialism 204, 212
   economy 147
   white 103, 114, 121, 124, 143,
      147, 152, 154, 196, 226
Seychelles 163
Sharawy, Helmi 54–55
sharecropping 47, 126, 139, 149
Sierra Leone 64, 175
Simons, Jack 207
social democracy 164, 226–227
social democrats 175
social formations 62–63, 71, 96,
      176–177, 189, 201, 211
   African 15, 59–100, 137, 197
   agrarian 146
   communal 90, 93
   conditions of 45
   ethnic 26
   interlacustrine region 60–71, 87, 95
   Latin American 65
   sub-Sahara 90
   tributary 89, 93
social science(s) 3–4, 29–30, 36–38,
      41–43, 49–57, 59, 87, 137, 205
   a critique of 1–100
   African 32, 57, 59
   bourgeois 42, 48, 52, 56
   conventional 136
   Eurocentrism *see* Eurocentrism,
     in social sciences
   functionalist-positivistic 42
   imperialist *see* imperialist, social sciences
   indigenisation 202
   liberal bourgeois 240 (n 53)
   metropolitan bourgeois 37–38
   radical 3–28
social scientists xi, 10, 19, 32,
      35, 41–42, 49, 79
   African 42, 56, 105, 136, 146
   colonial 35

European 4, 10–11
   from the global South 56
   liberal 25, 79
   Marxist 79
   radical 30, 50–51, 53
socialism 178, 181, 187–188, 191, 214, 216,
      218–219, 221, 224–227, 242 (n 17)
   Chinese experiment 85
   history 203
   international 42
   South Africa 203
socialist
   anthropology 37
   concept of national democratic
     revolution 220–223
   democracy 214–220
   Fabian 156
   ideology 182
   liberation 220
   politics 202
   revolution 159, 183, 216
   struggle(s) 215, 217
   transformation/transition
     188, 192, 216, 227
socialist-orientated
   economies 177
   regimes 186
   states 189
sociality 49
socio-historical zones 145
sociological individualism 40
sociologists
   functionalist 31–32, 39
   pluralist 14
   positivist 31–32
   Western 56
sociology
   classical 20
   historical *see* historical, sociology
   Marxist *see* Marxist, sociology
   of knowledge 10, 30–36, 42, 44, 48–49
   of religion 30–31
   positivist 39
Soludo, Charles 133
Somalia 64, 66–67, 189
Sotho 99
South Africa: From Soweto to Uitenhage 213
South African Communist Party (SACP)
     204–207, 211–216, 220–226

South Korea 175–176
Southern African Development
	Community (SADC) 144
'Soweto and Its Aftermath' 173
Soweto uprising 201
Speke, John Hanning 68
Spencer, Herbert 38–40
state capitalism 90, 112, 173–199
'State, Democracy and Development:
	An Exploration of the
	Scholarship of Professor Archie
	Monwabisi Mafeje' 195
The State of World Rural Poverty 168
'Strategy and Tactics' document 220
structural adjustment programmes
	(SAPs) 121, 132–133, 155,
	166–167, 169, 215
struggle(s)
	anti-comprador 224
	historical (European) 219
	liberation see liberation, struggles
	political 223
	revolutionary 159, 183
	socialist 215, 217
Studies in Imperialism 49
styles of thinking
	emergent/new 99
	free 97
'Subaltern Studies in South Asia and Post-
	Colonial Anthropology in Africa' 53
subsistence 46, 96, 113, 118, 195–197
	agriculture 148, 150, 156
	black producers 139
	crops 146
	declining levels 158
	economy 14
	farmers/farming 34, 48, 115, 119, 131
	for black people 150–151
	labour of women 110
	needs 120, 146, 151, 165
	production/producers 87,
		90, 114, 119–121, 157
Sudan 22, 116, 135, 189
Swaziland 114, 148, 150–151, 153
Sweezy, Paul 188, 191

T
Tanganyika 189, 209, 213
Tangatha system in Malawi 148

Tanzania 128–129, 135, 140,
	169, 190, 242 (n 17)
taxonomic categories/categorisations
	60, 92, 145, 184, 205
taxonomy 60
Tembuzi 66
Thailand 175–176
The Invention of Women 52
The Theory and Ethnography of African
	Social Formations xiv, 3, 20, 59–100
The Ties That Bind 213
thinking see styles of thinking
Thiong'o, Ngũgĩ wa xi
Third International see Comintern
Third World 51, 65, 168, 182–183,
	188, 194, 217, 224
Toro 66, 72, 75, 80
'totalising critique' 30–36
traditionalism 13, 197
transdisciplinarity 54
transformation
	agrarian 103, 154
	economic 215
	historical 31
	socialist see socialist, transformation
Transkei 9–10, 33–34
Transvaal 139, 149
tribalism xiv, 3, 20
	ideology of 3–4, 10–19
Trotskyist permanent revolution 222–223
Tutsi 67

U
UDF see United Democratic Front
Uganda 34, 67, 71, 106, 110, 112, 122,
	128–129, 136, 160, 169, 189–190
	see also Buganda
Uganda Agreement 107
Ujamaa policies 140
UMSA see Unity Movement of South Africa
underdevelopment 111–112, 137,
	157–158, 169, 173, 183, 199
	and neocolonialism 174–181
	colonial 190
	of African reserves 196
'Underdevelopment and Dependence
	in Black Africa' 209
unitary kingdoms 61, 71–72
United Democratic Front (UDF) 221

United Kingdom 27, 36–37
United Nations Development
       Programme 168
United States 27, 36, 107, 174,
       176, 183, 213, 239 (n 31)
Unity Movement of South Africa
       (UMSA) 3, 42, 203, 205, 220–221
universalism 161
USSR 183
utilitarianism 40

V

vernacular 201, 203–204, 211
    African political 203
    languages 202
Vietnam 178, 193, 215
Vilakazi, Benedict Wallet xi
voluntarism 157, 185–186, 194

W

Wales 8
Washington Consensus 133
Watutsi 82
Weber, Max 36, 39
Weberian concept of status 94
Western
    capitalism 138, 198
    dominance 156
    imperialism 169
    individualism 156
    powers 28
    sociologists 56
Western European liberals 184
'Western way of life' 12, 33–34
'Westernisation' 33
white-collar workers 178–179
white liberal 226
    ideology 34
    view 35
white minority rule 208, 212
Wilson, Monica 4–6, 30, 137–138,
       229 (n 3)
Wolpe, Harold 44–48, 94, 204
Woods, Roger 138
World Bank 132–133, 155–156,
       164, 166–168

X

Xhosa 7

Y

Yeros, Paris 104–105, 117, 143

Z

Zambia 12, 63, 124, 128, 152, 199
Zanu-PF Executive Committee 151
Zimbabwe 63, 114, 122, 126, 129, 143,
       150–151, 155, 170, 216, 224